W. L. WYLLIE

Marine Artist, 1851-1931

W. L. WYLLIE

Marine Artist, 1851-1931

Roger Quarm & John Wyllie

Foreword by Sir Hugh Casson, PRA

CHRIS BEETLES
LIMITED

Chris Beetles Ltd.
10 Ryder Street,
St. James's,
London SW1Y 6QB

Set in Monophoto Bembo
Filmset and printed in Great Britain by
BAS Printers Limited, Over Wallop, Hampshire

British Library Cataloguing in Publication Data
Quarm, Roger
W. L. Wyllie.
1. Marine painting, English
I. Title II. Wyllie, John
759.2

ISBN 1-871136-01-6

CONTENTS

LIST OF ILLUSTRATIONS

Photographs

Pages 29–32

Plates

Except where otherwise stated, all original works are at the National Maritime Museum, London and are reproduced by permission of the Director and Trustees. Measurements, in inches followed by millimetres, are sheet-size in the case of drawings and watercolours, plate-size in the case of etchings and drypoints, unless otherwise specified.

COLOUR

Between pages 88 and 89

BLACK AND WHITE

ACKNOWLEDGEMENTS

Thanks are due to Miss Aileen Wyllie for her support and encouragement; the Director and Trustees of the National Maritime Museum, London for allowing reproduction of the majority of the pictures, and use of the Museum's resources; Jane Dacey and Harley Preston for their practical help; Marie Richardson who took the majority of the photographs; Mrs Dorothy Beland for much typing; Denis Stonham, Bob Todd, Ian Craft, Laura Wortley, Sir Charles Madden, Peyton Skipwith of the Fine Art Society, Teddy Archibald, and many others.

R.Q.
J.W.

FOREWORD

by Sir Hugh Casson, PRA

I first met W. L. Wyllie when I was a schoolboy and he was in the last years of his life. To me he seemed the perfect man living the perfect life. I was passionate about boats but here was somebody lucky beyond belief who seemed to live entirely on behalf of (and *only*) for boats. He designed them, cared for them, sailed them and above all he never ceased to draw and paint them in every size and shape and in all weathers. He drew them as a seaman would . . . accurately, affectionately and above all with that deep practical understanding of the fact born of experience, that seamanship is fun but it is also serious, for a human life can often depend upon the curve of a hull or the angle of a cleat. And as if all this were not enough, he lived with his family in the most perfect house in the world, Tower House, with its toes in the water and great warships sliding past the window so close it seemed you could hand a biscuit to the captain on the bridge.

Although the creative output of W. L. Wyllie was prodigious, he managed to avoid the formula (so attractive to busy and popular painters) and treated every new problem with proper respect. This perhaps again was a sailor's training, for even to the most experienced no squall or wavetop is exactly the same as the last one. His place in the history of British marine painting – admirably assessed in the present book – is assured.

As the following pages relate, Wyllie began life as an illustrator – a profession demanding a sharp eye for detail, a decisive sense of dramatic composition, and above all a sense of occasion. These workmanlike qualities, inspired by his boyhood by the French seaside and enriched by a happy marriage beside the Medway and lastly old age at the gate of Portsmouth Harbour, are best exemplified perhaps in his quick shorthand watercolour sketches; they are not those of the contemplative, visionary or poetic painter. Wyllie dealt with facts . . . with one hand so to speak holding a brush, the other a tiller . . . but because he loved those facts he made from them an art that is lively, modestly aimed but truthfully accomplished, an art that is set *unmistakably* with the seal of the sea.

Hugh Casson
April, 1981

INTRODUCTION

'There are two main schools of Marine Art,' wrote Sir Geoffrey Callender, first Director of the National Maritime Museum, in his obituary of W. L. Wyllie in the *Mariner's Mirror*.

In the first the Elder Van de Velde stands as the grand exemplar, illustrating with matchless skill the dominion that man, with the vessels of his construction, has secured over the Sea. In the most beautiful examples of this artist's work, the sea and sky are subordinated, or subdued into a conventional pattern, so that there may be nothing to distract attention from the exquisite ships – the loveliest creations (to quote Ruskin) which the daring hand of man has produced. At the other end of the scale stands J. M. W. Turner in the final phase of his amazing career, when he gave to his ships in a seascape as insignificant, or purely decorative, a part as to his heroes of mythology in a landscape; when his main concern was no longer with ships as ships, but with the influence of light and wind, and the interaction of the two, upon the surface of ocean in storm and calm.

Midway between these two extremes may be grouped the outstanding masters of Marine Painting; those, that is to say, who have done full justice to the ship (and her exacting claims upon expert technical knowledge) without for a moment forgetting the conditions of weather; the effect of cloud-masses upon the distribution of light, and the effect of water-depth upon the shape of waves. First among these comes the Younger Van de Velde; and, not far behind him, the English eighteenth-century masters, Charles Brooking, Samuel Scott, and Nicholas Pocock.

To such great names that of W. L. Wyllie may be confidently added. . .[1]

A balanced assessment of Wyllie has long been overdue. In nautical circles he has always been popular, and to many, the work of the last two and a half decades of his life still stands for the whole: his depictions in etching, drypoint, oil and watercolour of the Navy and events of the First World War period, his work relating to the restoration of the *Victory*, and what Wyllie himself may have considered the culmination of his career, the Trafalgar Panorama in Portsmouth, completed and opened by George V in 1930. The pictures of his last, most prolific period were until recently acquired and collected, it would be fair to say, rather for the interest of their subject-matter, the vessels or types of vessel depicted, than for their qualities as works of art.

Wyllie's appeal on this level was summarised seventy-five years ago, when he was at the height of his career, by Admiral Sir Cyprian Bridge:

Sea faring folk, and not least, perhaps, those who can look back far into the olden days, can claim the right to adjudge to Mr Wyllie the possession of two distinguished qualities – viz., that of delineating with accuracy the craft of different epochs, and that of making the picture pleasing to those who look at it.[2]

Admiral Bridge, however, a specialist enthusiast writing on behalf of specialist enthusiasts, and self-admittedly 'ignorant of the rules of art criticism',[3] was in no position to tell the whole story.

Since the early 1970s new interest has grown in Wyllie's earlier work,* in his oils, watercolours and etchings of the 1880s and 1890s, expressing his response to the life of the Lower Thames and Medway, and the experience of his sailing and trips abroad. The present book is addressed to a public now becoming aware of the vast and varied nature of Wyllie's output over six to seven decades. Our examination of his art and life will uncover aspects of which many will hitherto have been scarcely aware – the early years spent on the northern French coast, the impact on his work of Turner and Whistler, the critical attention he received during his lifetime. The extent to which Wyllie's art deteriorated in the early years of this century will also be discussed, as well as the effects of the demand upon him of earning a living first as an illustrator for the *Graphic*, and then by commissions from shipping companies and the Royal Navy. It is our aim to reveal the full perspective of his oeuvre, which includes work that surely earns him the right to be acclaimed Britain's premier marine artist of the later Victorian and early twentieth-century era.

Many of the illustrations in this book are drawn from the Wyllie Collection at Greenwich, bought from the Wyllie family for the National Maritime Museum by Sir James Caird in 1931. This enormous collection contains items from all periods of Wyllie's life. Many of the five thousand or so drawings and watercolours which form the bulk of the collection are unfinished, and a large proportion are simply notes from nature on small scraps of paper, filed away for future use. The collection as a whole represents a reference system which Wyllie was able to consult when composing pictures. It is remarkable in its scope and size, containing, for example, many black and white drawings for the *Graphic*, studies for etchings and publications as well as for oil paintings, and a number of the beautiful black and white drawings and etchings of the Thames and Thames life for which Wyllie was renowned in his lifetime, as well as very many finished watercolours demonstrating the development of his brilliant technique.

*Evidenced, for example, by the exhibitions 'The Tidal Thames', showing Wyllie's paintings, drawings, watercolours and etchings, at the Malcolm Henderson Gallery, London, in 1973; and 'The Shadow of the Mainsail' at the David Messum Gallery, Beaconsfield, Buckinghamshire in 1977, which included work by Wyllie and Arthur Briscoe. The exhibition 'Wyllie the Artist', showing oils, watercolours and etchings from all periods of Wyllie's career, was held at the Royal Naval Museum, Portsmouth in 1981.

The collection is also of considerable subject interest, and according to Wyllie's fellow-artist Sir David Murray, 'a most reliable reference with regard to ships, the sea, and all he interested himself in'.[4] It is in fact impossible to discuss Wyllie's pictures without reference to the subjects depicted, whether some extant form of cargo-handling, the handling of a Thames barge, an unusual kind of naval craft, merchant shipping or sea-travel in the 1890s.

Wyllie was an artist of tremendous natural talent and drive, whose background and early training as an illustrator eventually led him to a degree of specialisation which may have inhibited stylistic development. In the mid-1880s the critics compared him with the foremost painters of the sea. Harry Barnett, writing in the *Magazine of Art*, held high hopes of Wyllie: '. . . As a painter of water his ability is not a whit less unquestionable. Here, however, he meets powerful rivals in men like Hook, and Henry Moore, and Colin Hunter . . . in certain departments – as a delineator of certain aspects of the river, and certain conditions of the sea – Mr Wyllie, it seems to me at least, stands alone.'[5] Working within these narrow confines he developed his skills to extraordinary levels, though as an artist he was no innovator.

Those artists whose work shows an affinity with that of Wyllie were all marine artists, specialists, lacking Wyllie's broader based training and outlook. The most distinguished of them, Charles Dixon (1872–1934), twenty years younger than Wyllie, also an illustrator, produced work of extremely high quality including Thames scenes and First World War subjects. He too was an extremely accomplished watercolourist, frequently working on a large scale in that medium. His work bears a strong resemblance to that of Wyllie, but has a strength and individuality of its own. The same may be said of the work of the Scottish marine painter Frank Watson Wood (1862–1953), who with Wyllie and John Lavery was present to cover the surrender of the German High Seas Fleet in 1918. Frank Mason (1876–1965) and Charles de Lacy (*c.* 1860–1936) both worked as illustrators and produced work which closely followed Wyllie's later style of the First World War period. Roland Langmaid (*c.* 1897–1956) at first received lessons from Wyllie, and during the War Wyllie himself produced work based on sketches by 'Lieutenant Langmaid', but later, it has been suggested, the relationship soured when Langmaid's etchings were thought to rely too precisely on Wyllie's, even to the detail of his handwriting. The paintings of A. B. Cull (1880–1931), an artist who also worked in the Portsmouth area, have a close similarity with Wyllie's fleet pictures of the First World War, but they are, if anything, more meticulous than Wyllie's. The American painter William M. Birchall (b. Iowa 1884), who settled in England, also painted pictures which closely resemble Wyllie's work of the First World War period, and is said to have been a friend of Wyllie. It must also be realised that, being a 'popular artist', Wyllie had a considerable effect upon the work of many amateur artists and illustrators of his period.

In discussion of Wyllie's art an overriding theme emerges and recurs. It is that of the effect upon his work of the places, the people and the things that immediately surrounded him. Thus there arises a natural division of his career as an artist into three phases broadly equivalent with the three geographical locations in which his life was spent.

1851–79. The earliest and most influential years, from his birth until his marriage, were spent between London where he was born, and more importantly, the coast of northern France around Boulogne. During this period Wyllie's art was at its most charming and sensitive; his interest in painting the sea and ships had not yet fully developed, and his early work exploited the more atmospheric aspects of landscape, seascape and coastal views.

1880–1906. Soon after their marriage the Wyllies went to live in the then beautiful surroundings of the Medway estuary near Rochester. While living there Wyllie firmly established his reputation as an artist and settled down to the necessity of earning a living from his work. He responded to and developed the subjects of his surroundings, the lower Thames and the Medway, bringing a new poetry to the mundane aspects of the new industrial age. It was during this period that the final direction his art would take was established, and he developed links with the Navy and the merchant shipping companies as sources for subjects and commissions.

1907–1931. The years after Wyllie moved to the house at the entrance of Portsmouth harbour in 1906, until his death in 1931, were years not of great artistic development, but rather of consolidation and prosperity pursued with unrelenting industry. During this period naval and travel subjects occupied a large part of Wyllie's time, and he became something of a grand old man, painting, exhibiting and sailing to the end.

This book is divided into two main parts. In the first, a brief account is given of W. L. Wyllie's life and career, with a grandson's boyhood memories. The second sets out to trace Wyllie's development as an artist, and to assess his achievement in various media. The illustrations have been chosen to reflect the variety of his work, and are arranged broadly chronologically. It is our hope that in these pages Wyllie's true standing in British marine art may emerge.

R.Q.
J.W.

NOTES

1 G. Callender, 'In Memoriam W. L. Wyllie', *The Mariner's Mirror*, 2 April 1931, p. 101.
2 C. Bridge, 'W. L. Wyllie, R.A.', *The Art Journal* (Christmas November), London, 1907, p. 13.
3 Loc. cit., p. 1.
4 M. A. Wyllie, *We Were One*, London, 1935, p. 30.
5 H. V. Barnett, 'By River and Sea', *The Magazine of Art*, May 1884, p. 314.

LIFE

by John Wyllie

The house we lived in during the ten years of my youth which I spent with my grandfather, W. L. Wyllie, RA, stood on the entrance of Portsmouth harbour with the sea as its nearest and most influential neighbour. At high tide the waters glittered, or raged, no more than six feet from the front of the building where a narrow terrace separated us from the element which dominated my grandfather's life.

When south-westerly gales blew the waves broke green over the windows on the ground floor and sent spray up three storeys to drum on the windows upstairs. By contrast, on a quiet summer's day when the afternoon sunlight bounced off the sea to make the ceilings of the rooms ripple with reflections, the house breathed the kind of tranquillity that is usually to be found in the presence of still water.

It was a tranquillity which seldom lasted very long because the tideway separating the house from HMS *Dolphin*, the RN submarine base, was a narrow one and all the traffic entering or leaving the harbour had to use it. When aircraft carriers were developed and grew to have more and more freeboard they would blot out the sky as they steamed slowly by barely a hundred yards from the house.

In the summer small launches full of tourists, using the slack water close to the shore, would pass near enough for us to hear the skipper tell his passengers: 'That is the old Round Tower built for the protection of the harbour by Henry the Eighth . . . and next to it is the house that belongs to Mr Wyllie, the famous marine artist. If you look in the bottom window,' the man would point, 'you can see the old gentleman at work.'

'Old gentleman.' When I went to live in Portsmouth, in 1920, my grandfather was not quite seventy. Age, however, meant nothing to him. He worked a full day at his painting every day of the week unless commitments to various voluntary institutions claimed his attention. One activity could and did distract him from his painting though it was as much a part of his living and being as his art; indeed, it was a very part of it. That activity was sailing or, more frequently at that time in his life, racing a

14-foot international dinghy which he had himself designed. He had watched it being built, frame by frame, by a local boat-builder who was one of his keenest competitors when they were both sailing in local races.

From the age of nine or ten until I was sixteen I was often the 'old gentleman's' crew. Dinghy sailing is an occupation which can tax the reflexes and energies of a seventeen-year-old, let alone a seventy-year-old. Yet my grandfather continued in the sport, competing with such able rivals as Uffa Fox, Tom Thorneycroft and Morgan Giles, until he was over seventy-five.

The old man liked to win, but what gave his attitude to the sport its special impetus was a compulsive pursuit of excellence and perfection. The game was not played for the award, but was a matter of sailing a race in which seamanship mattered above all else and in which every element had to be considered – tides, wind, fine tuning of sail and rigging, tactics – so that, with this combination as nearly correct as he could make it, he could feel he had got the best out of his boat.

A most vivid memory of my grandfather is of seeing him, during the winter of 1924, standing in front of his easel at work on a wet-back watercolour. The subject was a fierce gale that was whipping the tops off the waves creating the illusion that the surface of the sea was smoking.

It was a study, in fact, of what was happening just the other side of the big plate-glass window of his ground floor studio. The conditions on that day were not the worst he had experienced since he moved to Portsmouth nor was it the first time he had made such a study. On an earlier occasion when the terrace was actually breaking up during a similar storm, he had gone out to rescue a new boat, had been knocked down by a wave and had broken his ribs by falling on a stone bollard. It has always seemed to me that trying to catch and record the ferocity of the wind as it tore the sea apart was his way of diverting his mind and energies from the helpless anxiety that such tempestuous conditions caused to a constructive purpose.

During spring tides, even in calm weather, the level of the sea was barely four feet below the level of the terrace. When it blew a force nine or ten gale and there was a spring tide, as there was on the day I have in mind, the waves broke in solid brutal shoulders of water against the studio's teak doors. Fortunately they were stout enough to withstand this onslaught. In no way, however, could the jambs and the joints between the doors be made sufficiently watertight to prevent the sea forcing its way through them in jets. So the routine of buckets and swabs was put into action and while my white-haired grandfather painted bare-footed, with his trousers and long-johns rolled half way up his shins, standing on a thick boat's grating, his youngest daughter Aileen and I bailed furiously to maintain an effective level of flood control.

We sustained our efforts for three or four hours while the tide reached its peak and then fell off. Throughout that time as the artist's study took shape he encouraged us, whistled snatches of Gilbert and Sullivan and said half a dozen times, 'I hope the wind does not drop. I hope the wind does not drop.' It was an attitude that was typical of the man in that he would subject himself to almost any discomfort or sacrifice if it meant that he could produce a record that might stand on its own as a dramatic or simply an accurate record of a scene, event or object which caught and held his interest. On occasions like that storm in 1924, the execution of what quickly became a finished picture took no more, from start to finish, than a few hours.

Whether he was sailing or painting, William Lionel Wyllie, 'W.L.' to many of his friends and acquaintances, was a man who under a quiet, modest exterior was as single-minded with regard to his work as any master-craftsman must be if he is to be successful. But this compulsive dedication was neither exclusive nor narrow. It ranged over the sea and the sky and every mood that possessed them both. W.L. had a scientific interest in the form of every ship he saw and in every device used to propel it from the earliest days of sail to the latest Scott, Paine and Vosper power boats of his day. He mixed and cultivated friendships with all men who went to sea, whether in dinghies or transatlantic liners, whether skippers or deck-hands, Admirals or ABs. He was acquainted with many marine architects and designers as well as with the carpenters, riggers and welders who took the blueprints from the drawing offices and turned them into battleships or barges, coasters or racing cutters, merchant marine leviathans or fishing luggers. His studies included everything he could find that had been written about the ships which sailed the oceans and coastal waters and the men who had learned to cope with the sea's disorderly ways. As he examined these subjects he wrote notes and made thousands upon thousands of studies of scenes and objects in small sketchbooks, using a two-inch stub of pencil and a little wedge of soft green india-rubber which went everywhere with him in one of the pockets of his waistcoat. Even in the warmest weather, though he might shed his coat and thus appear in his shirt-sleeves, I can never remember seeing him without his waistcoat.

Leafing at random through the sketchbooks one finds, for instance, a quick impression of the tall pinnacle of water sent up when a sixteen-inch shell strikes the sea, the steeple of a Wren church in London, men lifting shrimping nets, sailors out on the to'gallants'l yard-arm furling canvas, three men on the vulnerable-looking conning tower of one of Britain's earliest submarines, a sheet of paper covered with studies of sea-gulls, brilliant sketches of First World War aircraft, and uniquely, drawings made of the shothole-filled sails of HMS *Victory* which were found one day in a loft in a Portsmouth dockyard where they had been stored ever since the ship had returned from Trafalgar. No details of items that interested him were too insignificant to be jotted down, and some of these drawings catch more meaningful action in a few lines than could be caught with a camera.

Later these sketches would be used as the foundation for pictures of London and the Thames, of places around the world from Spitzbergen to Trinidad, of battles at sea and in the air during the First World War when W.L. was an accredited war artist, of historical scenes such as the Battle of the Nile, of state occasions such as

Queen Victoria's funeral cortège, with her coffin aboard the Royal Yacht *Alberta* being escorted through the fleet on its way from the Isle of Wight to Portsmouth. And there were many pictures of a more commercial nature which he painted for the big shipping companies, and over three hundred others executed to illustrate books.

With all this work in hand, which involved him in a great deal of travelling, W.L. still found time for other activities. He corresponded, for instance, with the Astronomer Royal about the nature of the craters on the moon, and the sketchbooks came in handy again when he followed his keen interest in palaeontology. He founded, and ran to his last days, the first Sea Scout troop in Portsmouth. He taught map-making to the Territorial Army. He was commodore of a number of yacht clubs, sometimes holding this post in two or three clubs at the same time. Besides being a Royal Academician he became a member of the Royal Institute of Oil Painters and the Royal Society of Painter-Etchers and Engravers. All these appointments involved committee work. He chaired the first meeting of the group which eventually formed the Society for Nautical Research and was elected that organisation's Honorary Vice-President. Deriving from this appointment he became a very active member, and never missed a meeting of the committee which was organised first to raise the necessary funds to restore HMS *Victory* to the condition she had been in at Trafalgar, then to see the project through to its conclusion. In the end, W.L. became the committee's biggest single contributor.

As quite a young man, in the 1870s, he had been the leader of a trio, the others being his father and his half-brother, who initiated a campaign against the 'closed shop' attitude of the Council of the Royal Academy. The three men pushed their protest as far as a private member's bill in the House of Commons, and W.L. was sitting in the visitor's gallery when the protest was quashed personally by Gladstone. Twice he played the rôle of pavement artist to raise funds for important charities; for Westminster Hospital he succeeded in flushing gold sovereigns out of the pockets of visiting royalty. Once, such was his expertise in navigation and the rule of the road at sea, he was called upon to act as assessor in a case in which two vessels had been in collision in Newhaven harbour.

The foregoing should be regarded as no more than a sample of Wyllie's many and varied activities inside and outside his profession. When taken in conjunction with his many other ventures, some of which will be described in more detail, it will be understood that he was a man who rarely wasted one 'unforgiving minute' of his time. The sheer quantity of sketches, etchings, watercolours and oil paintings which he left behind him may be compared in its extent to Turner's prodigious output.

And yet, in all the years that I lived in his house I found, as did everyone else, that he was always approachable and seldom, if ever, seemed to be in a hurry.

In the matter of inherited talents, W. L. Wyllie was obviously rich. His mother, not herself an artist, married one in William Morison Wyllie and was the mother of three more, two of whom became Royal Academicians and the third an Associate of the Royal Academy, all three having work purchased for the nation by the Tate Gallery: Lionel Percy Smythe (1839–1918), William Lionel Wyllie (1851–1931), and Charles William Wyllie (1853–1923).

William Morison Wyllie came from a reasonably well-to-do family with major land-holdings in Tobago. He went to school at Harrow and acquired a further education from various sources as his parents wandered about the Continent. He was a well-read man and he was, we are told by W.L.'s wife-to-be Marion Amy Carew who was herself fluent in the language, 'an excellent French scholar'. He studied art in London at Carey's School of Art, at Heatherly's in Newman Street (otherwise known at the time as Leigh's School of Art), and the Royal Academy Schools.

William Morison Wyllie had been brought up in the anticipation that he would inherit the family plantation in the West Indies which, until 1833, had had slaves and a slaving brig. However, when he was twenty there was a legal dispute within the family which his side lost. So in the late 1840s W.M. moved to Paris where he took up art at an atelier and lived the life of the student *quartier*.

There he met Katherine Benham, the sister of a London solicitor, who already had two children, Lionel and Minnie, with the surname of Smythe. Presumably they were born out of wedlock★ because when W.M. married Katherine, in St Pancras Church on 28 January 1851, the certificate states that she was a spinster. Since she was beautiful, talented and sweet-natured it is a pity that no more is known of her.

She gave birth to W.L. at 67 Albany Street, Regent's Park on 5 July that same year. Despite the indisputable facts that result from simple arithmetic, it is also indisputable that W.M. made an admirable choice in the woman who bore and mothered the boy. Katherine had a strong influence on the family, and possessed the gift of being able to keep what became a houseful of artists happy. Later her fourth-born, a son named Charles, christened her 'Goody'. It was a name that was immediately adopted by the rest of the family.

It is worth noting that the year after W.L.'s birth his father had for the first time a picture hung in the Royal Academy. W.M. was a tall, athletic man with a forceful character and, in the Bohemian fashion of the age, a head of long black hair and a beard. He was known in the family as the governor, or 'Guv', and he encouraged his sons and his step-son in every way possible to develop their natural talents as artists. He hoarded every painting they made from their earliest childhood and drove W.L. with particular fervour, perhaps because he found in his elder son a responsiveness to such intense encouragement.

After their marriage the Wyllies lived for some years in a house that belonged to Katherine, 36 Gloucester Crescent, London, which at that time was newly built and still had open fields nearby. In 1853 'Goody' was delivered of her fourth child, the

★Since the above was written a letter dated 7 March 1944 written by Lionel Smythe's daughter Minnie has come to light, stating that Katherine was 'married' to Percy Sydney Smythe; also that Katherine and her two sisters, all professionally trained as singers, supported their father, John Benham, after the collapse of his weaving business, by singing.

already mentioned Charles. Soon after that, because W.L. in his first years tended to be sickly (probably with a bronchial condition largely attributable to the dense London fog), it was decided to return to France. Perhaps, also, W.M.'s and Katherine's common experience of life in that country, away from the superficial proprieties of London society, had some influence on their choice. It was only a partial move, however, because the family continued to winter in England.

First they lived in Boulogne, which at that time supported a considerable colony of English residents amongst whom was General Sir John Bennet Hearsey, KCB, a hero of the Indian Mutiny and the grandfather of the woman W.L. would eventually marry. The Wyllie mode of spending the summers in France and winters in England continued for well over twenty years and, once they moved away from Boulogne to the sandy wilderness around Ambleteuse and Wimereux, it suited W.M. and his sons and step-son admirably.

Here more detailed mention of Lionel Smythe and Charles is necessary because Lionel, particularly, must have contributed to W.L.'s development as a painter. He was ten years older than his elder half-brother, a strong and colourful personality in his own right. Had he possessed the same fierce compulsion to paint that inspired W.L., he might have equalled him and even outstripped him in their pursuit of recognition as painters. Lionel's work, unlike W.L.'s, was slowly executed and limited in quantity. He etched and painted landscapes and compositions which featured the country people and fisher folk who lived along the coast of Pas de Calais. Since his mother had lived in Paris amongst art students, Lionel's father too could have been a painter, or at least a student of art. Whatever the facts, Lionel was fortunate that a man of W.M.'s talent and strength of personality became his step-father.

Charles, the youngest painter in the family, must have had some struggle to escape the dominance of his father, elder brother and step-brother. His paintings show that he was obviously talented and flexible, and when he turned to marine painting it is often hard to tell his work apart from W.L.'s. He was, on the other hand, more successful in finding some individuality when it came to landscapes and figure-painting. In pictures with the same or similar subjects to those painted by W.M. and Lionel, he shows a tendency to move away from their naturalistic approach to the kind of symbolism and mysticism to be found in the work of Burne-Jones.

Records of the Wyllies' lives in Wimereux from around 1860 to 1880 suggest that it was an Elysium for young and old alike. Roger Quarm discusses later in this book what the environment meant to W.L. and the others as painters. As for additional influences it had on W.L., there was in the first place the sea air to help build up his health and to give him the wiry strength which never deserted him thereafter. The effect on his character must also have been strong because he grew into a young man in an ambience that was free of almost all forms of confinement or restriction. With

Lionel and Charles he lived an indulgent, care-free family life. He did not have any formal schooling but had as a tutor, in his early years, along with Charles, a 'fairy-like mite of twelve', Alice Gunyon, who later became Lionel's wife. She taught her charges reading, writing and music, undoubtedly with the aid of Goody who was an accomplished musician. No doubt, too, their father, the old Harrovian, French scholar and traveller, aided in their education, though it is true that to the end of his days W.L. had no concept of or feeling for elementary arithmetic let alone any advanced form of mathematics. If a problem could be put in geometric terms – for instance, matters of perspective – he could master it sufficiently to write, as he did, a definitive book on the subject (*Nature's Laws and the Making of Pictures*, 1903). For all other calculations he would, I believe, have been amongst the first to welcome today's pocket calculators. In his day he solved his difficulties with numbers by enlisting the aid of others.

When W.L. was fourteen the family moved from a row of cottages that had been built as billets for the officers of Napoleon's troops to an old Napoleonic guard-house. It was built right down on the shore line so that, at spring tide, the moody sea licked or pounded the foot of the narrow bastion which protected the foundations of the house from direct contact with the waves. To the north and south of the house lay twenty miles of empty beaches and sand dunes stretching from Cap Gris-Nez to the Pointe de Lornel. In the house on the shore the Wyllie family spent many very happy days.

Goody sang and played the piano almost as professionally as her offspring painted. Her husband had a deep rolling voice in which he was wont to deliver 'Care can never reach the soul who deeply drinks of wine' while the others joined in, though in fact they were a rather abstemious family. These convivial evenings took place at the end of the long summer days when the boys sat at the table drawing along the edges of newspapers or on anything else that came to hand. They were also drilled by their mother in operatic airs by Mozart, Weber and Bellini as well as part songs such as Bishop's 'Chough and Crow'. The three artists-to-be became quite capable musicians and learned to whistle together, according to Lionel Smythe, 'the same tune very correctly and in strict time, but each in a different key'.

Most important to the boy who was to become a marine artist was the constant challenge of the ebb and flow of the Channel tides which in rough weather roared at the family doorstep. In their youth and adolescence the boys were as agile and capable of surviving in any sea, no matter how rough, as porpoises. It was a talent which enabled them on a number of occasions to save lives because the coast, southwards from Gris-Nez, was a graveyard for schooners and other larger vessels of that age of hemp and canvas. The disasters came about because the tides in the area were tricky and the prevailing winds often turned the coast into a lee shore.

No one ever logged the number of lives saved by Lionel Smythe and the young Wyllies but at a later date the Mayor of Wimereux successfully opposed a motion to change the name of the street which led to the Wyllie home from Rue des Anglais to

Rue du Capitaine Faber by recalling the many lives 'ces Anglais' had saved from the wrecks which occurred on the sands and rocks, particularly Les Crans des Oeufs, to the south of Gris-Nez.

The most remarkable rescue the amateur life-guards carried out was when a topsail schooner ran aground and subsequently broke up in one of the fiercest gales anyone could remember. The crew, who could not swim, had already lost the ship's boat and were being watched helplessly from the beach by a crowd which had assembled to witness the spectacle. Lionel, W.L. and Charles when they arrived with their father at once headed into the sea. The local newspaper, *La France du Nord*, told the story on 17 September 1869.

> The three young men, aged 16, 18 and 28, charged into the water. They were knocked down, battered and thrown back. Many times they disappeared into the waves and everyone thought they were lost. The youngest one eventually had to return to the beach but the other two continued to battle on . . . just before they reached the wreck they seemed to falter. Then, with a last effort and to the frenzied cheers of the crew, a rope was thrown to them from the ship and with it they returned to the shore.
>
> Throughout their efforts, which must have seemed to him like eternity, their elderly and worthy father followed, with his eyes and his heart, the endeavours of his intrepid sons ready, all the time, with his own coil of rope to go to their rescue.
>
> Finally, a link was established with the shore and the lives of the seven men aboard the ship were saved. Nor was the rescue effected a moment too soon for almost immediately the ship was rent asunder.

In essence this account is true according to W.L.'s own version of what happened. Amongst those who witnessed the rescue was Prince Jerome Napoleon, a nephew of Bonaparte, who was accompanied by the actress Cora Pearl. Subsequently he invited the rescuers aboard his yacht in Boulogne for a glass of the best brandy in the world.

On the day of the rescue the Wyllies had only just had time to get home and change into dry clothes when they saw, in W.L.'s words, 'another vessel [this time a brig] going headfirst for the shore. Her foresail and foretopsail were blown right out of their bolt ropes. Only the staysail was set on the bowsprit and she ran, in a smother of spindthrift, with glistening sides, before enormous breakers.' The ship, which eventually beached safely enough for the crew to get ashore, was the *Wheatsheaf* of Guernsey. Since no rescue mission was required, W.L. in this case made a study of the event and painted an oil titled *Wreck of the 'Wheatsheaf'*, which received favourable comment in *The Times* of 26 October 1869.

Three years later, in 1872, during another big storm, the house on the shore was washed away and Goody, who was very ill, had to be taken from her bed in a hastily extemporised carrying chair slung between two oars. Wrapped in blankets she was transported across the dunes to the refuge of a friend's house. Sadly she never fully recovered from her illness, which cannot have been improved by the forced retreat from the house she loved. Before the year was out she was dead. She was buried in the cemetery at Wimille.

During the winters in London, and despite his lack of formal education, W.L. had been going to art school. He was first enrolled, at the age of twelve, at Heatherly's and at fifteen he moved on to the Royal Academy Schools. Two years later, in 1868, his first picture was hung in the Academy's Summer Exhibition. He was seventeen and the following year he was awarded the Turner Gold Medal for Landscape.

There seems never to have been any doubt in W. M. Wyllie's mind that his sons were going to earn their living as painters. They were talented; it was his own chosen profession which he enjoyed and I believe he saw no reason why they should not enjoy it too. Nor is there any evidence that they disputed this assumption.

In W.L.'s case there seem to have been only two rather brief periods in his life when he regretted his choice of career. The first occurred when he was twenty-four. It is recalled in a letter written to his wife by the landscape painter Sir David Murray, RA. Wyllie, Sir David said, had told him that he 'was giving up Art altogether for a sea life for which he was sure he fitted'. His reason for renouncing his passion for painting was that, in 1875, the Academy, for the first time in seven years, refused both his submissions for the Summer Exhibition. He had spent two years, he told Murray, working on the pictures. Very handsomely Murray, wanting to encourage an artist in whose ability he had complete faith, bought both pictures sight unseen.

The second occasion that Wyllie ran into hardship was protracted and a lot more painful. It followed his marriage to Marion Amy Carew, the daughter of a Captain in the Royal Indian Marine and granddaughter of the already mentioned General Hearsey. The wedding, in Switzerland in 1879, followed a nine-year courtship which started when little Miss Carew was a girl of ten and W.L. was nineteen. In turn the wedding was followed by a honeymoon which ended with the newlyweds sailing across the Channel from France to England in a fourteen-foot, flat-bottomed, centre-board punt, both being very seasick on the way. They started their married life in a small house at 70 Carlton Hill in London but spent most of their time in the yawl *Ladybird*, a boat which Wyllie had had built in Boulogne. *Ladybird* was a good sea-boat but comfort down below had been sacrificed to the need to make her into a miniature floating studio.

Living aboard this little vessel must have been a tremendous test of the newlyweds' devotion to each other. Marion is on record as saying that at one time she gave up and wept with her head on her hands on the narrow cabin table. Her despair was not without reason, for she was pregnant with her first child. The accommodation was almost as confining as that being experienced by the child she was carrying and it was a lot less comfortable. She and W.L. were also in serious financial difficulties and, for a time, had to live on a diet of gritty hardtack and whelks. The hardtack, the cheapest thing they could buy, was gritty because the large paper sack in which it was delivered had been dropped, had split open on the sandy foreshore and the biscuits had to be picked up and brought on board in a bucket.

The cause of their financial hardship had been a picture dealer who had given promissory notes for the pictures he had received and then failed to honour them.

Wyllie had had to go to a money-lender and had then insisted that this debt be given priority and cleared before anything else. With an iron will he reduced them both to bare subsistence level to achieve this objective.

By the end of 1880 the pair were free of debt and their first son was born to W.L.'s happy cry, 'Mim, dear, I've sold a picture!' It was the first thing he said, before congratulating his wife on her own accomplishment. Thereafter their affairs took an enormous step in the direction, if not of fame and fortune, at least of wide recognition for Wyllie's talents and enough money to enable him and his family to forego, for the rest of their days, a diet of whelks and ship's biscuit.

Working from *Ladybird*, Wyllie was producing a flood of paintings and studies of the London River upon which, initially, his reputation was to be consolidated. He was also doing an increasing amount of work as an illustrator for the *Graphic*. It was an occupation in which he had been engaged, on and off, since the early 1870s. With his debts cleared and growing family responsibilities, he was producing a black and white sketch or more a week for the magazine which had been established to compete with the *Illustrated London News*. Thanks to the Franco-Prussian war coinciding with its launch the *Graphic* was making excellent progress.

Three years after his marriage, now the father of three sons, Wyllie painted the oil picture '*Toil, glitter, grime and wealth on a flowing tide*', which was bought by the Chantrey Bequest for the Tate Gallery and launched him into a close friendship and business relationship with the art dealer Robert Dunthorne, which was to prove most profitable to both of them. Dunthorne commissioned Wyllie to make a big etching of his picture. The subject was the crowded reaches of the Thames below Tower Bridge, and the fascination that this stretch of waterway held for artist and writer alike may be glimpsed in Conrad's description: '. . . in the part called the Pool, the vessels moored stem and stern and in the very strength of the tide formed a solid mass like an island covered with a forest of gaunt leafless trees.'

In 1885 the Wyllies, now with four children, achieved sufficient financial stability to move into the first of their two large, superbly sited homes, Hoo Lodge, which stood on high ground with a sweep of orchards below it ending on the banks of the Medway, with Gillingham and Chatham facing it across the tideway.

At thirty-four, Wyllie was approaching the peak of his creative powers. Like an otter he hunted the Medway and the Nore day after day in *Ladybird*, painting and sketching. In 1888 he took the boat and his wife and eldest son Harold to Holland to sail the rivers and canals, returning to Hoo with fifty, sixty or more paintings. *Ladybird* had already made two voyages on the Dutch canals and knew Holland almost as well as her home river. We have a brief glimpse of her crew at work in this excerpt from a log 'Mim' kept of the yawl's third voyage. *Ladybird*, with her conventional hull and sail plan, narrow-gutted and deep-keeled, was truly amongst strangers in the bluff-bowed Dutch boats of shallow draft.

The day starts with a double reefed mainsail. Tore up the Zuidvliet, which was like a seething cauldron. The water boils under our bow and spray from the crests of the waves makes our faces white with salt. We were soon miles away from Veere. In the gale the sheets seem to turn to iron bars and run through one's hands like fire. One strained at the helm with all one's might yet the boat insists on coming to the wind.

Thinking enough wear has been taken out of the gear for one day we pass the night at Zandkreek. At low tide we are on a soft and shining bed of mud surrounded by curlews, gulls and herons, all as tame as barn door fowls.

As she shows in this log, 'Mim' was no dunce in a boat, a fact she was amply to prove a little later. The only other member of *Ladybird's* crew, seven-year-old Harold, was himself to become a marine artist of distinction.

This third visit to Holland was undertaken as a commission for Dunthorne and, relating to the quoted excerpt from the log, pictures numbered 12, 13, 14 and 15 in the exhibition were titled, respectively, *Gale in Zandkreek*, *After the Gale in Zandkreek*, *Veere, a Dead City*, *Veere from Veergat*. The exhibition, 'Watercolours of the Netherlands Waterways', was held at the Sign of the Rembrandt Head in Vigo Street, London. These entries from the catalogue show both the speed with which Wyllie worked and the way he married the pleasure he got from boats and sailing to his work as an artist. In his love for a wind-driven craft and the snarl or whisper of water under its bow, he was indeed a passionate man. From his childhood days at Wimereux he had been an intimate of the sea.

Before Hoo Lodge the Channel traffic, which had sailed intermittently past Wimereux, formed much busier scenes. On the Medway and the Thames Wyllie saw battleships from Chatham and Sheerness, ocean liners from Tilbury and Surrey Docks, freighters and coasters of all shapes and sizes and, most important of all, the tan sails of Thames barges with which he so often filled his pictures. Barges were his favourite subject, and he knew them in every state of dress and undress, wearing, during high winds, no more than a jackyard topsail, a foresail and a partly brailed mizzen, or during a Thames barge match carrying close to half an acre of canvas. In 1897 the game and hardworked little *Ladybird* went into retirement and was replaced, inevitably, by a Thames barge, *The Four Brothers*, bought in partnership with H. O. Arnold Forster, who later became Minister of War. From this date onwards to his death, Wyllie's life was crowded with incident, almost all of it related to painting, the sea, the 1914–18 war, and warships.

On his arrival at Hoo Lodge, Wyllie's instinct for the sea was converted into a powerful interest in war at sea. While he lived at Hoo he made his first major study of the battle of Trafalgar, painted the Spanish Armada, the battle of the Nile and Blake's engagement with Van Tromp, and exhibited pictures of all these subjects at the Royal Academy in 1891, 1892, 1899 and 1900 respectively.

What awoke such a keen interest in history might well have been the fact that he knew Sir Francis Drake had spent his boyhood aboard a hulk during Edward VI's time, moored off neighbouring Upnor. There it would have been within sight of Hoo Lodge had the building existed at that time. Wyllie also knew that Pepys had noted: 'On June the 10th, 1667, comes news that the Dutch are come up as high as the Nore.' In fact the Hollanders came much further. They were only turned back at Upnor Castle and the impression their action and their fire ships must have made on anyone watching the events from the top of the hill where Hoo Lodge now stands would have been spectacular. There too, as close as the telescope could bring them, were Chatham and Sheerness, on the other bank of the Medway, stiff with warships and hulks bearing memories of prisoners of war from the Napoleonic period. Both are reflected in Wyllie's watercolours of that time. Maritime history was to be his burden for the next thirty and more years.

When daylight waned, Wyllie – who never painted by artificial light – buried himself in Hakluyt, Pepys and the works of a host of other authors such as William Smith who wrote of Rochester in 1588 and authorities such as Barham, Collingwood, Dillon, St Vincent and other seamen-autobiographers as well as naval historians too numerous to mention. When he painted battle scenes his concern was always to render on canvas the historical truth. The position of every ship was plotted by endless cross-referencing, and its specifications checked with studies of old sail and rigging plans and blueprints. This obsession with historical accuracy reached its ultimate fulfilment in Portsmouth in the last years of Wyllie's life, with the painting of the vast *Panorama of the Battle of Trafalgar*.

Before making his final move, however, Wyllie continued to work like a man possessed. He was made an Associate of the Royal Academy in 1889, and between 1888 and 1906 he exhibited no less than sixty-three pictures at the Summer Exhibitions at Burlington House. In 1888 alone he exhibited in Dunthorne's and the Fine Art Society's Galleries 131 new watercolours made on the trip to Holland and during a cruise aboard HMS *Black Prince*.

The next year he sailed along the west coast of Scotland in a new yacht, *Grey Mare*, and sold all the resulting watercolours to Brown and Phillips who exhibited them in a gallery in Glasgow where they were 'a great success'. The next year's paintings were done in the Pas de Calais and Italy. Year in year out, Wyllie was also always in demand by the shipping companies and many of his cruises* were paid for with paintings of the cruise lines' ships. At the same time the cruises yielded a profit in pictures sold to passengers. Thus he sailed on their maiden voyages aboard the *Majestic* and the *Teutonic* (on the latter, in 1889, in select company to attend the review at Spithead where the Prince of Wales visited the ship). He cruised to the West Indies, when some of the passengers and crew died of yellow fever. He went to Norway and the Baltic and made at least two cruises in the Mediterranean. He sailed to Santa Pola to witness and draw the total eclipse of the sun. In 1883 he had been to Alexandria to make studies for a picture of the bombardment of the approaches to that city by a British fleet under Admiral Sir Beauchamp Seymour. For the *Graphic*, for which he continued to make black and white sketches, he painted the opening of

*See Chronology beginning on page 39 for dates.

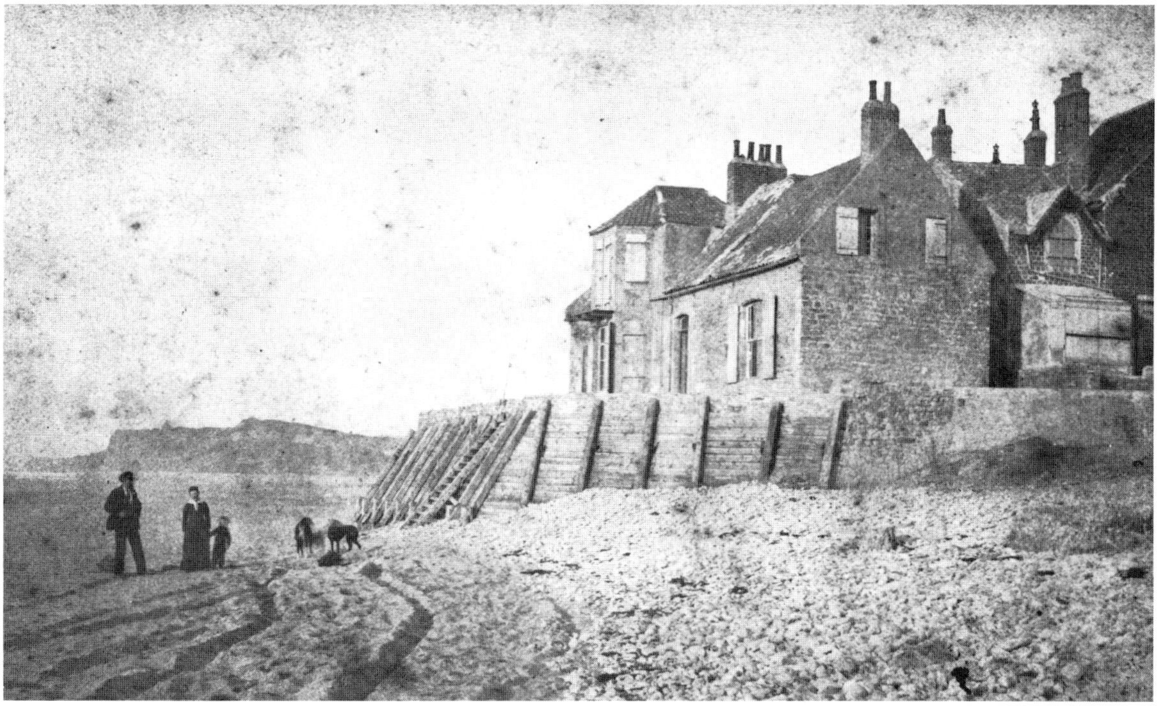

The Wyllies' house at Wimereux, early 1870s; the figures on the left are probably Lionel Smythe and his family

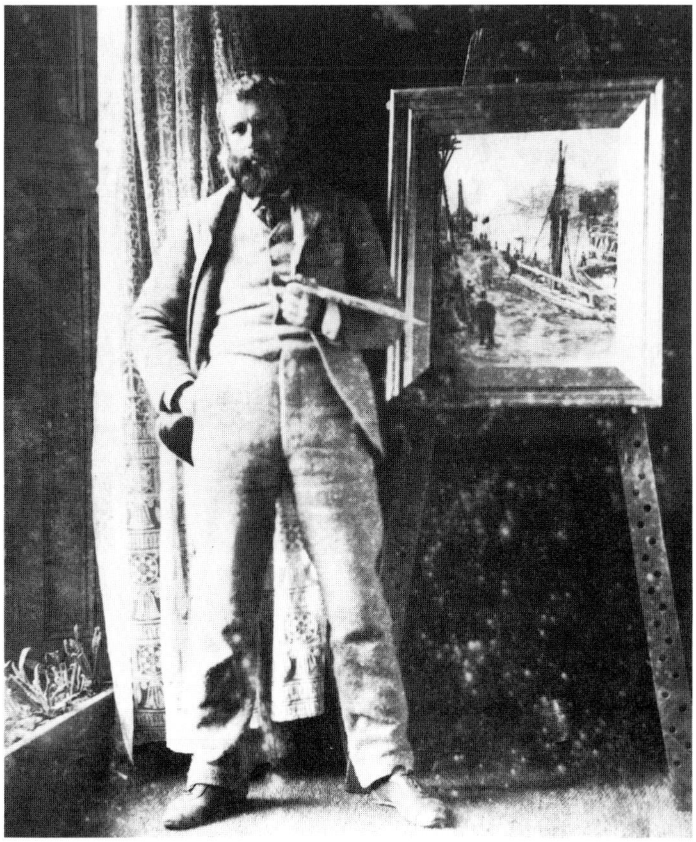

W. L. Wyllie with his painting *Gabriel's Wharf*, exhibited in 1886

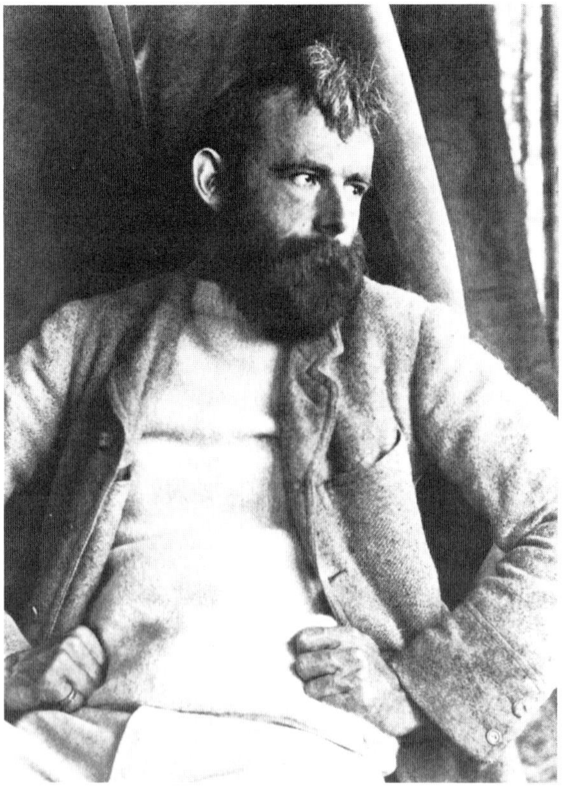

W. L. Wyllie, *c.* 1889

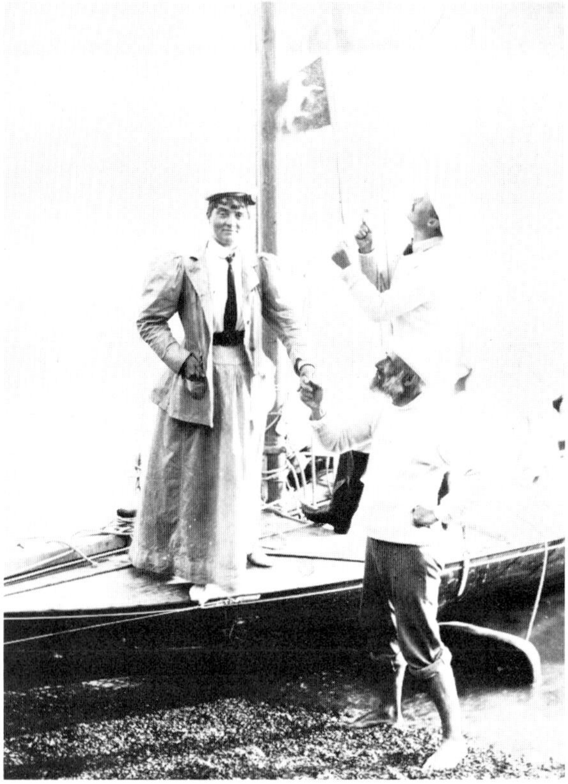

After a race: Wyllie congratulating his wife, *c.* 1898

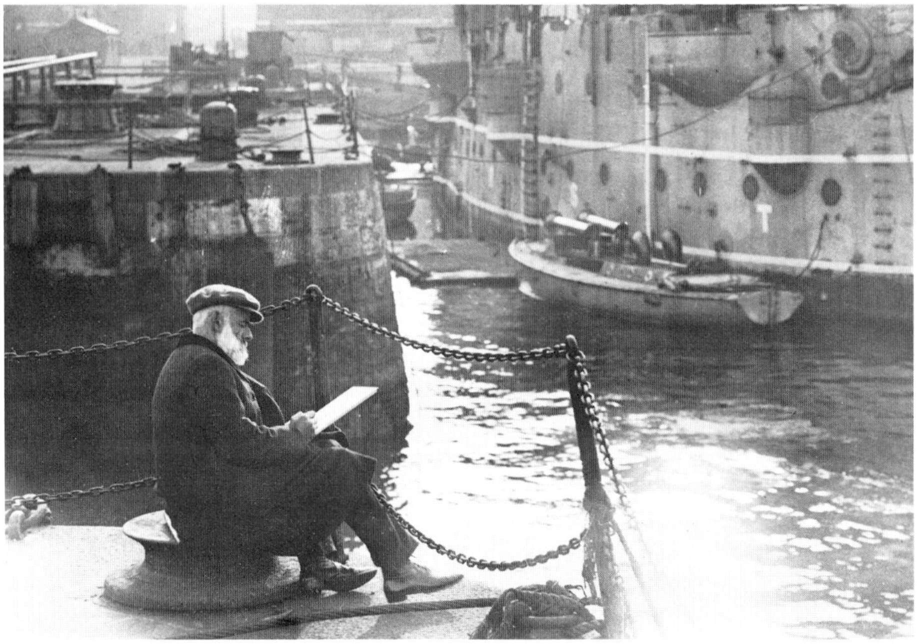

Wyllie drawing HMS *Hero* – later blown up in gunnery practice – at Portsmouth, winter 1907/8

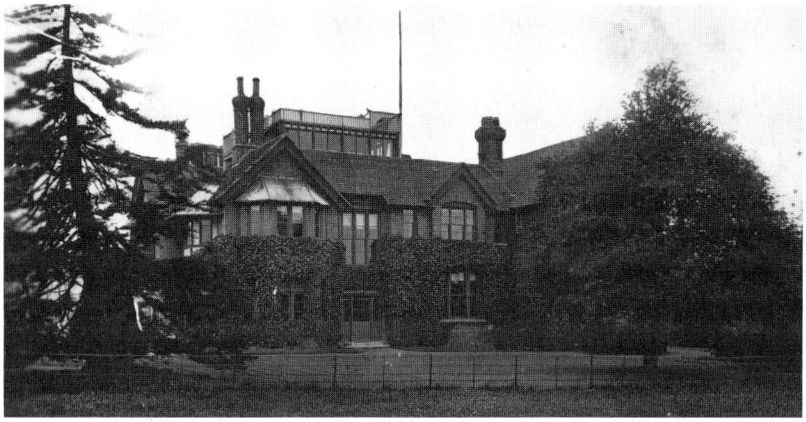
Hoo Lodge, *c.* 1910, showing Wyllie's studio at the top of the house, from which the artist had a commanding view of the Medway

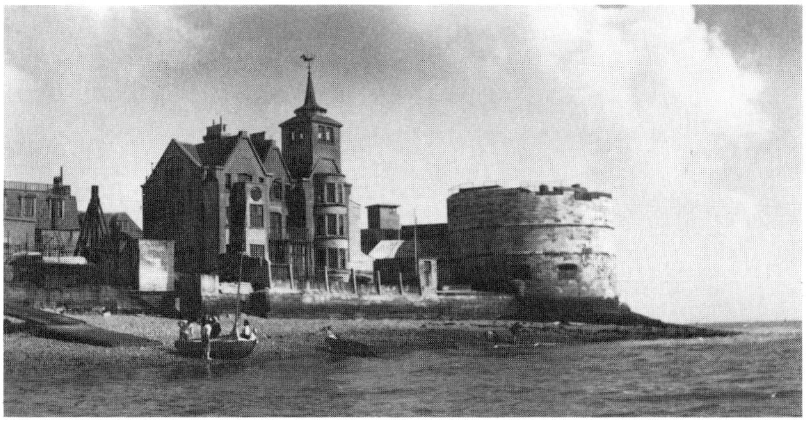
The Tower House, Portsmouth at low tide

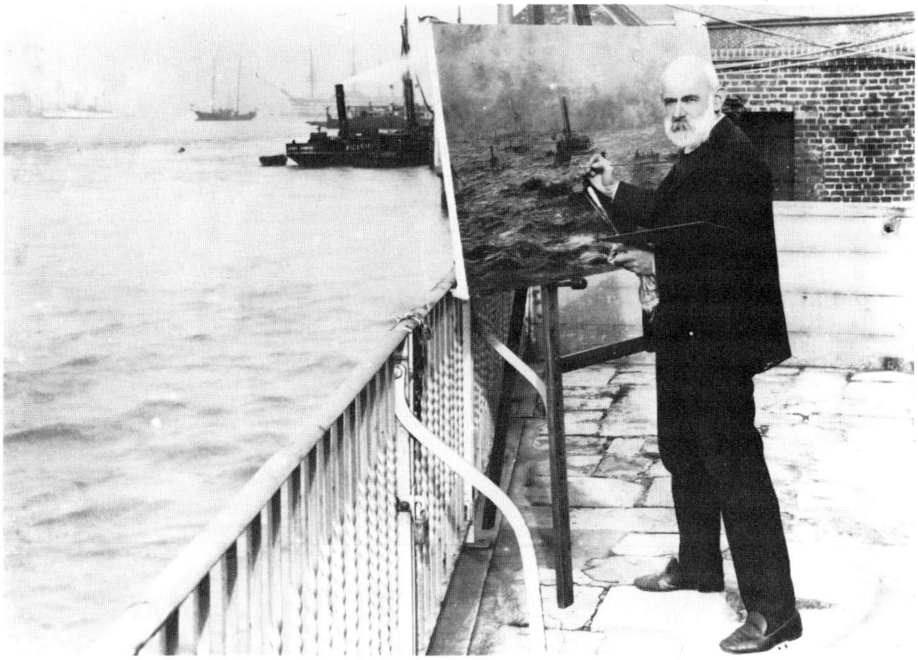
Wyllie painting on the terrace of the Tower House, *c.* 1912

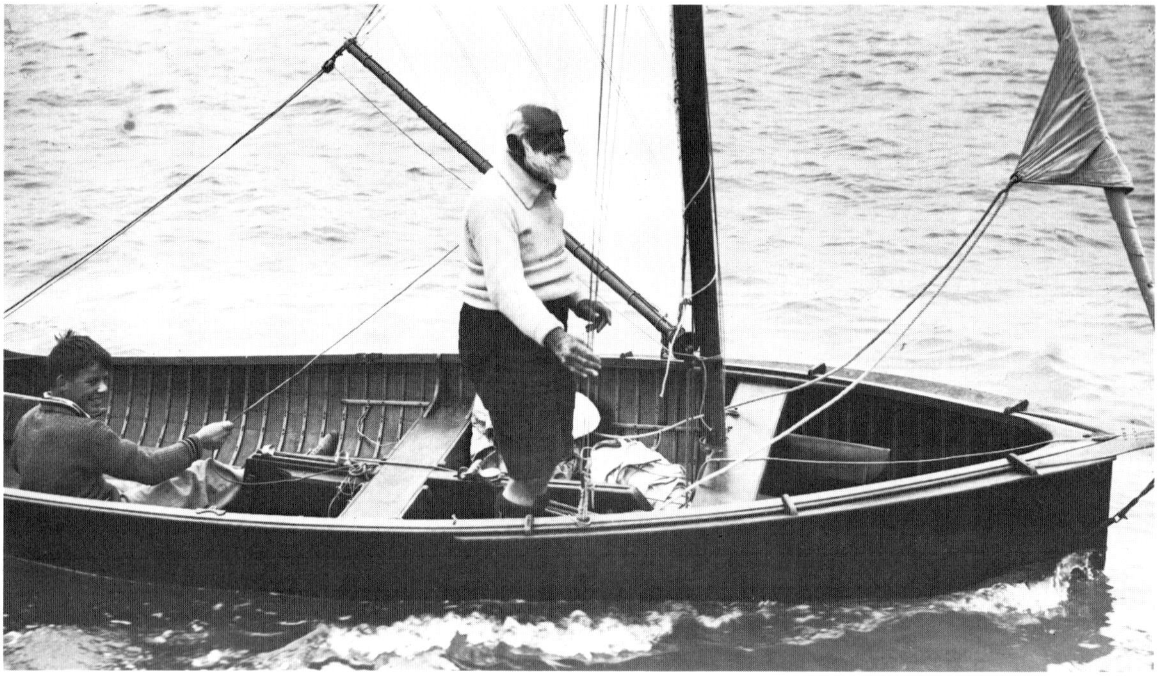

W. L. in one of the 14-foot International dinghies he designed, after winning a race at Cowes in 1927. His grandson John Wyllie, co-author of this book, is sailing the boat

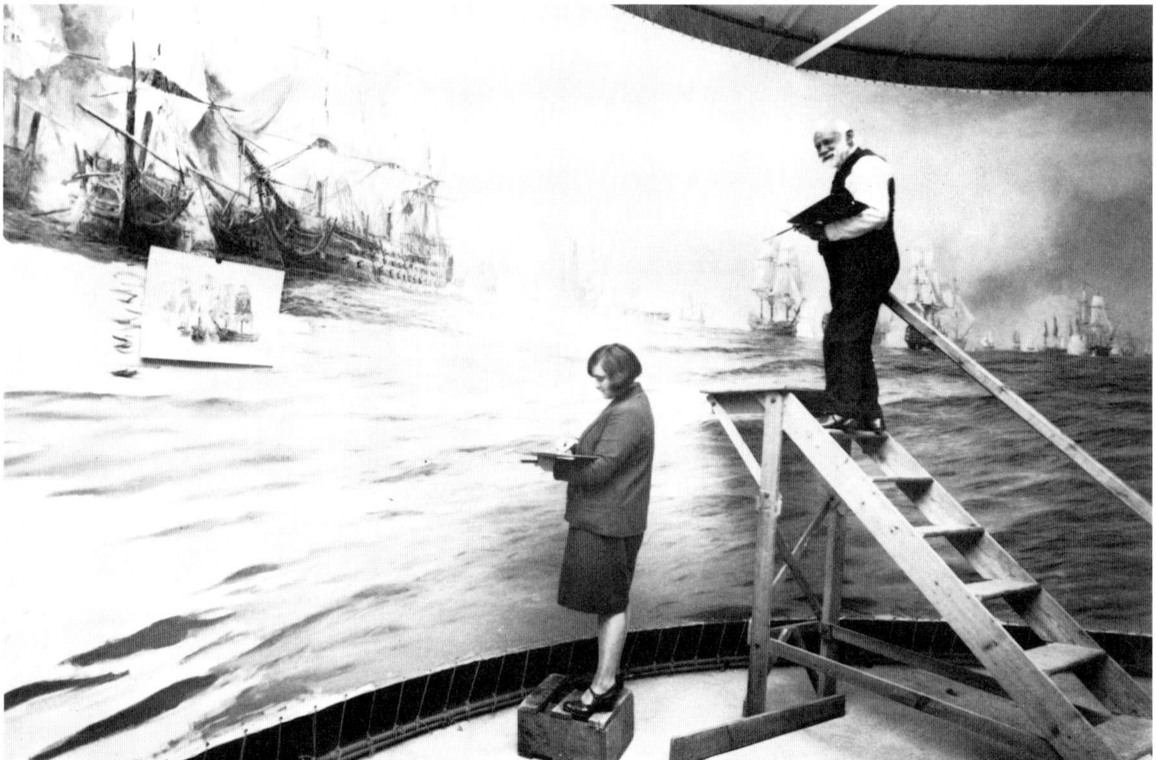

Painting the *Panorama of the Battle of Trafalgar*, Portsmouth, 1930; W. L. with his daughter Aileen

Tower Bridge (he also made an oil from this study for the Academy and for Sir John Wolfe-Barry, the designer), the opening of the Kiel canal and the marine aspect of the ceremonies relating to the funeral of Queen Victoria. Earlier, for Victoria and for the Princess Royal (both commissions came at the same time), he had painted pictures of the new Royal Yacht *Britannia* and a third picture of the same subject called *Butterflies and Working Bees*, now in the Royal Corinthian Yacht Club, showing *Britannia* competing against the Kaiser's *Valkyrie*.

This last subject brings this account of Wyllie's life around the turn of the century back to Hoo and a sailing race in which he played the principal part as co-designer of the boat and as her skipper. The race caused a considerable stir at the time and led to special trains being run from London to Chatham to accommodate would-be spectators.

The contest resulted from a challenge issued by an Australian, Mark Foy, owner of the champion Sydney Harbour boat *Irex*. On behalf of British yachtsmen generally, and as Commodore of the Medway Yacht Club specifically, Wyllie accepted the challenge, designed with Lynton Hope a boat he called the *Maid of Kent*, and had it built in a month by Gill & Sons of Rochester who were famed for their construction . . . of Thames barges!

Given that the event took place in an age when it was generally held that a woman's place was anywhere but in small boats, the most unique aspect of the whole affair was that, while Wyllie was sailing-master and skipper, the hand on the tiller was his wife's. This outraged the Australians who were afraid that if they lost it would be a day of infamy for them. They lost. Mrs Wyllie sailed *Maid of Kent* to victory in three straight races despite the fact that her boat carried only 500 square feet of canvas to the 4,000 square feet of the challenger. The Australians might have been a little less contemptuous of their crop-headed female opponent in her 'skimming dish' (which, of course, met all the rules they had laid down for the design) and her painter/yacht-designer husband if they had studied their competitors' form sheet. They would have seen that in another Wyllie-designed boat they had had fourteen wins and one second place in their last fifteen races.

Wyllie's work was largely an extension of the man. He lived what he painted and did not seek to abstract himself from the general body of the people who surrounded him. Politically, and to a large degree culturally, his values were similar to those of the educated middle class among whom he lived. He thought well of Kipling (who also had problems with arithmetic), Stevenson, Dickens and Galsworthy and in his lighter moments he read Conan Doyle, Buchan, 'Bartimeus' and Rider Haggard as people today read Deighton and Le Carré. He believed without reservation in the Imperial power of Britain, in the Empire and, most importantly, the Royal Navy.

When in 1907 he and his family moved to a house in Portsmouth, the event had the smooth rightness and finality of a well greased bolt shooting home. The new

Wyllie home was called Tower House; the basic street plan around the house had not changed for at least 500 years, and indeed it is still the same today. The narrow alley backing the house runs as it would have run in 1418 when construction started on the massive Round Tower which stands adjacent to the house on the southward side.

Beside this fortress, in 1522, the first of several 'mightie chaines of yron' closing off the mouth of the harbour was hauled home on capstans, and Capstan Yard still stands separating Tower House from its massive neighbour. It was there that, some time in the eighteenth century, the man who became William IV of England, then a young prince and midshipman, is reported to have had a bloody fist fight. In a pub he had provocatively drunk a glass of beer that belonged to a young waterman. The latter, not knowing the identity of the thief, challenged the king-to-be to a bout of fisticuffs and left him with a black eye and a bleeding nose.

Wyllie rented Capstan Yard from the municipality and made it an extension of his property. He also rented a narrow strip of beach on the other side of the house as a storage place for his boats. One day, when I was ten years old, my grandfather took one of them and rowed across the entrance of the harbour and back while I swam beside him. It was the test I had to pass before I was allowed to go sailing alone in a dinghy which bore the ominous name of *Sudden Death* because it turned over so easily.

The quarter-mile wide strip of waterway across which I had swum had seen the passage of Phoenicians and, after them down the ages, uncountable types and numbers of ships of war. Inevitably, enemies came to Old Portsmouth, as the Germans came in the Second World War, and attacked the entrance of the harbour where the Round Tower and the Wyllie house still stand; the first of such assaults to be recorded took place in 1337 when Nicholas Behuchet led invaders ashore at the beginning of the Hundred Years War.

From the dawn of his interest in maritime history, Wyllie had been an admirer of Nelson, and now he lived within a stone's throw of the Sally Port where that indomitable little man had embarked many times. Five minutes up the road from his house was the inn where Nelson had quite often stayed as a senior officer. Less than five minutes down the road the other way was another inn where Nelson as a very junior officer had, as was the custom of the time, used a diamond ring to cut his name on one of the windows. Both inns were demolished by German bombs. Finally, the house was in sight of the *Victory*, which then lay to a buoy a short distance up the harbour.

Wyllie, then, was surrounded by historical sites and lived in a neighbourhood which in the early 1900s was dominated by the Navy, the Marines and the Army. There was obviously something about the military that appealed to him. In the furore of patriotism whipped up during the Boer War he had joined the Territorials – there was no RNR in those days – and he continued with them when he moved to Portsmouth, becoming a Captain in the Hants RE(T). At that time he was close to sixty, and he retired in the early summer of 1914 to make room for younger volunteers. It was as well he did, otherwise when the First World War broke out in August he might have found his loyalties divided, for it is certain that the sea was his first and only true love. It is also certain that he had the same instincts which made Cartier-Bresson and Margaret Bourke White great battle photographers. He wanted to be personally involved in the action so that, as he showed with his paintings of Trafalgar and other sea fights, what he set down in paint on paper or canvas was as near the truth as possible. Unhappily during the First World War he had to settle for second best, getting the stories of the battles at second-hand. He could, however, do what neither Cartier-Bresson nor White could do, visually reconstruct the battles after they had been fought.

To this end, and since he already had the reputation to reach such people, he developed contacts not only with the men who fought the battles but, more essentially, with the men who commanded those who did the fighting. Such was the strictness of the censorship at that time that without the co-operation and permission of such men he would not have been allowed to go to sea, or to visit the battlefields in France. Indeed, without permission he would not even have been allowed to paint the pictures. Amongst the remnants of his correspondence (most of his papers and over forty large paintings were destroyed by bombs in the Second World War), there are letters he received from Jellicoe, Beatty, Haig, Trenchard and other military and naval leaders.

The 1914–18 war, therefore, saw Wyllie painting with redoubled energy and output, and always he was badgering eyewitnesses for details of the events he had chosen or had been commissioned to paint. The 101 illustrations made with this attention to detail included in the two books he illustrated and co-authored about the sea battles of the First World War* are only a fraction of the work he did in this field. It is interesting to note that the preface to the second volume states: 'Mr W. L. Wyllie RA cruised in all types of craft of the Royal Navy from the largest and newest of the Super-Dreadnoughts and battle cruisers to submarines, "Q" ships and motor launches.'

A list of the titles of the pictures exhibited at the Royal Academy in 1915 and 1916 gives some indication of the variety of his subjects:

Bringing in the wounded Lion. A damaged battle-cruiser being towed into Scapa Flow.

Portsmouth in war time: mine sweepers putting to sea.

The fighting line from Ypres to the sea. A bird's eye view from about 5,000 feet of an air battle going on over the salient and such infamous places as Hill 60 and the British and German fire trenches; those at the bottom of the picture were drawn from maps issued to the men engaged in the fighting. For the pictures he painted of air battles Wyllie also had on-the-spot sketches made by his son Harold, who as a pilot survived the war in the air, with distinction, for over three years.

*See 'Books Illustrated, Written or Co-Authored by W. L. Wyllie', page 139.

The armed liner 'Carmania' engaging the 'Cap Trafalgar' off Trinidade. A battle between two armed merchantmen. On one of his pre-war cruises the ship in which Wyllie was travelling had docked near the *Cap Trafalgar*, the German vessel in the fight, and he had made sketches of her.

Spotting for the Fleet, Dardanelles. Another bird's eye view showing an early type of sea-plane flying over the Turkish coast in the vicinity of the narrows.

Master of the Sea. Ships of the British Fleet in being.

A fight to the finish: off Coronel, 1st November 1914. An early naval engagement in which the British lost two obsolescent cruisers. For first-hand information on the battle Wyllie had access to a letter written by Lieutenant Count von Spee, the son of the Admiral, who was gunnery officer aboard the cruiser *Nürnberg*, one of the German cruisers engaged in the battle.

The Hooge salient. Another perspective of the fighting in France with another air battle being fought, at eye-level, between British and German aircraft. In all a total of twenty-two of Wyllie's war pictures were exhibited at the Royal Academy.

After the end of hostilities, though he had passed the peak of his creative capabilities, Wyllie occupied a pinnacle which was far removed from that of any of his contemporary Academicians. He was still a master craftsman in the use of watercolours and etching tools but he was also, now, a recognised authority on everything pertaining to the sea. Evidence underlining this fact had already been signalled when he was asked to take the chair at the first meeting of the nascent Society for Nautical Research in 1910. In post-war England he was often called upon to contribute his knowledge to various nautical projects. For him, the most important of these was his being asked to sit on the committee to study what steps should be taken to restore Nelson's *Victory* to the condition she had been in in 1805. This resulted in a recommendation signed by W.L. and his son Harold, a simple, straightforward and impressive document which proposed over twenty major alterations.

My grandfather's interest in painting the picture he called *A Panorama of the Battle of Trafalgar* had been expressed as far back as the centenary of the action in 1905. Then the suggestion was that a fitting place for it to be displayed would be Trafalgar Square and there is still an echo of that suggestion in the fact that there is a copy of the work he eventually painted on the wall of the present Trafalgar Square post office. The painting was not commissioned but was the work of a 79-year-old man executed entirely on his own initiative as his contribution to what became the Victory Museum, an institution which helped to pay for the famous flagship's reconstruction and her maintenance today by attracting fee-paying visitors. The work, which was unveiled by King George V in 1930, measures 42 feet by 12 feet and it took the artist thirteen months to complete it.

He was helped in the painting by his daughter Aileen and by Captain Hugh

Taylor, RN who planned and made diagrams of the whole battle, spending months reading French, Spanish and English accounts of what each ship was doing at the particular moment of battle depicted in the scene. The Panorama is viewed through the carefully depicted stern cabin of the French ship *Neptune*, which was built by local shipwrights and carpenters. This immense canvas stands as a memorial to a man who always found self-fulfilment in stretching his mind and skills to recreate in line and paint the world he saw about him and all men, past and present, who 'occupy their business in great waters'.

My grandfather died as he was putting the finishing touches to one of the three pictures that were hung, after his death, in the 1931 Summer Exhibition at Burlington House. He was 80 years old and his funeral was invested with unusual ceremony. Appropriately, given that the victorious Admiral at Trafalgar was one of the most passionate interests in his life, HMS *Nelson* provided a cutter. It was manned by the Sea Scouts from the troop which he had founded, many of them by then grown men. Thus his coffin was rowed up the harbour to Porchester Castle where he was buried in the graveyard of the little Norman church which stands within its walls.

His wife said of him, 'Extreme simplicity was the keynote of Bill's life.'

To that view I would add that he was a man without false pride, and one who took his social and family responsibilities very seriously. From his early youth, when his earnings were put in the family coffer by his father, to the end of his days when his wife, with his consent and co-operation, followed virtually the same course, he was a very frugal man who spent his comparative wealth on others but not himself. At the same time he had a great compassion for any of his fellow men when they were physically handicapped, suffering and in need of help. To them the door of his house was always open; to such an extent that beggars instinctively knew him for 'a soft touch'. He also had a strong sense of what might be called 'other men's rights'. Finally, he had a vigour and vitality that were exceptional but never flamboyant. This was a feature of his character that I remember best from one particular incident. We were racing at Cowes and lying second to Uffa Fox, the prince of all dinghy sailors at that time.

It was a day of strong winds which were blowing against the tide and churning up a nasty steep lop. The lee gunnel was in the water and W.L., seventy-five or seventy-six at the time, and I were both sitting the boat up. It was before the days of the trapeze and I was as far out as I could get while he was still urging me to get out further. My head was below the level of the weather gunnel and all I could see between the sheets of spray was the old man, looking surprisingly burly in the two or three sweaters that my grandmother had insisted he wear.

'That's a good boy. That's good. We are pointing better than he is.' We were gaining. Uffa Fox, however, had no intention of letting us improve our position.

We heard a warning shout from his boat, 'I'm going about.' We had not established an overlap, barely fifteen feet separated the two boats and we were both on the port tack. Uffa Fox's manoeuvre meant that we would have to bear off and then match his swift swing through something rather less than ninety degrees to maintain our advantageous position on his weather quarter.

'You heard him,' my grandfather shouted, eased the sheet a fraction, bore away and then put the helm down. Dinghies, when they go about, pivot almost instantly on their centreboards. For a fraction of a wild moment, there was slatting canvas and scramble as the boat came about. Somehow I made it. It meant jack-knifing my body to get under the boom, across the boat and up on the other gunnel, letting go and then hauling in the jib sheet as the boat picked up way on the other tack, and again getting as far out as I could. My grandfather had accomplished the same feat of athleticism, and when I looked his way I saw him, as ever, through sheets of spray. He was laughing out of sheer exhilaration. A white-bearded old pirate trading broad-sides with a smart and much respected younger enemy and enjoying every second of it. We did not win but now, over fifty years on, that memory of him typifies, for me, a characteristic of the man with which anyone who knew him must have been most familiar – his single-minded zest for whatever occupation he had in mind or in hand.

CHRONOLOGY

1851 Born 5 July; Albany Street, London. Son of Katherine (née Benham) and William Morison Wyllie. Katherine Benham already had a son, Lionel Percy Smythe (1839–1918), and a daughter, Minnie. W.M.W. well-read and educated at Harrow. Later, date unknown, the family moved to 36 Gloucester Crescent, London, then a newly built house in green fields.

c.1853 Charles William Wyllie (brother, 1853–1923) born.

c.1863 Takes lessons at Heatherly's Art School in Maddox Street, London.

1865 For reasons of W.L.'s health the Wyllies spending the summers in Boulogne and in this year W.M.W. buys a Napoleonic guardhouse overlooking Ambleteuse harbour.

1866 Enters Royal Academy Schools of Art.

1868 First picture *Dover Castle and Town* hung in the RA.

1869 Wins Turner Gold Medal for Landscape with *Dawn after a Storm.* When brig is wrecked near Wimereux, takes part in dramatic rescue of crew. Later a second wreck on the same day provides him with subject *Wreck of the 'Wheatsheaf'*.

1870 Meets Marion Amy Carew then ten years old, later to become his wife, in Boulogne. Starts drawing for the *Graphic.*

1871 Visits and sketches scenes in Portsmouth where he finally makes his home.

1872 The Wyllie residence 'on the shore', bought some years after the Napoleonic guardhouse, collapses into the sea. Katherine Wyllie (mother) dies.

1873 *Ladybird,* Wyllie's first substantial yacht, a yawl, built and launched at Boulogne. Soon afterwards makes his first cruise to Holland in her.

1875 RA refuses two pictures and Wyllie declares that he is going to give up art and go to sea.

1876 Officially engaged to Marion Amy Carew. She is 16. Walker Gallery, Liverpool purchases *Blessing the Sea.*

1877 Again cruises and paints in Holland.

1878 Joins M. A. Carew in Switzerland.

1879 Marries M. A. Carew in Switzerland. They set up house in London at 70 Carlton Hill.

1880 First son, Harold, born in London. Wyllie cheated by picture dealer and suffers financial hardship.

1882 Second son, Bill, born in London.

1883 *'Toil, glitter, grime and wealth'* bought for the Chantrey Bequest. Begins long association with the dealer

Dunthorne with the commission of an etching of this picture. Commissioned by the Fine Art Society to paint the bombardment of Alexandria and makes studies on the spot. Third son, Dick, born in London.

1884 Family moves to Gillingham House, Chatham. Holds one-man exhibition at Fine Art Society, Bond Street. *Tidal Thames* illustrated by Wyllie and written by Grant Allen, published by Cassell, coincides with exhibition of the same title of 73 pictures at Fine Art Society. Doing much of his work from *Ladybird* as has been his practice over the past four – five years. May issue of *Magazine of Art* eulogises his work. Wyllies return to live in London at the end of the year.

1885 Daughter, Eva, born. In June family moves to Hoo Lodge in the Hundred of Hoo, Kent. Paints landscapes for RA.

1886 Son, Robert, born. Designs class of yachts for Gillingham YC 'for men who have no money to spend on expensive boats': these were single-handed, said to have been 'very wet'. During this and the next two years devotes much time to developing designs for small yachts. Also develops a friendship with Sir Philip Watts, designer of war ships.

1888 Makes his third trip to Holland in *Ladybird*, accompanied by his wife and son Harold as crew. M.A. writes *Log of the Ladybird* and Dunthorne shows sixty-two watercolours made on this expedition. Three pictures submitted to the RA for the Summer Exhibition are rejected.

1889 The Wyllies cruise the West Coast of Scotland in the new Glasgow built yacht *Grey Mare*. All pictures resulting from this cruise are sold to the Glasgow dealers Brown and Phillips. Sixty-nine watercolours made on the cruise aboard HMS *Black Prince* are shown at the Fine Art Society. Elected ARA.

1890 The Fine Art Society commissions a visit to the Pas de Calais for an exhibition which eventually includes drawings made in Italy earlier in the year. Colour-lithograph poster of SS *Dunottar Castle* sent to the Great Exhibition, Chicago, and placed amongst the watercolours in the Exhibition Art Gallery.

1891 Receiving many commissions from steamship companies and given free accommodation aboard the *Majestic* and *Teutonic* on their maiden voyages. Starts long association with the RNLI as painter and influences choice of colours for their new lifeboats.

1893 Cruise aboard Orient Line *Garonne* to West Indies nearly ends in disaster when some passengers and crew die of yellow fever. Cruise is extended to Mediterranean as compensation to passengers and results in watercolours of the Mediterranean in addition to those made crossing the Atlantic (twice) and in the West Indies.

1894 Major exhibition at Bond Street galleries of Dowdeswell shows pictures of West Indies, Atlantic, Mediterranean, Solent, Thames and includes two pictures of the Royal Yacht *Britannia* painted, one for Queen Victoria and the other for the Princess Royal, as gifts for the Prince of Wales. *Butterflies and Working Bees* (now at the Royal Corinthian YC), showing *Britannia* competing with *Valkyrie*, is painted this year, as is *London's Water Gate* (the opening of Tower Bridge). The latter results in a life-long friendship with the Tower Bridge architect Sir John Wolfe-Barry who will commission and buy many of his paintings.

1895 Represents the *Graphic* at the opening of the Kiel Canal and in partnership with Arnold Foster purchases the Thames barge *New Zealand* which is reconstructed and renamed *The Four Brothers*.

1896 Makes studies of Thames barges and other shipping trapped in the ice on the Medway and paints his first major picture of Trafalgar for the RA. Visits Italy with wife and father.

1898 Accepts, on behalf of Medway YC, a challenge to meet *Irex*, champion Sydney Harbour boat, in a series of five races. Designs and has *Maid of Kent* built and with M.A. at the helm defeats the challenger in three straight races. The contest attracts much public interest and special trains are run to Chatham to accommodate would-be spectators.

1899 Second picture, *The Battle of the Nile*, bought for the Tate Gallery.

1900 Joins expedition to Santa Pola to witness total eclipse of the sun. Paints Blake's battle with Van Tromp for RA.

1901 Makes studies of pageantry surrounding Queen Victoria's death. Major oil of subject bought by Walker Gallery, Liverpool. Also makes big etching of the subject and scores critical success with RA painting entitled *Bolivar*. Agnews holds exhibition (including nine studies of Queen Victoria's funeral and nine pictures of Manchester Ship Canal). Cassell's publish *Marine Painting in Water-Colour*. Fifth son, Eric, born.

1902 Celebrates end of Boer war with painting of apple blossom with Medway in the distance, *Blackberry Square*. Writes and illustrates *Nature's Laws and the Making of Pictures*, published by Edward Arnold.

1904 Second daughter, Aileen, born.

1905 *London to the Nore* published by A. & C. Black. Wyllie marks Trafalgar centenary with painting of the battle and etchings. Cruises Norway with M.A. to produce text and illustrations for another book, *Norway and its Fjords*. Edition de luxe of *London to the Nore* presented to King Edward VII. Also published this year is a biography of J. M. W. Turner published by George Bell. Makes studies at Spithead and paints oil of French fleet's visit to England, titled *L'Entente Cordiale*.

1906 Paints a large (4 by 12 foot) historical tableau for the 4th Batallion Queen's Own Royal West Kents. Wyllies now move to Portsmouth.

1907 Entire issue of Christmas edition of *Art Journal* is devoted to Wyllie and his work following his appointment as RA. Establishes first troop of Sea Scouts in Portsmouth. On second cruise to Norway reaches Spitsbergen and the North Cape. Appointed Captain, Hants Fortress, RE(T). Makes studies, carries out experiments and does drawings relating to his theories about origin of craters on the moon and sends results to Astronomer Royal.

1908 Cassell publish *Sketchbook*.

1914–19 Few precise dates for his period. Resigns commission in Territorials a few weeks before war breaks out and throughout the war years paints, etches and makes studies without remission. Twenty-two pictures of the war are exhibited over six years at the RA. Goes to sea with the Navy; fights storms which frequently swamp the ground floor of his home; visits the rear echelon areas of the Western Front where he makes studies; writes and illustrates two books, *Sea Fights of the Great War* and *More Sea Fights of the Great War*; paints a panel of the landings at Zeebrugge for the Royal Exchange and innumerable other pictures of sea, air and land battles. Over a hundred watercolours, drawings and etchings are included in the two books mentioned above.

1920 Commissioned to paint the arrival of the Japanese Fleet in British waters. Picture and Wyllie are presented to Prince Hirohito. Another painting has been presented earlier to the Heir Apparent, on his marriage, by officers of the Imperial Japanese Navy.

1922 Invited to join the 'Save the Victory' Committee.

1924 Starts making studies for the 42 by 12 foot panorama of Trafalgar. Cruises to France and along the south coast on barge yacht *Cawana*.

1929 At age 78 is still selling very well despite the Depression. Sells all three RA paintings. Meets Prince Takamatsu at the latter's request. Continues to design and sail dinghies. Golden wedding celebrated. Starts work full-time on *Panorama*. Elected Hon. Vice-President of the Society for Nautical Research.

1930 King George V unveils *Panorama*. RA shows studies made for the picture.

1931 While in London putting finishing touches to three pictures for the RA Exhibition, staying with friends who have taken over Heatherly's Art School, collapses and dies of heart failure. Buried in the graveyard of the Norman Church inside Porchester Castle.

ART

by Roger Quarm

1

'On the Shore': 1860-1880

The remarkable Wyllie family of artists – the father, William Morison Wyllie, the stepson Lionel Percy Smythe, and the brothers William Lionel Wyllie and Charles William Wyllie – and the life they led in the summer months during the 1860s on the northern coast of France, have already been described by my co-author in the first part of this book.

William Morison Wyllie knew both the 'handsome, curly headed boy' Millais, 'who painted wonderfully spirited pictures partly in the style of old Frost the Academician', and Dante Gabriel Rossetti who 'used to try to draw like John Gilbert' and made several drawings in W.M.'s sketchbook.[1] But he was not in England when the Pre-Raphaelite brotherhood was formed in the autumn of 1848, and whether or not his ideals coincided with those of the brotherhood is not clear. One suspects from his gruff nature that such pure ideals may not have been to his taste. In 1848 he left England to study in Antwerp, making copies after Rubens, and in Paris he learned to paint in 'the fashion of Le Jeune' though 'traces of the teaching of Cabanel' showed themselves.[2]

The Wyllies' decision, soon after their marriage, to spend half of each year on the French coast near Boulogne, which was easily accessible from London, provided an environment which was to have an enormous influence on the young W. L. Wyllie. The journey itself offered the child his first taste of sea, ships and shipping, as W. L. Wyllie himself recalls:

> *Panther* or *Rainbird* would carry the family for 12s.6d. each all down the crowded reaches of the Thames. What a different river it was in those days! Tiers of colliers six and eight abreast lined both sides of the waterway, and the brigs and schooners of that faraway time banked and filled up what was left of the channel.[3]

W. M. Wyllie is best known for the large pictures he later painted of the members of the House of Lords and Commons in 1879, but his real interest was genre (sometimes of a humorous kind) and he was capable of painting extremely sensitive landscapes and seascapes.

In the mid-1860s the landscape and genre painter Charles James Lewis (1830–92) came to live near the Wyllies in France. Lewis seems to have been a stimulating force for the whole group of artists, not only for W. M. Wyllie, but also Lionel Smythe and the 'boys' William and Charles. Lewis was an 'enthusiastic worker from Nature, had a very refined eye for colour and drew with great feeling, though he was a weak draughtsman when he ventured on figure subjects, never having had proper training.' According to W. L. Wyllie he produced his best work when working directly from nature, and was 'so loud in his praises of the beauties of Nature that it was only natural that the younger man [Smythe] should try to follow his teaching'.[4] And it is very likely, too, that Lewis's attitudes should have affected the young Wyllie who throughout his life was an unrelenting worker from nature.

Despite Smythe's eleven years' seniority, he and the young W. L. Wyllie were particularly close both as brothers and as artists during the 1860s. Smythe influenced his younger half-brother both stylistically and by example. He first exhibited at the Royal Academy in 1863, when Wyllie was twelve. During the 1860s, when Smythe was in his twenties, he joined Lewis and W. M. Wyllie on their long sketching excursions along the French coast. His subjects, genre and landscape, or more precisely figures in landscape, were poetic, meticulously observed and delicately painted, and he is linked 'in thought, sentiment, and to some extent method' with his friend J. W. North and with Frederick Walker.[5]

It is against a background, then, of a small community of artists, with common training and ideals, who for a greater part of the year ranged the coast of Northern France on long sketching excursions drawing and painting similar if not identical subjects, landscape and coastal views, that the vigorous, determined character of Wyllie may first be glimpsed.

Wyllie's ease and fluency of production were evident very early, although the artistic family in which he was brought up did not immediately take his efforts seriously:

> Willie was . . . about four; Lionel was sixteen, and had begun to paint in earnest. He had the greatest admiration for his small half brother, who, as soon as he could hold a pencil, began to draw. He used to state what the subject was going to be and then set to work, but was not taken seriously until his drawings were seen to be really like the object they claimed to represent.[6]

At the age of about twelve, Wyllie was making very competent efforts. That this is so may be seen in a small, dramatic watercolour, *Salvaging* (Plate 1) dated 1863, which strongly reflects the idiom of the English watercolourists of the previous two decades. Very likely copied from an engraving, it is sophisticated work for a boy of twelve, reflecting the physical environment in which he lived, and foreshadowing in its subject and preoccupation with atmosphere the mature artist's work.

In London during the winter months at this time, following the example of his father and of Lionel Smythe in attending Heatherly's School of Art, Wyllie received 'a very sound education in Art', although 'because he was so young he was not immediately allowed to attend the Life class'.[7] At the Royal Academy Schools,

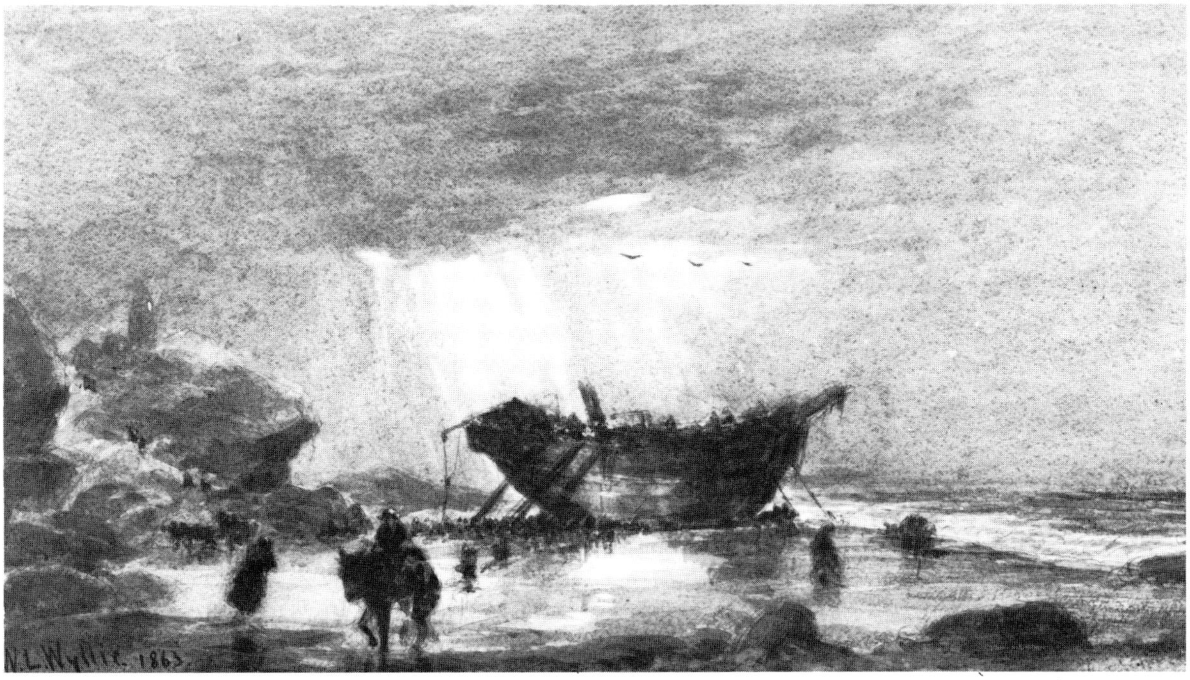

1. Salvaging, 1863
watercolour, $17 \times 9\frac{1}{4}$ (432×235)
Private collection

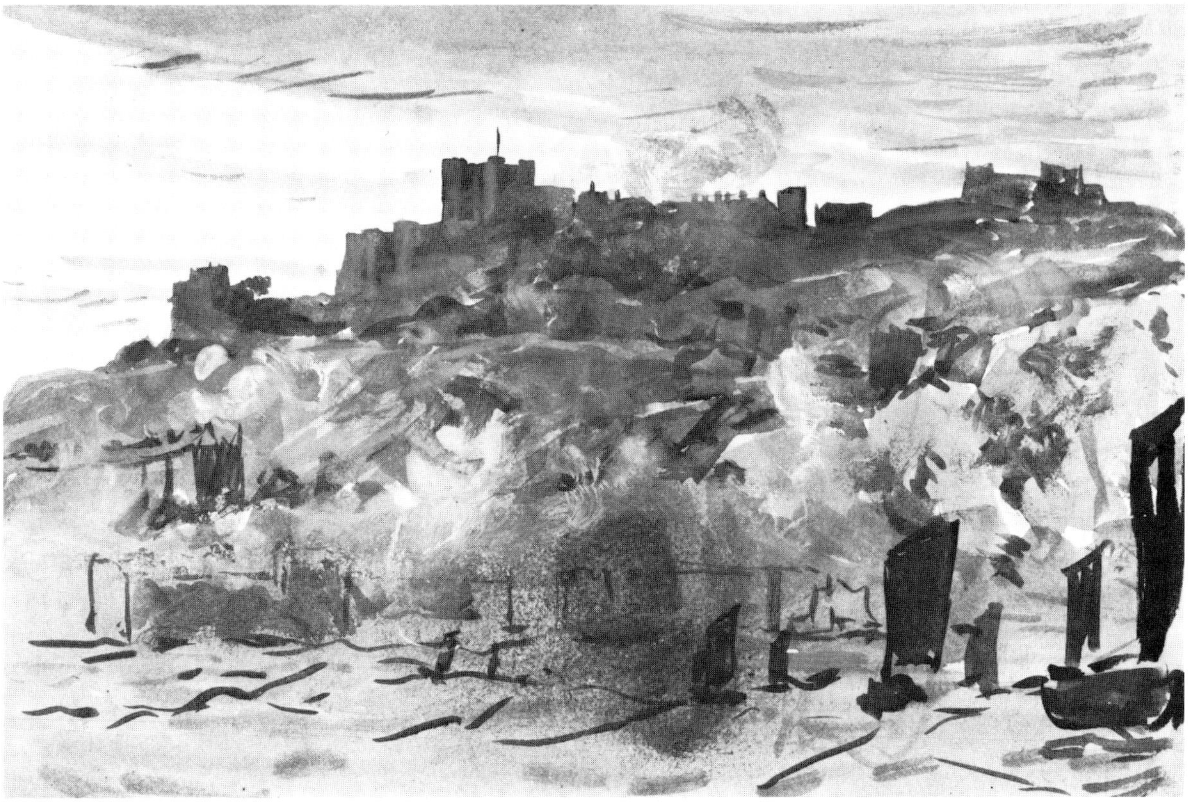

2. Dover Castle from the sea, *c.* 1868
grey wash with white heightening, $7 \times 9\frac{7}{8}$ (177×252)
National Maritime Museum, London

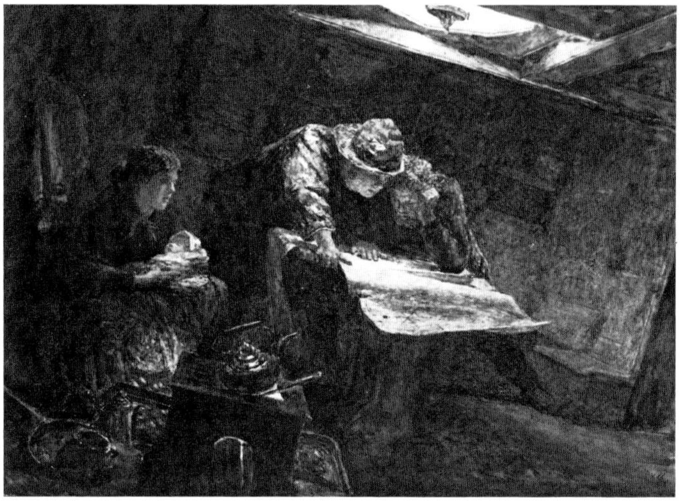

3. L. P. Smythe: A thick night off the Goodwins, 1869
watercolour, $12\frac{1}{4} \times 16\frac{1}{2}$ (311 × 420)
National Maritime Museum, London

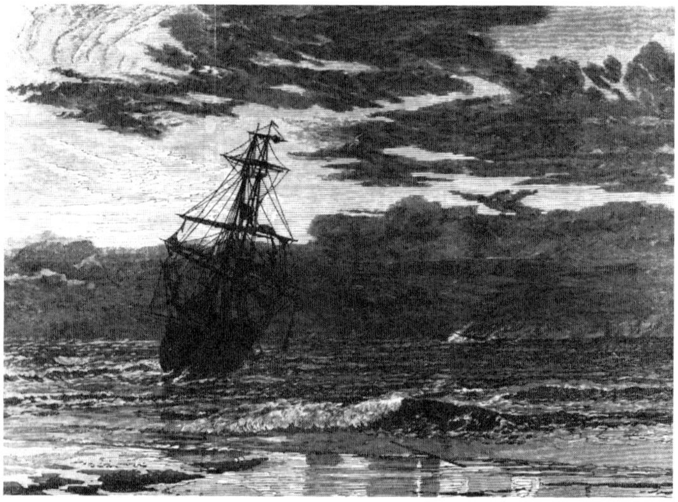

4. Dawn after a Storm
wood-engraving after the oil painting which won the Turner Gold Medal: from the *Illustrated London News*, 1870

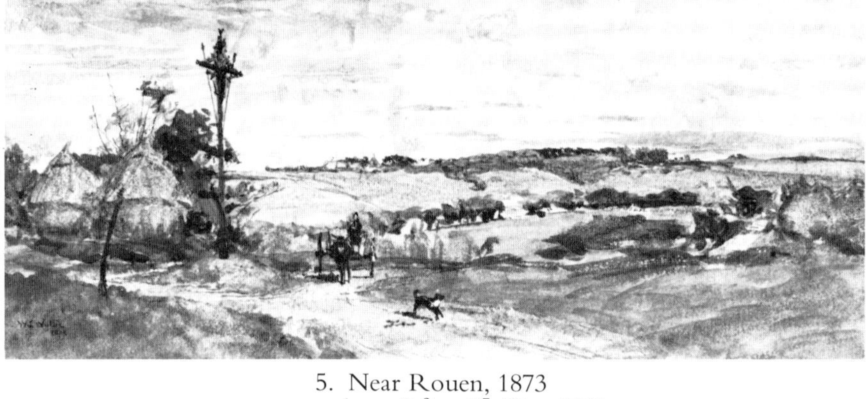

5. Near Rouen, 1873
watercolour, $3\frac{9}{16} \times 7\frac{7}{8}$ (91 × 200)
Private collection

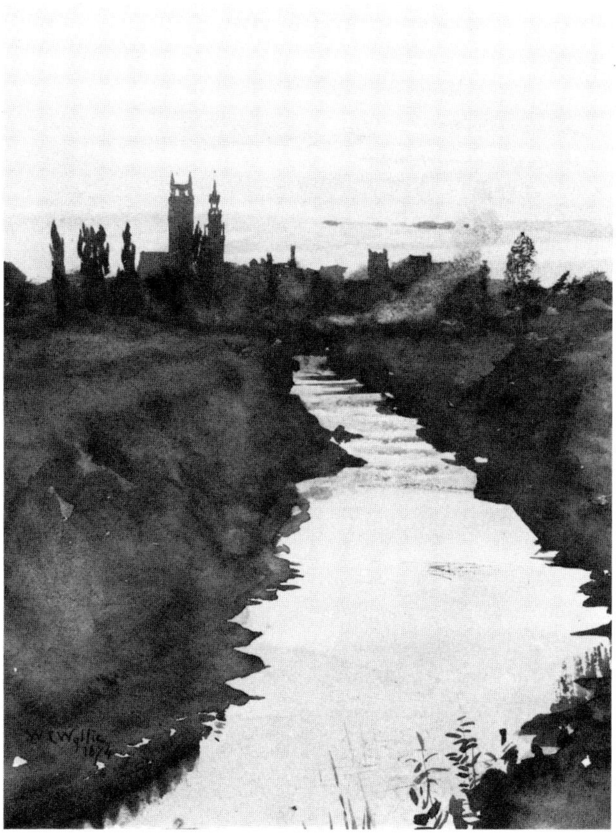

6. View of a town in the Netherlands, 1874
watercolour, $5\frac{3}{4} \times 7\frac{7}{8}$ (145 × 200)
Trustees of the British Museum

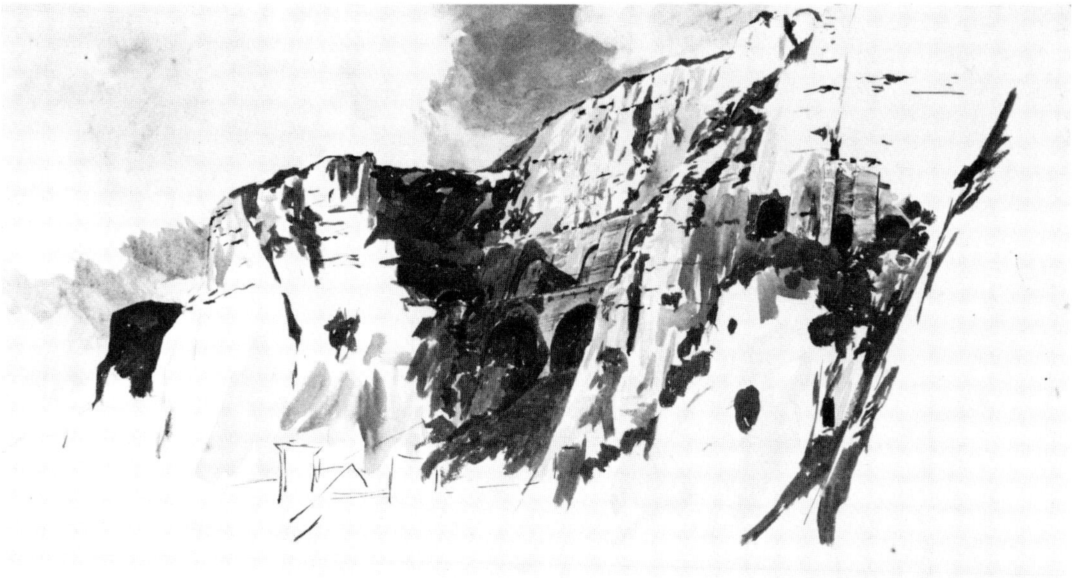

7. Study in the French Alps, *c.* 1879
watercolour, $8 \times 12\frac{3}{4}$ (203 × 325)
National Maritime Museum, London

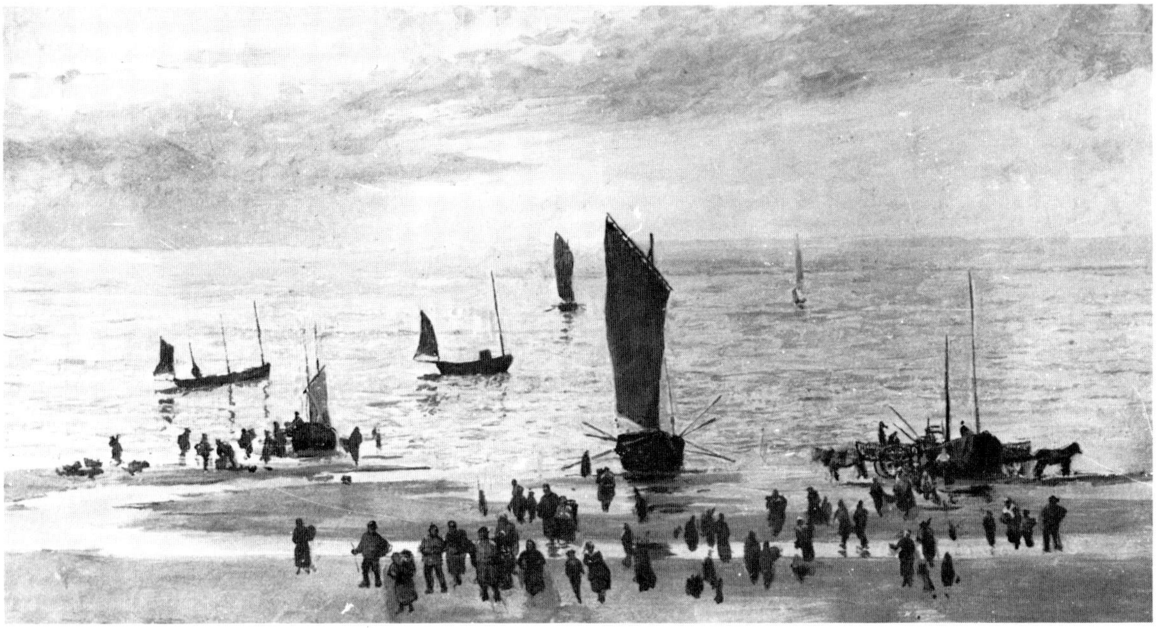

8. W. M. Wyllie: Bringing in the catch, Northern France, *c.* 1875
oil on paper
South London Art Gallery, London Borough of Southwark

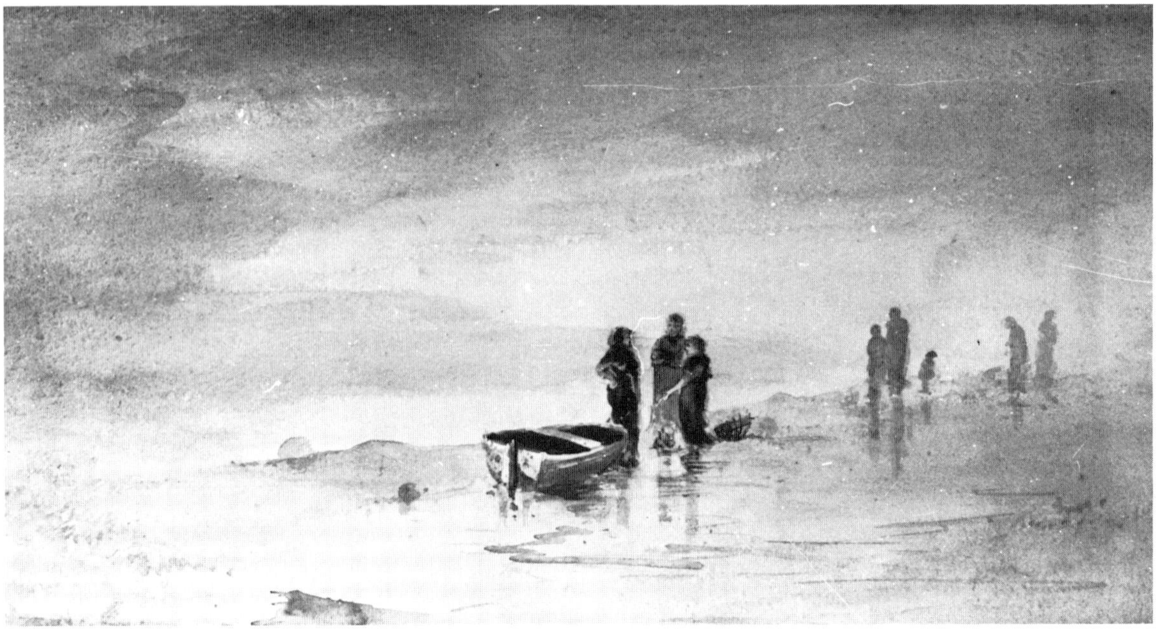

9. W. M. Wyllie: Fisherwomen on the beach, *c.* 1875
grey wash
South London Art Gallery, London Borough of Southwark

where he was enrolled in the spring of 1866 at the age of only fifteen, he worked alongside students much older than himself. It is significant that in later years Wyllie recalled with gratitude 'Mr Boulger's' lectures in perspective, which no doubt contributed to his ability to handle spatial problems with such skill.

At the age of seventeen, in 1868, Wyllie exhibited his first picture at the Royal Academy, then in Trafalgar Square, where it was hung at the highest possible point. It was a view entitled *Dover Castle and Town*, 'a very finished work of Dover Castle partly hidden in a sea mist, the Castle standing out above it, with snow in patches, tinged with pink from the rising sun.'[8] Plate 2 shows a small sketch of Dover made from the sea at this time which is quite probably a sketch for this picture.

In the following year *Dawn after a Storm* won Wyllie the Royal Academy's coveted Turner Gold Medal for Landscape, and his reputation began to be made. It is significant that in 1869 the critic writing of Lionel Smythe's oil painting *A Thick Night off the Goodwins*, exhibited at the Dudley Gallery (Plate 3), writes of the eighteen-year-old Wyllie as 'a companion . . . another rising young artist.'[9] The *Times* critic writing of the same exhibition refers to Wyllie as 'the rising young painter of the clever sea studies here'.[10] Wyllie, in fact, helped Smythe in the composition of *A Thick Night off the Goodwins*, the subject of which was suggested by an article in *Household Words*.*

An engraving after the picture *Dawn after a Storm* appeared in the *Illustrated London News* in January 1870, and provides clear evidence of Wyllie's early debt to the marine paintings of Turner (Plate 4). The critic wrote of Wyllie's youthful works:

> The young painter, Mr Wyllie . . . has given unmistakable indications of an original gift in art – of possessing the power to look at nature for himself and faithfully record his original observations . . . yet two years ago his picture painted in the last competition for the Turner medal brought him into notice. And since that, his 'Friend of All Nations', in the last winter exhibition at the French Gallery; his 'Below Bridge' and 'Sou'wester', at the Dudley Gallery; his 'Shoal in the Offing', at Suffolk-street; and his 'Outward Bound', at the Royal Academy, have proved at once his originality and industry. . . . The present prize picture, entitled 'The Sea-Beach after a Storm – Time, Dawn', beyond question represents a scene and an effect witnessed by the artist himself. The scale of colouring closely resembles that of most of the works already named, the subject being not widely dissimilar and is limited almost entirely to greys – a slatey hue largely predominating. The execution, too, is the same, showing a tendency to haste and dash, which, while it preserves the freshness of the impression, must be carefully watched in so young a painter, lest it should degenerate into 'fatal facility', or slovenliness.[11]

By 1873, Wyllie's reputation seems to have been more firmly established and W. M. Wyllie, exhibiting *A Leisure Hour*, again at the Dudley Gallery, is described in the *Illustrated London News* as 'the father of two young and promising painters, whose sea coast and shipping subjects are already favourably known to the public'.[12]

*Smythe made studies in the cabin of a schooner moored at the Surrey Commercial Docks. A sloping platform was then constructed in the back parlour at Gloucester Crescent, where Smythe and Wyllie took turns sitting to each other. There is a watercolour version of the subject at Greenwich.

At this period Wyllie and his brother Charles spent a great deal of their time roaming, sailing and sketching together. The titles they exhibited at the Royal Society of British Artists in the early 1870s are sometimes almost identical. In 1873/4, for instance, as a result of a sailing trip up the Seine to Rouen, Charles exhibited *Roche Guyon on the Seine* (No. 405) and W.L. *Roche Guyon from the Cliffs* (No. 414). The brothers continued to exhibit side by side until well into the next decade, and often too together with their father. In 1884 the *Illustrated London News* was to comment on their contributions to the exhibition of the Institute of Painters in Oil Colours 'as shewing the treatment of very similar subjects by two talented members of the same family. Both have a fondness for accentuated effects of light and shade . . .'[13] The delicate watercolour shown in Plate 5 dates from the 1873/4 trip to Rouen. It is typical of the meticulous watercolours which Wyllie produced during the 1870s.

Much of Wyllie's early work, the coastal views and landscapes, relates very closely to that of his father in subject-matter, and in preoccupation with keenly observed atmospheric and meteorological effect. Both used the oil sketch for making small direct studies from nature. The oil sketches produced by W. M. Wyllie, probably in France, during the 1860s and 1870s are painted with confidence and gusto, and reveal an artist with a sensitive response to landscape and natural effects. A knowledge of the work of Whistler is suggested in the large wash of his drawings, broadly painted and atmospheric (Plate 9).

W. L. Wyllie's oil sketches of the period, displaying a close affinity with those of his father, are painted with even greater sensitivity and panache. In the sketch depicting the cliffs at St Margaret's Bay, Kent (Plate 10) Wyllie's handling is enormously deft and free, and the patches of sunlight on the cliffside are painted with great virtuosity. The oil sketch of figures on a terrace (Colour Plate 3), however, depicting members of the artist's family, is reminiscent of similar subjects by Boudin, although Wyllie never attempted to imitate Boudin's freedom of approach.

An example of the kind of *plein air* paintings which Wyllie produced at this time can be seen in the 'moon studies' painted around 1870 presumably in the dunes around Wimereux (Plates 12, 13). Like the sky studies of Constable, they contain sky with a small strip of land. They are concerned not so much with the effect of light upon surfaces, but with light itself. Wyllie's concern was to produce precise effects, so that in three small oil sketches, each of roughly the same dimensions, the moon occupies the same position; only the skies vary. They are carefully and sensitively painted. They suggest the 'scientific' attitude in Wyllie's work which was to last his entire life, and which later manifested itself in the publication of *Nature's Laws and the Making of Pictures* (1903), and in the more bizarre experiments of later life when he experimented by dropping wet plaster of Paris down the stairwell in his house in an attempt to discover the nature of the moon's craters.

The influence of Whistler may be detected as early as 1870 in Wyllie's work, and was to remain, although he was never a professed follower, as Clausen and Sickert,

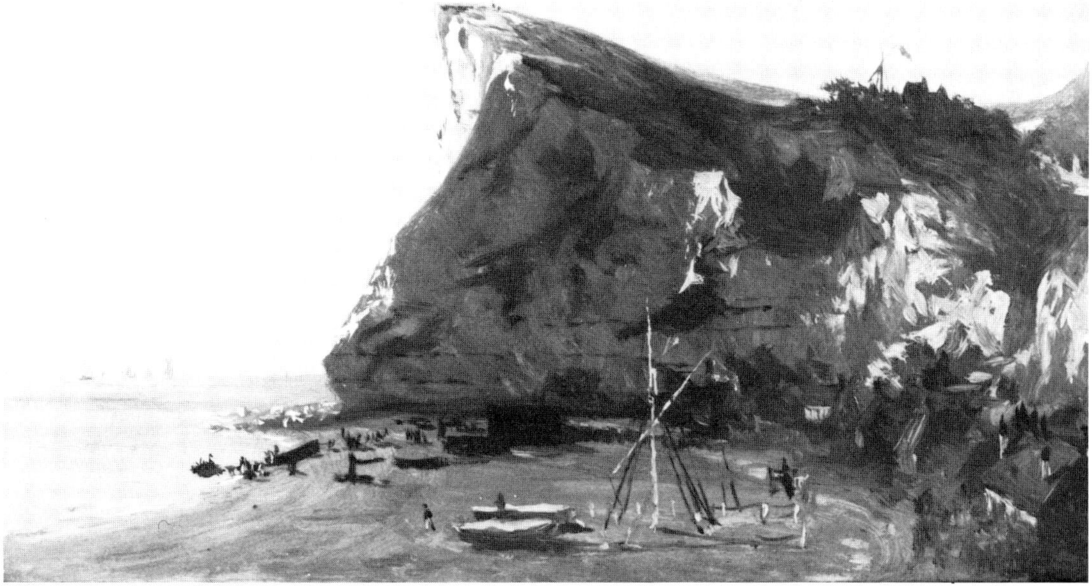

10. A cove, St Margaret's Bay, Kent, *c.* 1875
oil, $4\frac{1}{2} \times 6\frac{3}{4}$ (115 × 171)
Private collection

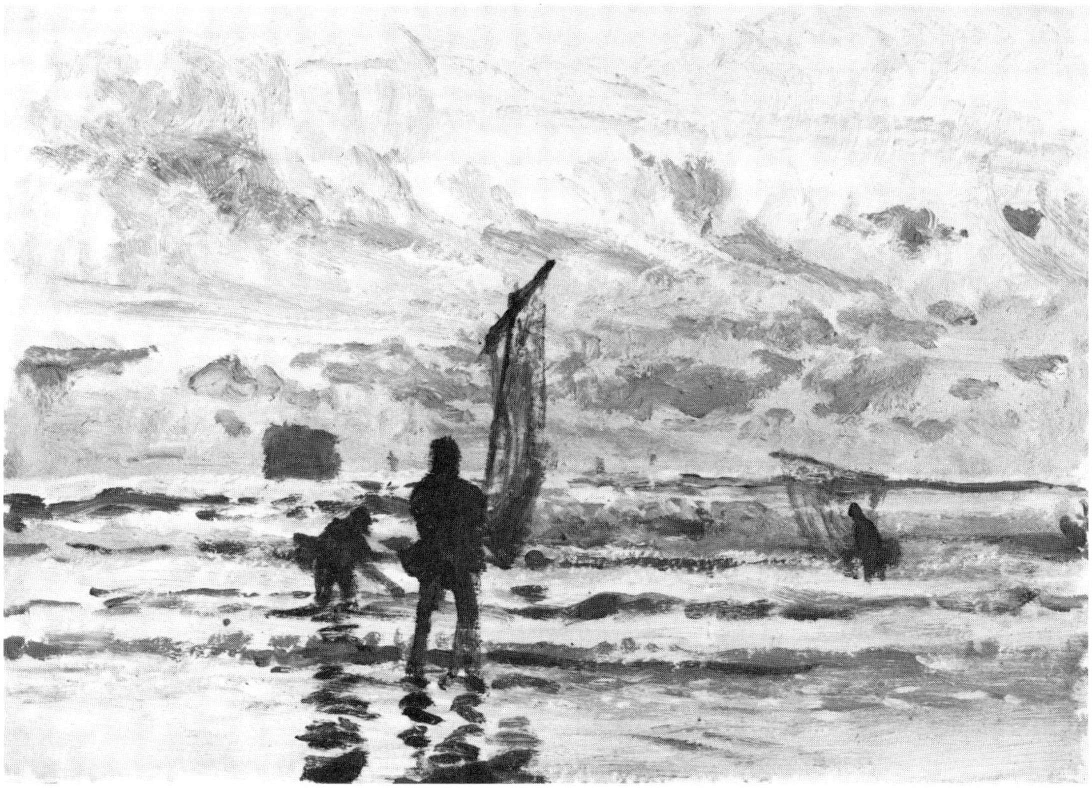

11. Shrimpers, near Boulogne, *c.* 1870
oil on paper, $10 \times 13\frac{15}{16}$ (254 × 349)
National Maritime Museum, London

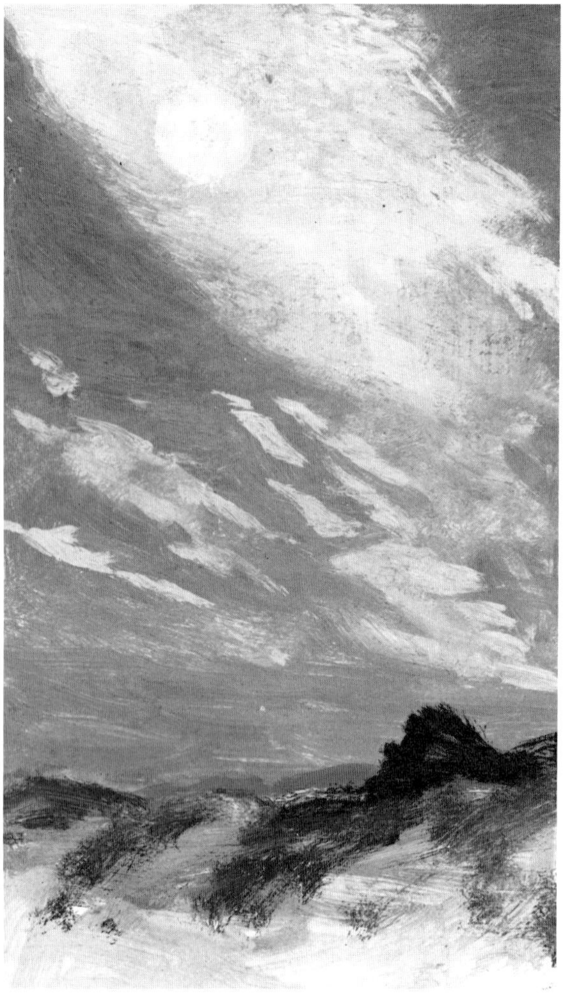

12. Moon study, *c.* 1870
oil on paper, $8\frac{3}{4} \times 5\frac{3}{16}$ (222 × 132)
Miss A. D. Wyllie

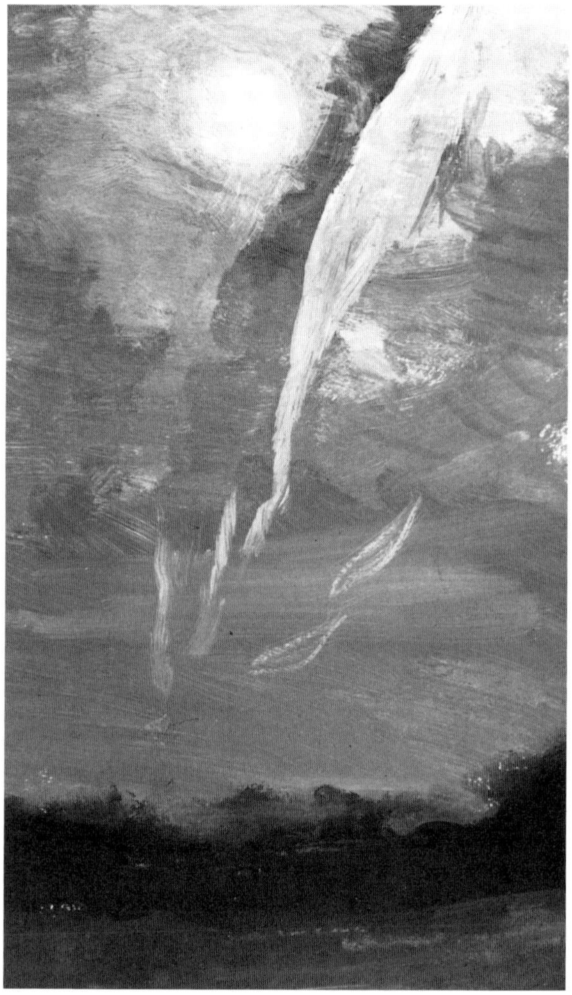

13. Moon study, *c.* 1870
oil on paper, $9\frac{1}{8} \times 5\frac{5}{16}$ (231 × 135)
Miss A. D. Wyllie

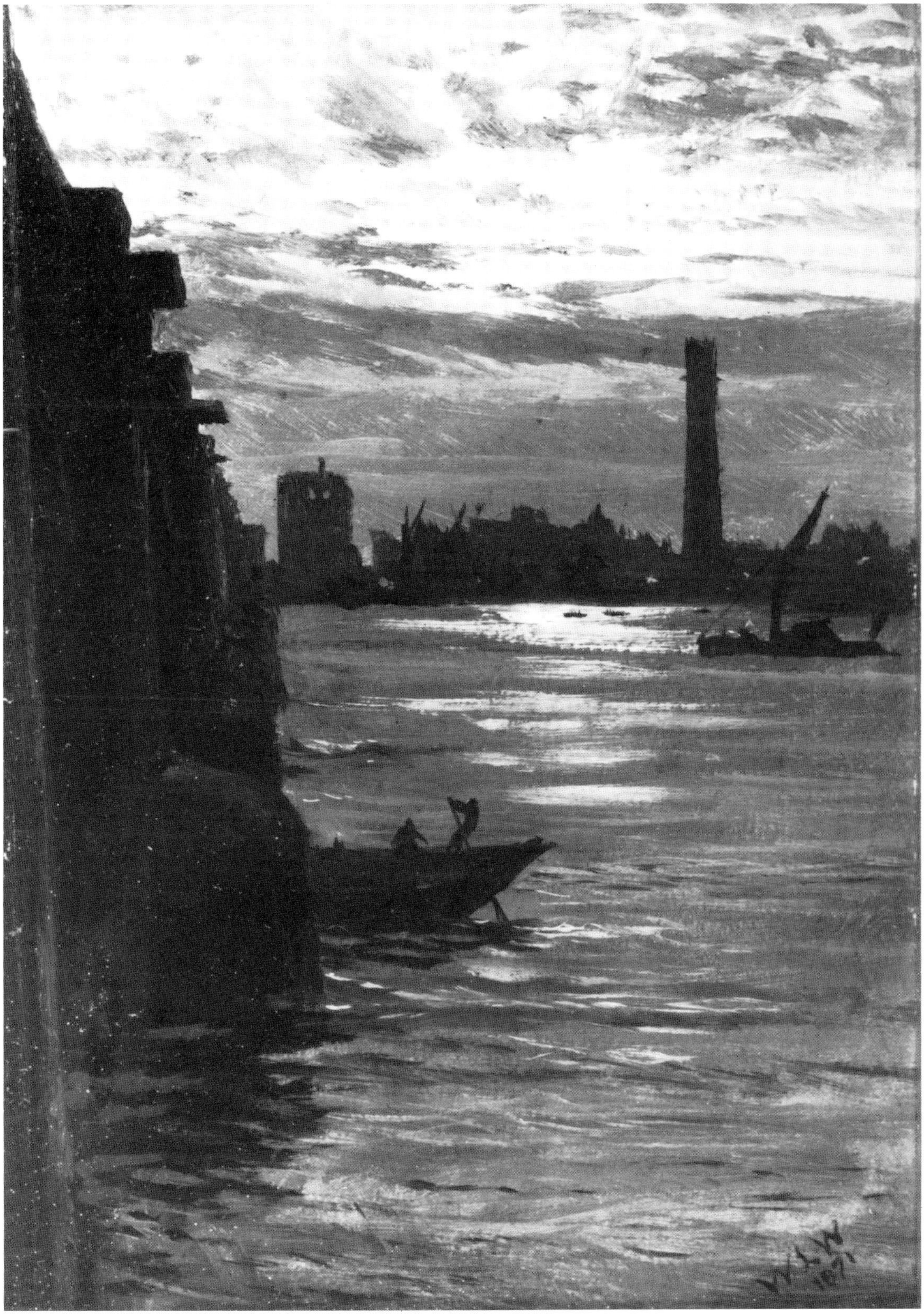

14. A view of the Shot Tower from Waterloo Bridge, 1871
oil, $4\frac{13}{16} \times 5\frac{9}{16}$ (122 × 141)
Private collection

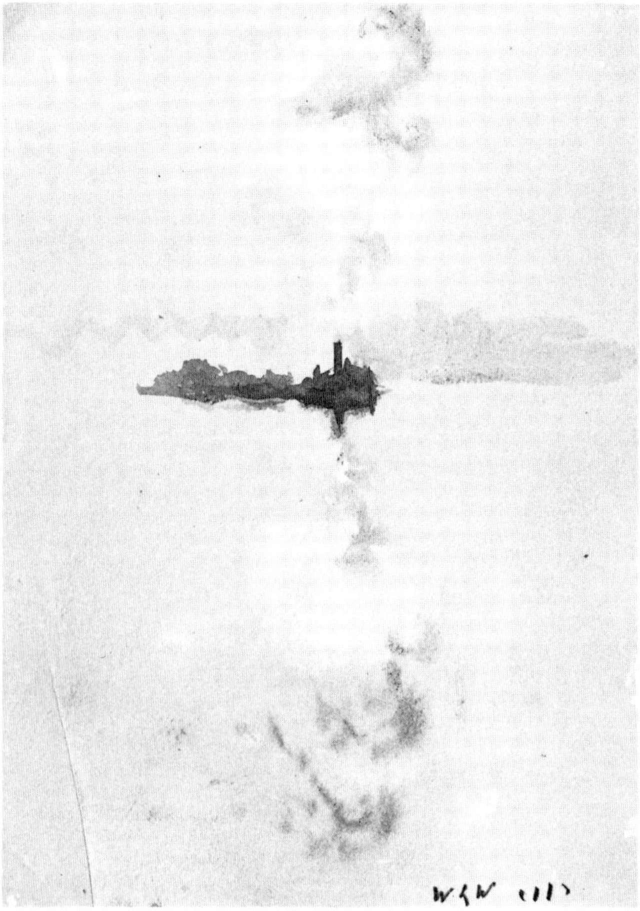

15. Steam tug in a mist, *c.* 1875
grey wash, $5\frac{1}{8} \times 3\frac{5}{16}$ (130 × 91)
National Maritime Museum, London

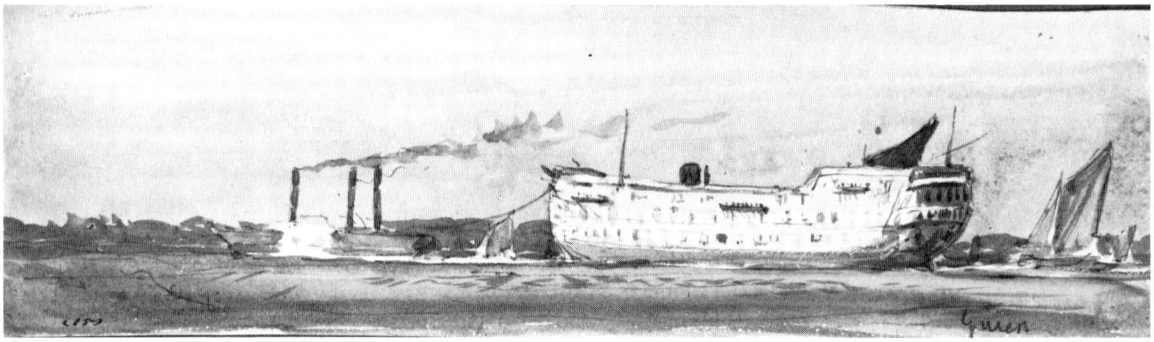

16. HMS *Queen* (1839), *c.* 1870
pencil and watercolour, $2\frac{7}{8} \times 9\frac{7}{8}$ (72 × 252)
National Maritime Museum, London

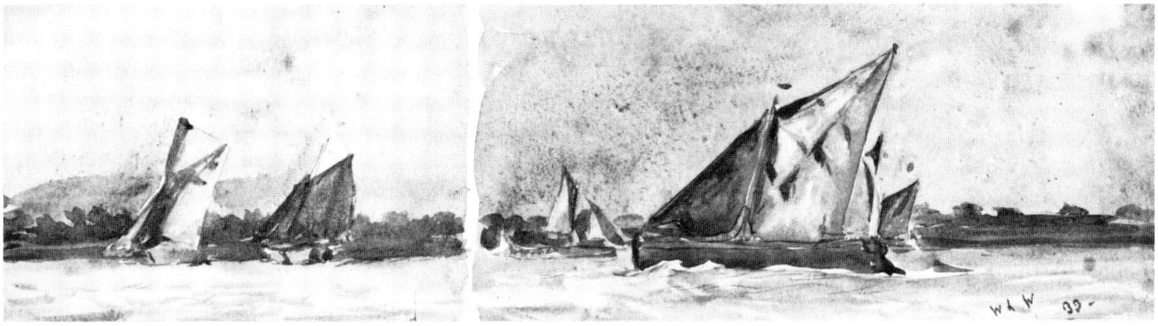

17. Thames sailing barges and a gaff-rigged vessel, 1870s
watercolour, $2\frac{3}{4} \times 9\frac{7}{8}$ (69×251)
National Maritime Museum, London

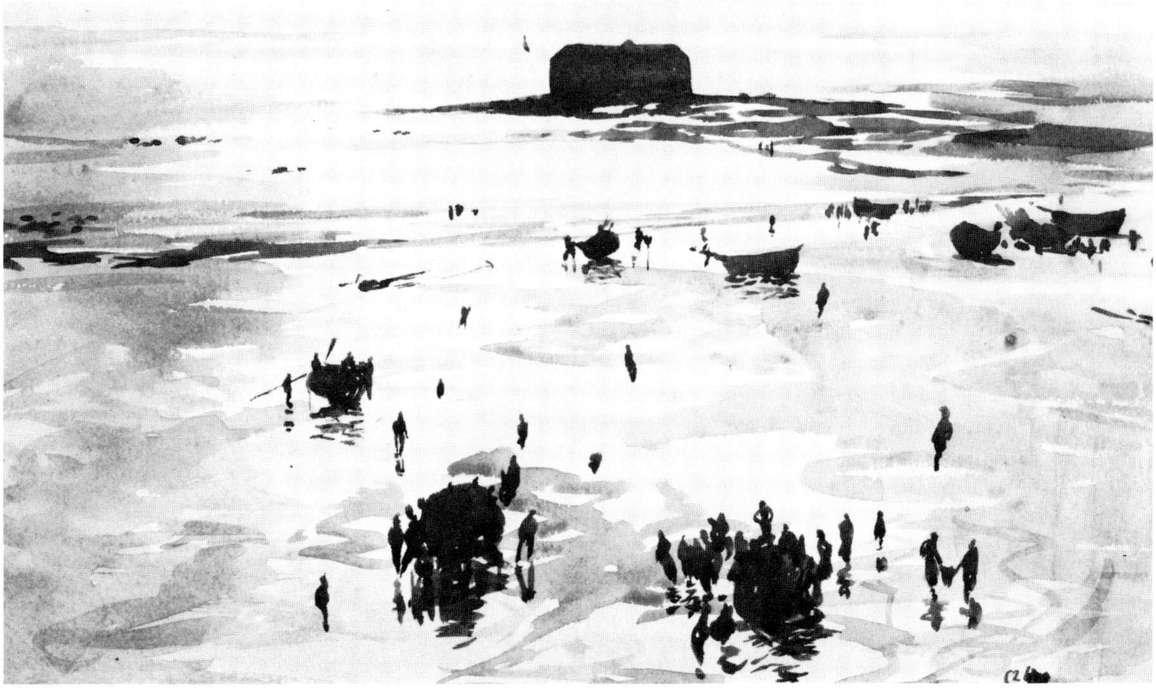

18. Fisherfolk and their boats on the beach, Northern France, *c.* 1873
watercolour, $5\frac{15}{16} \times 9\frac{15}{16}$ (151×253)
National Maritime Museum, London

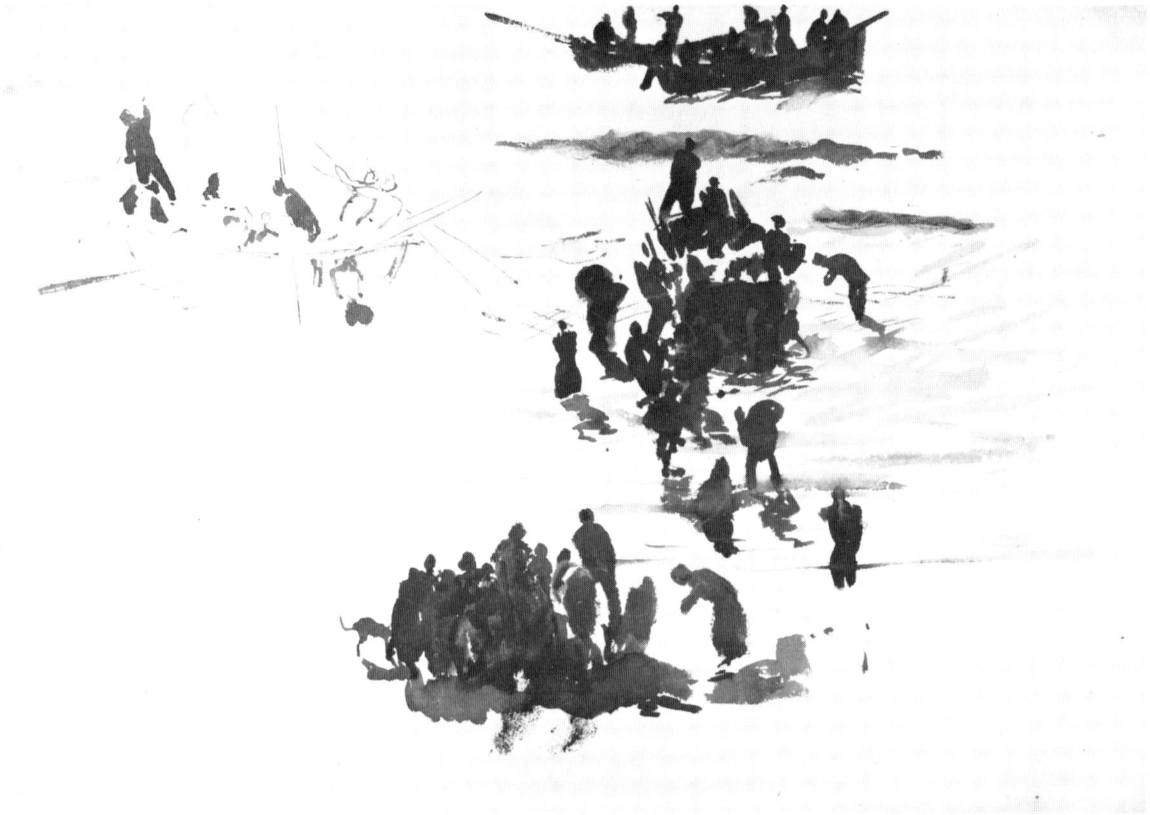

19. Landing fish, *c.* 1875
sepia wash, $8\frac{1}{8} \times 11\frac{1}{2}$ (208 × 292)
National Maritime Museum, London

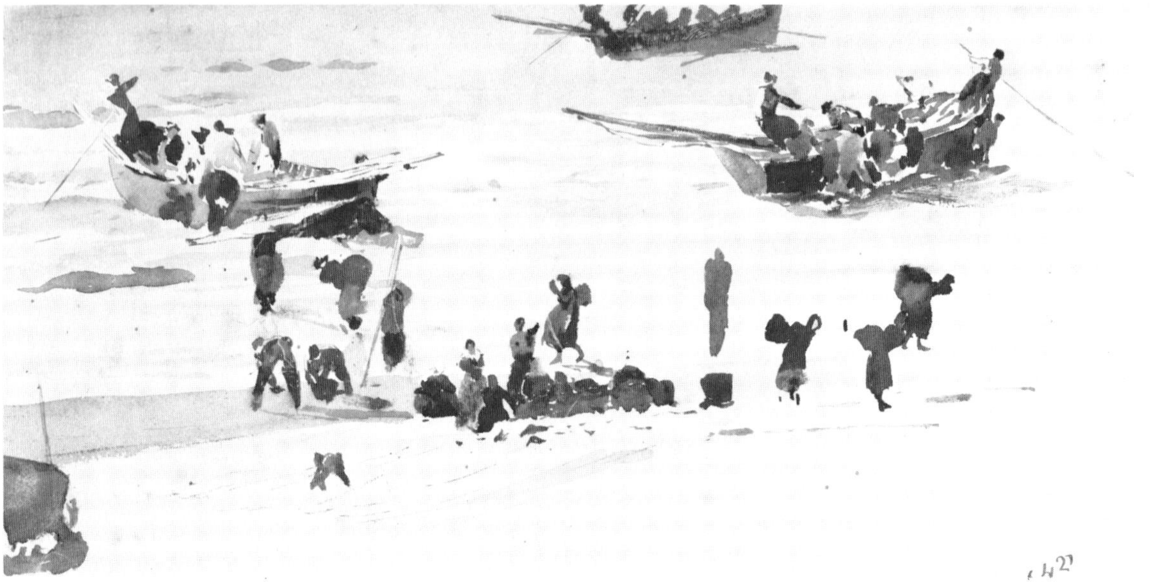

20. Landing fish, *c.* 1875
sepia wash, $5\frac{7}{16} \times 10\frac{7}{8}$ (139 × 277)
National Maritime Museum, London

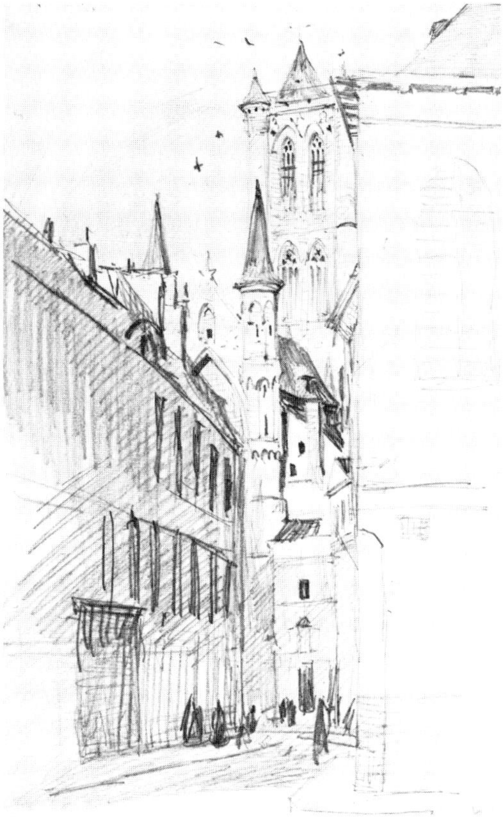

21. Ghent, *c.* 1874
pencil, $8\frac{1}{8} \times 4\frac{15}{16}$ (207 × 125)
National Maritime Museum, London

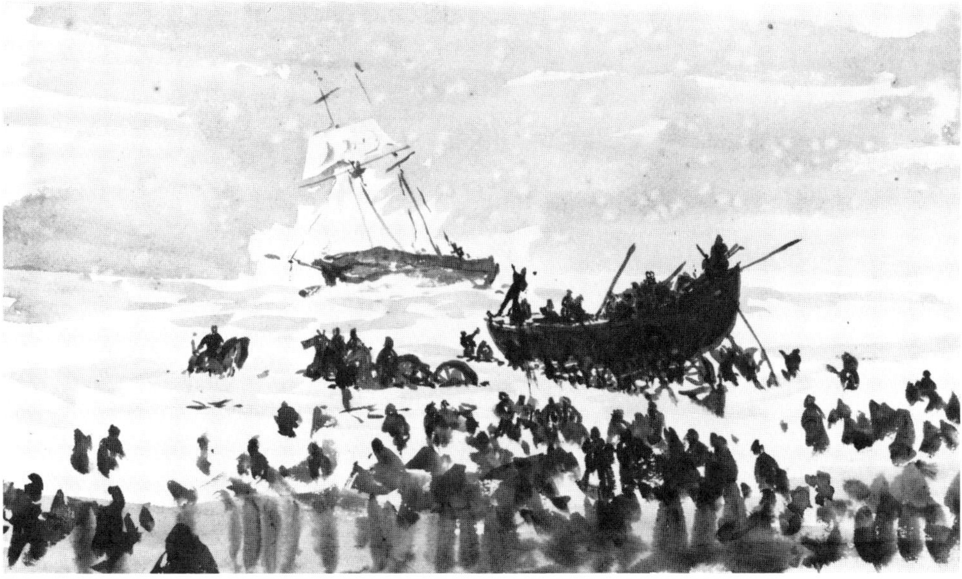

22. Study for the 1873 Royal Academy picture: 'She does no work by halves, yon raving ocean! Engulfing those she strangles.'
watercolour, $6 \times 10\frac{1}{4}$ (153 × 260)
National Maritime Museum, London

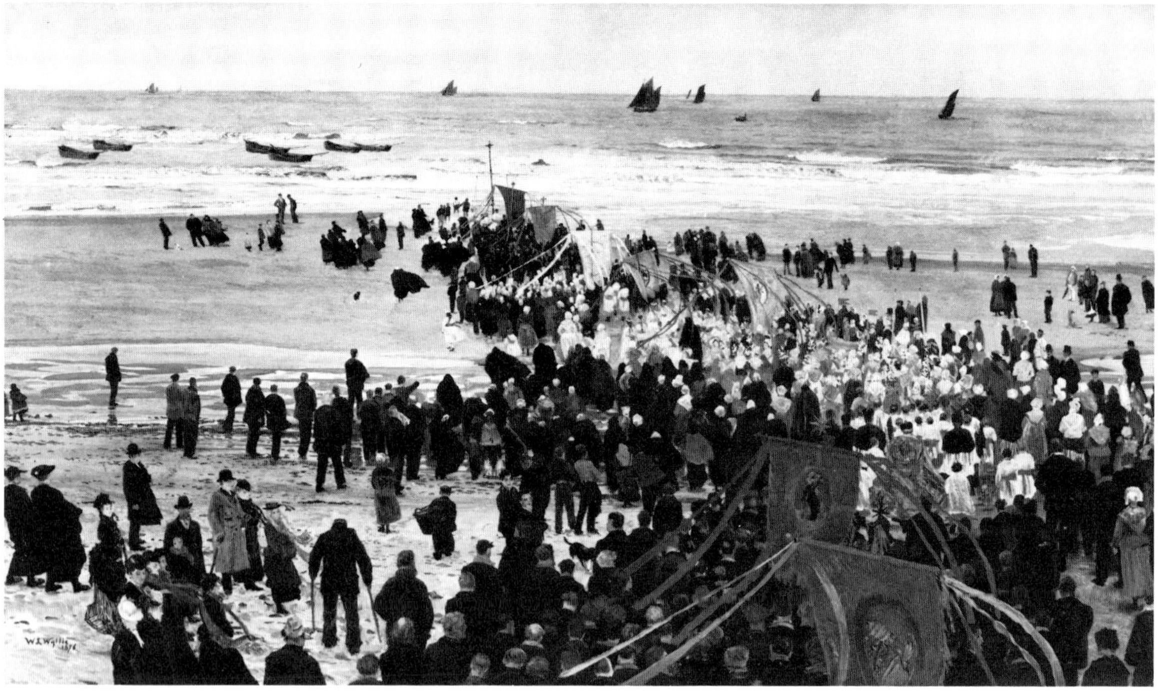

23. Blessing the sea, 1876
oil, $30\frac{1}{8} \times 50\frac{1}{8}$ (765 × 1273)
Walker Art Gallery, Liverpool

24. A procession, 1875
watercolour, $4\frac{7}{8} \times 8\frac{1}{8}$ (123 × 205)
National Maritime Museum, London

for instance, were. It affected Wyllie not only in the way he responded to atmospheric effect, particularly in the Thames night scenes (Plate 14), but resulted in some loosening of his rigid formality in composition. This is best appreciated in the small delicate watercolour sketches with which he filled his reference albums (Plate 15). They show clearly his admiration of Whistler's art, which was to manifest itself in his etchings as late as the 1920s.

From the 1870s Wyllie produced many watercolour studies of fisherfolk and their craft on the coast of Northern France, a not uncommon subject for artists of his period (Colour Plates 1, 2, 5). It was a subject with which his father also experimented. They represent the most poetic and sensitive aspect of his early work. The subjects are usually set against a background of sky and sea in their varying moods, and depict such subjects as fisherwomen bringing in the catch or fishing boats going to sea. The worked-up watercolours have fine atmospheric and spatial effects achieved with a closely controlled watercolour technique. Wyllie's small sketches of the same subjects drawn from life have a spontaneous calligraphic quality which is rare in his work (Plates 18–20). It was only in such works, when confronted with a subject which had to be drawn quickly, that he was able to relax from a compulsion to include detail.

The picture exhibited at the Royal Academy in 1873 '*She does no work by halves, yon raving ocean! Engulfing those she strangles*' embodies the experience of Wyllie's childhood in France, but the scene of a lifeboat rescuing a stranded brig is set on the English coast, and it is very likely that the event was actually witnessed and sketched by Wyllie. It is a dramatic picture full of action, with a sense of wetness, even of noise, from the foaming sea. The painting of the sea is full-blooded. Plate 22 illustrates a sketch for this picture.

Blessing the sea, exhibited in the Royal Academy in 1876 and in Paris in 1878 (Plate 23), has been regarded as a charming picture but untypical of Wyllie.[14] Untypical that it is of Wyllie's mature work, it demonstrates many of the preoccupations of his early years with its subject of fisherfolk, the horizontal sea, land and sky composition, and atmospheric effect precisely recorded. The picture, with its high vantage point, is composed from separately observed and carefully drawn elements using studies from life such as the one illustrated in Plate 24. It is certain that the effect of spatial recession of the beach to the windy sea was worked out with the same precision which Wyllie later employed to plot the positions of barges and steamers in the Thames, or ships in action during battles of the First World War.

2
'The Tidal Thames': 1881-1906

To the credit of our artist, the picturesqueness of the lower part of the stream, the beauty that is to be found in ships and wharves, and even, in the clouds of smoke that fall from the funnels of steamers, is not allowed any longer to be ignored; and Mr Wyllie is among the leaders who, having discovered these artistic qualities, are determined to bring them to the Public mind.[15]

The subjects described by the critic of *The Times* are those which occupied Wyllie in the years immediately after his marriage, and which very soon made his name. He brought them to the public eye single-mindedly, with a great force and directness. His pictures caused a stir. Between 1880 and 1885 Wyllie exhibited exclusively Thames and Medway subjects at the Royal Academy. In the late 1880s these began to give way to subjects of a similar nature which also included merchant steamships (such as the Orient steamship *Ormuz* fitting out in 1887), but it was not until 1890, at the age of nearly forty, that he exhibited at the Royal Academy an exclusively naval subject.

The Thames and Medway now became a part of Wyllie's life, as has been described earlier in this book, and his knowledge, not only of tide and wind, but of ships, their cargoes and local industries, was increased with an insatiable curiosity and industry as he explored the Thames in his small boat *Ladybird*, in what was a mobile studio. In 1880, for instance, he spent the entire month of May in *Ladybird* off the Gas Light and Coke Company's Beckton gas works, recently constructed (1868–9) in Galleons Reach, Barking. In 1880 the subject of a gas works was an unlikely one for an artist to paint, but for Wyllie it provided the subject of his 1881 Royal Academy picture, and was a subject which always fascinated him (Plate 70).

The first of Wyllie's one-man exhibitions, *The Tidal Thames*, was held at the Fine Art Society in the summer of 1884, following a Whistler one-man exhibition. It consisted of seventy-three drawings, some of which were Thames subjects, which later that year appeared in photogravure in a large volume entitled *The Tidal Thames*, with narrative by Grant Allen. The exhibition was received with enthusiasm by the art critic of the *Illustrated London News*, who wrote that the collection which comprises the studies of the last year only, furnishes remarkable evidence of the great industry, the original unconventional observation, and the great technical skill, to which we have frequently borne witness, and which brought the artist into prominent notice when displayed in his picture of the bombardment of Alexandria, exhibited in these same rooms, a year or so back. It was studies such as these that resulted also in the very vigorous and striking picture of the Thames 'below bridge', in the last exhibition at Burlington House which the Academicians bought from the Chantrey Bequest.[16]

This exhibition was the first of four of Wyllie's work at the Fine Art Society. It is interesting to note that the total of works exhibited by Wyllie in commercial galleries was greater than the average achieved by most artists of his generation, and is indicative not only of his compulsion to produce, but of his commercial motives. He also exhibited on the Continent, for example in Paris in 1878 and 1889, and at the Munich Exhibition in 1890. When in 1885 he exhibited a landscape, *Sheep Dipping*, at Tooth Galleries the *Illustrated London News* concluded that 'in Mr Ernest Parton, Mr W. L. Wyllie and Mr T. Collier, we have landscape painters who would find appreciation abroad as much as at home'.[17]

'*Toil, glitter, grime and wealth on a flowing tide*' (Plate 25) was hung in the Royal Academy in 1883, and today it is the best known of Wyllie's oil paintings. And yet it is only one of a series of paintings of similar subjects produced by Wyllie in the 1880s depicting men and boats at work on the London River, Lower Thames and Medway. In these pictures Wyllie describes with an intimate knowledge and affection not only the precise nature of the labour being carried out, but also its setting, the two elements in equal balance. Work is not viewed from afar off for its picturesque qualities, but at the closest possible quarters. Landscape painters of the period, such as Walter Greaves, Seymour Haden, or Wyllie's old friend C. J. Lewis, also painted or etched the Thames at this time, but none showed its life so intimately.[18]

Writing in 1889, the art critic of the *Magazine of Art*, Harry Barnett, an enthusiastic supporter of Wyllie's art, was loud in his praise of the Thames picture:

The small fry of contemporary water-painters have taken the silver Thames under their special and presumptuous patronage; they have libelled its glory with dulness, its beauty with colour which is hypothetical, and its romance with an atmosphere that does not exist. The Thames they paint was never seen outside those harbours of the commonplace, their own studios. The Thames Mr Wyllie paints is the Thames as it is, with all its grime and much of its wonder, all its business and something of its pathos, and suggestions (always right and often vivid) of its contrasts of hurry and rest, its minglings of dignity and degradation, its material embodiment of British supremacy and prosperity, and its enormous testimonies to the dark romance of these coal-and-iron times. In all this he is unrivalled by living men; and even if he had done nothing else he would be entitled to a front position in the van of modern English art.[19]

The picture was begun in London in the autumn of 1882, and its progress was closely watched by John Bagnold Burgess (1830–97), Wyllie's friend and admirer, a painter of Spanish genre subjects who was enthusiastic about it. He brought along his brother-in-law, Sir Joseph Pulley, MP, already a patron of Wyllie, who expressed a wish to purchase the picture. Although he was prevented by the Hanging Committee of the Royal Academy who required it for purchase from the Chantrey Fund as picture of the year, Wyllie painted him a replica.

Like many of Wyllie's large oil paintings, it succeeds despite a certain laboured quality and 'greasiness' in the handling of the paint. Wyllie's effects, whether of moving water or billowing smoke, were rarely achieved with any degree of ease or spontaneity in his oil paintings. The whole process of laying in a picture was a deliberate, methodical one, although occasionally he is known to have painted an Academy picture without first making studies. At this period he seems to have painted his oil paintings, as well as his watercolours, piecemeal, with the result that if a section of painting happened to be incomplete when he finished work for the day, it was scraped out, and begun afresh the next day. Of his technique Harry Barnett in the *Magazine of Art* noted that 'His water-colours were always good; and if at first his oils were inclined to be leathery in tone and texture and heavy in colour, the war pictures at the Fine Art Society and "Toil, glitter, grime" showed that to a great extent he had mastered those defects, and could paint with a better sense of colour and with a freer hand.'[20]

In the case of '*Toil, glitter, grime and wealth . . .*' Wyllie began by laying a thick layer of flake white, smoothed on to the canvas with his palette knife. This was his custom, and family or friends were often employed at this stage. On this surface when dry the subject, thoroughly worked out, was painted usually in thick paint, but sometimes making use of glazes and scumbled areas.

In 1883 Wyllie made his first contact with the dealer Robert Dunthorne, and this was to be a long and happy business relationship. Dunthorne commissioned from Wyllie what was to be his first etching, a large plate of '*Toil, glitter, grime and wealth . . .*', the first of a large and varied *oeuvre* (Plate 26). Dunthorne subsequently published many of Wyllie's etchings. To undertake a large plate was certainly ambitious, but Wyllie succeeded in producing an extremely strong image, perhaps more atmospheric than the oil painting itself. It was exhibited at the Royal Academy in 1884 and was compared favourably with the oil painting by the *Illustrated London News*: 'W. L. Wyllie also puts in an appearance as an etcher with a capital version of his Academy picture of last year, bought from the Chantrey Bequest, which is quite as admirable in its way as the picture itself.'[21] As in many of the earlier etchings, some areas are deeply bitten, producing rich deep blacks, whereas others have not been touched by the acid at all and are completely light. The result is a plate of bold contrast, the figures in the foreground barges silhouetted darkly against the shimmering light on the river beyond.

As an illustrator for the *Graphic* since the early 1870s Wyllie had been called upon to render events pictorially in a realistic and detailed way. The illustrations were to be informative, and were used much as photographs are today in newspapers and

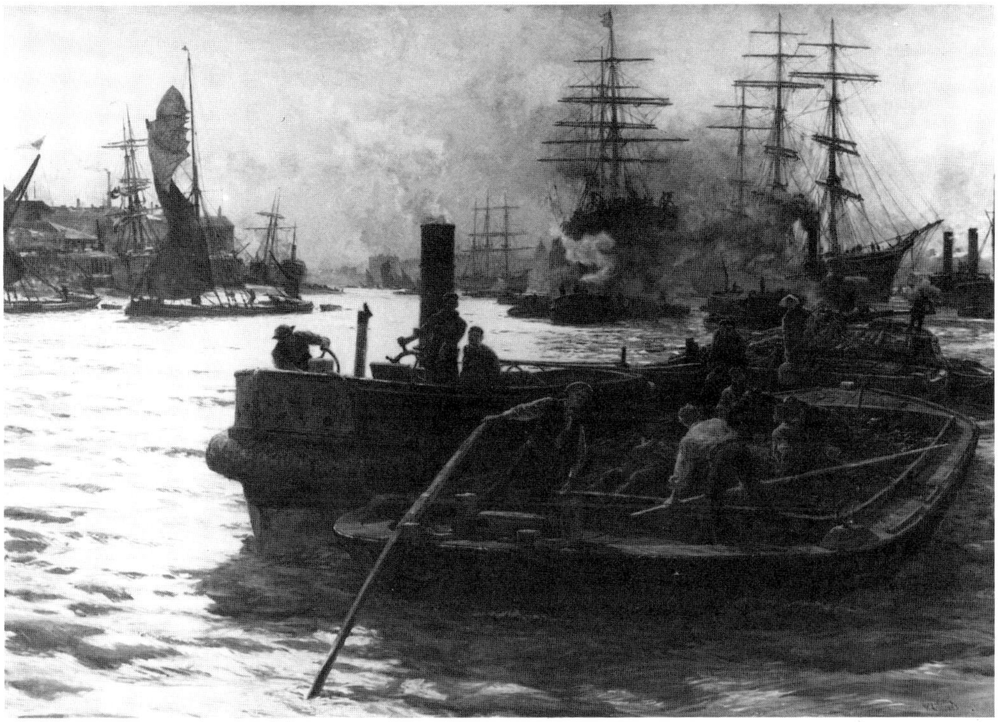

25. 'Toil, glitter, grime and wealth on a flowing tide', 1883
oil, $45\frac{1}{2} \times 65$ (1155 × 1650)
Tate Gallery, London

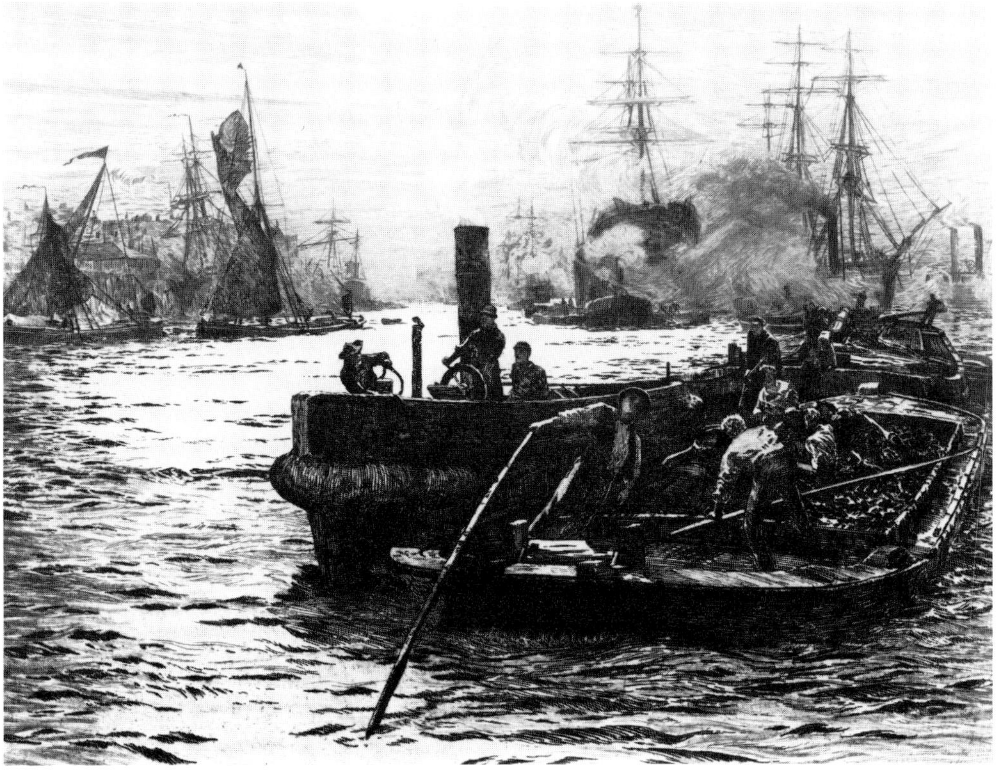

26. 'Toil, glitter, grime and wealth on a flowing tide', 1885
etching, $16\frac{7}{8} \times 21\frac{13}{16}$ (429 × 554)
National Maritime Museum, London

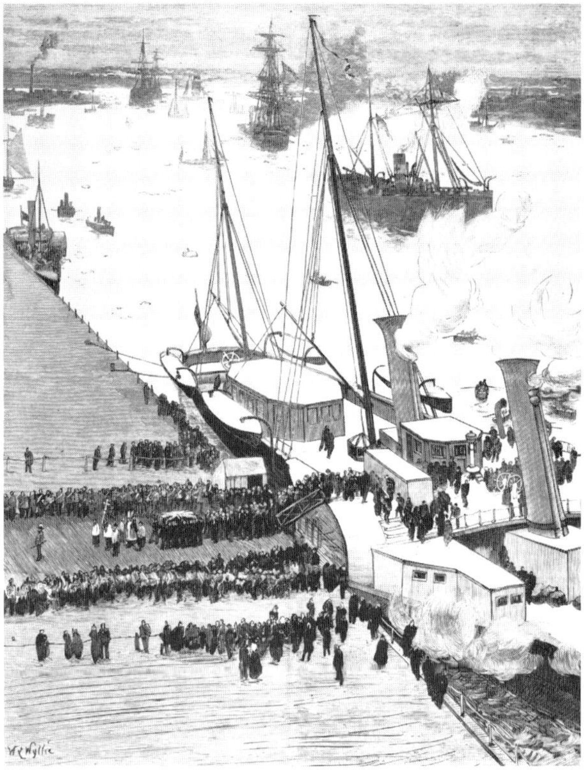

27. 'Funeral of the Late Prince Louis Napoleon – Debarkation of the Body at Woolwich', 1879
wood engraving
This is an example of the early work produced by Wyllie for the *Graphic*, when reproduction was by means of engraved wooden blocks

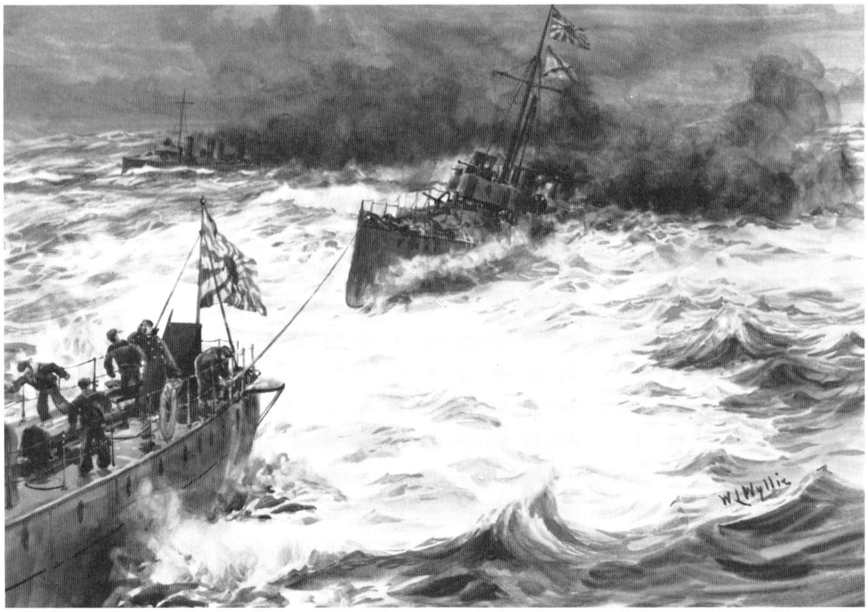

28. 'A Lost Prize: an incident of the Torpedo Attack at Port Arthur', 1904
grey wash, $10\frac{1}{8} \times 14\frac{9}{16}$ (270 × 320)
National Maritime Museum, London
This illustration for the *Graphic* shows an incident in the Russo-Japanese War in 1904. It is an example of Wyllie's later work for the magazine and demonstrates his enormous skill in the use of black and white.

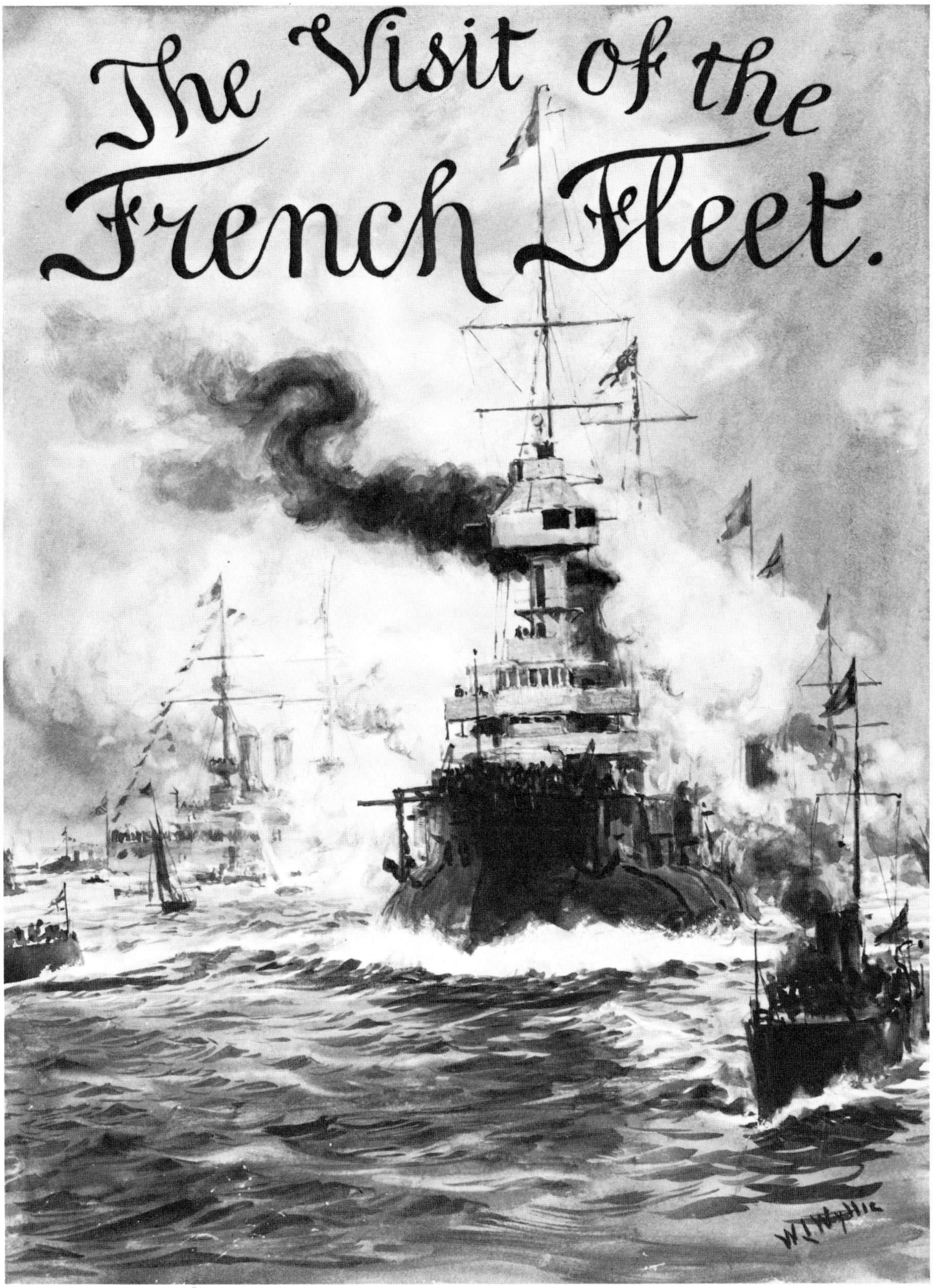

29. Visit of the French fleet to Portsmouth, 1905
grey wash, $13\frac{13}{16} \times 10\frac{1}{16}$ (351 × 255)
National Maritime Museum, London

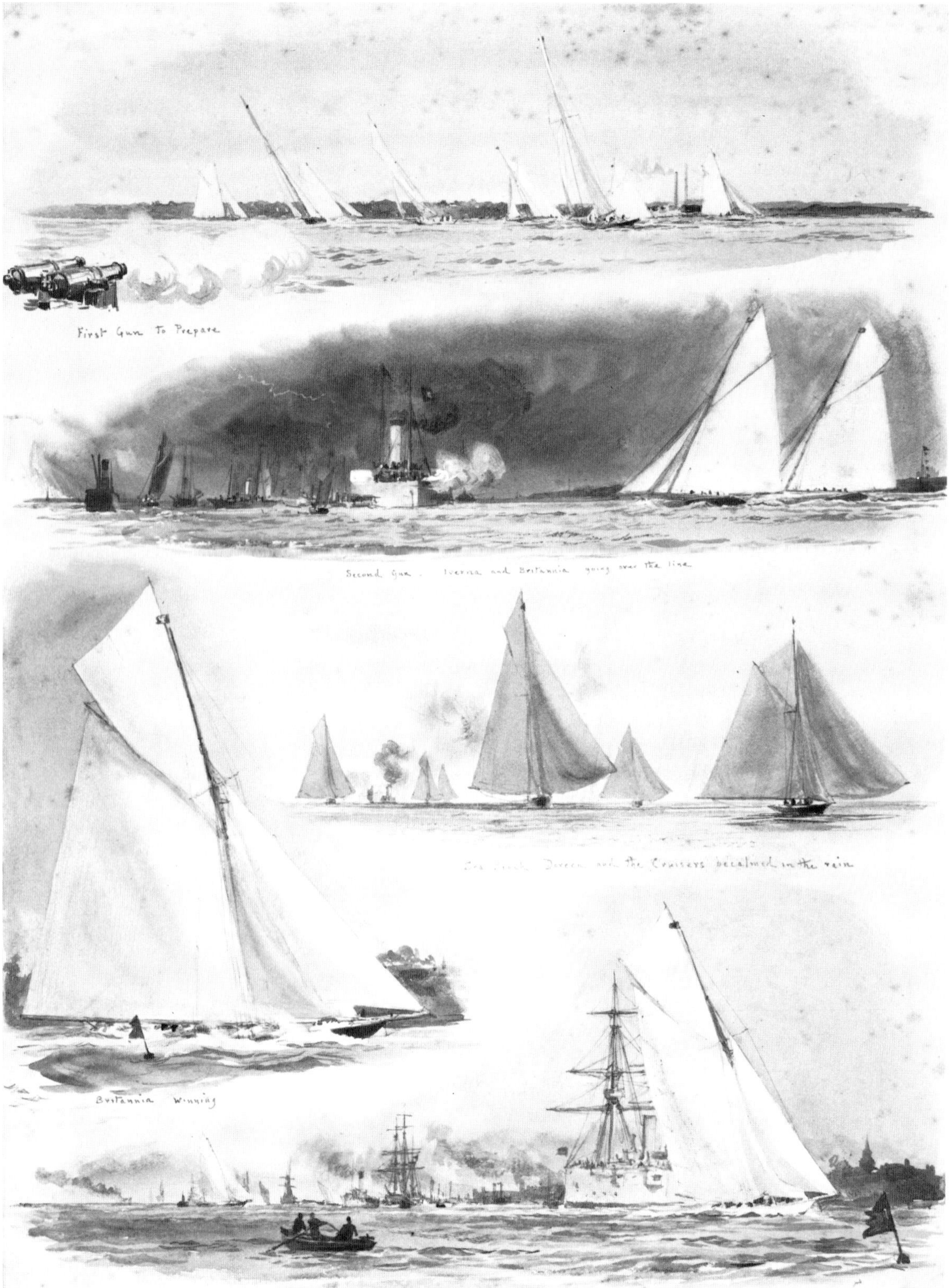

30. Yacht racing in Gravesend Reach, *c.* 1895
pen and ink, grey wash with white heightening, $13\frac{7}{8} \times 9\frac{15}{16}$ (353 × 253)
National Maritime Museum, London

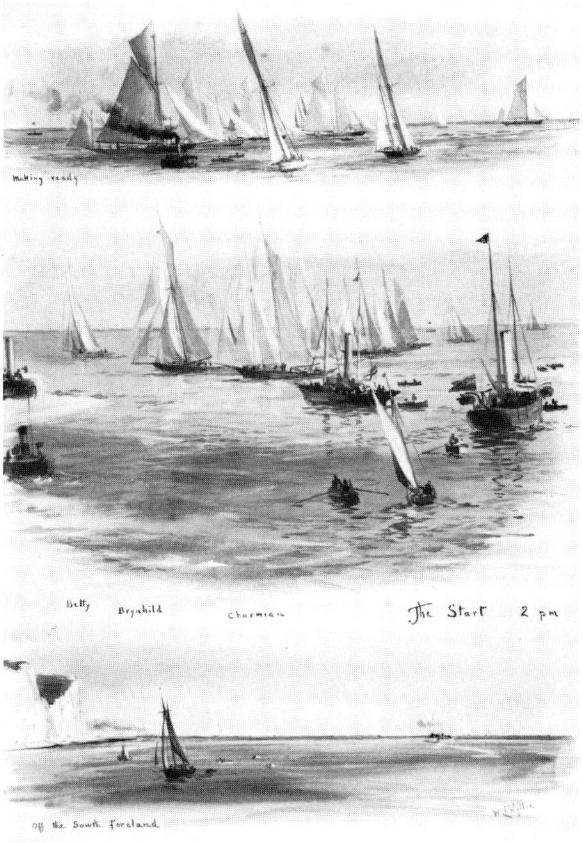

31. Yachts off Dover, 1899
pencil, sepia wash and white heightening, $9\frac{7}{8} \times 14$ (252 × 355)
National Maritime Museum, London
This drawing for the *Graphic* shows the start of the race to Heligoland for the German Emperor's Cup in June 1899

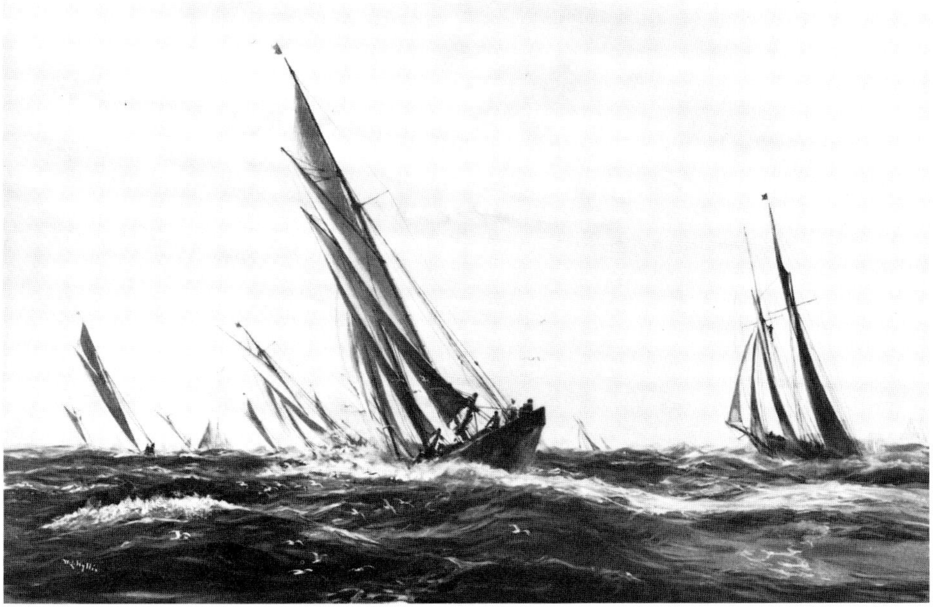

32. Out for a spin at the opening of the season: a sketch in the channel (for the *Graphic*, 1900)
pencil, grey wash and white heightening, $13\frac{3}{8} \times 20$ (340 × 508)
National Maritime Museum, London

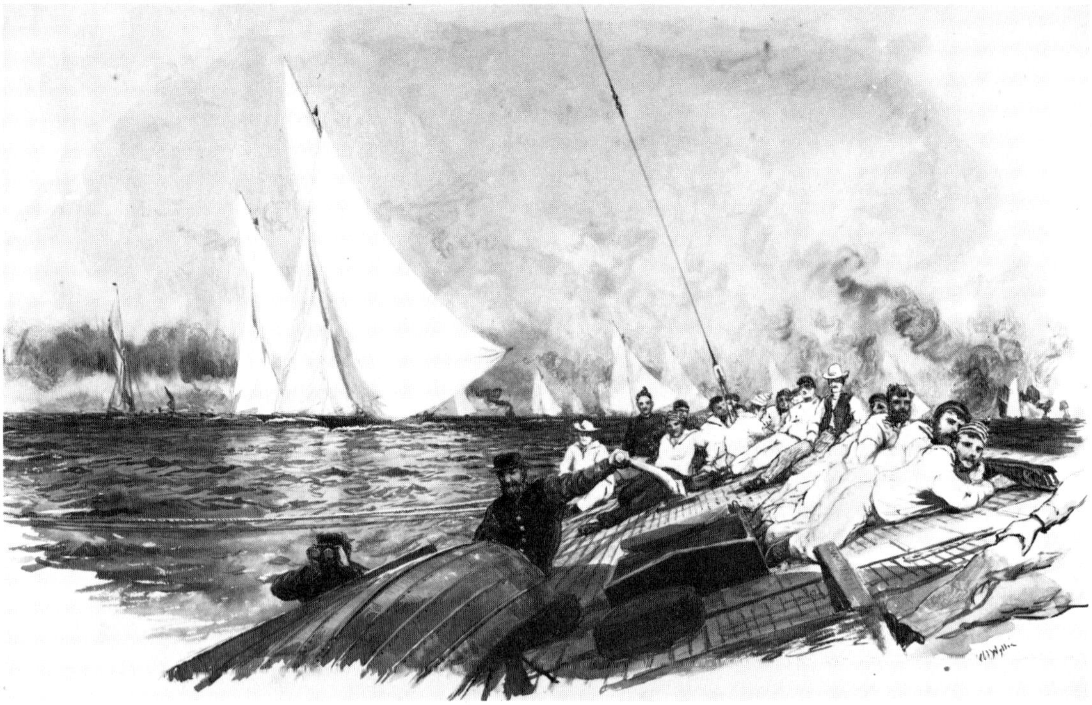

33. Lord Dufferin's yacht racing
pencil, pen and ink, grey wash and white heightening, $12\frac{7}{16} \times 19\frac{1}{4}$ (316 × 489)
National Maritime Museum, London

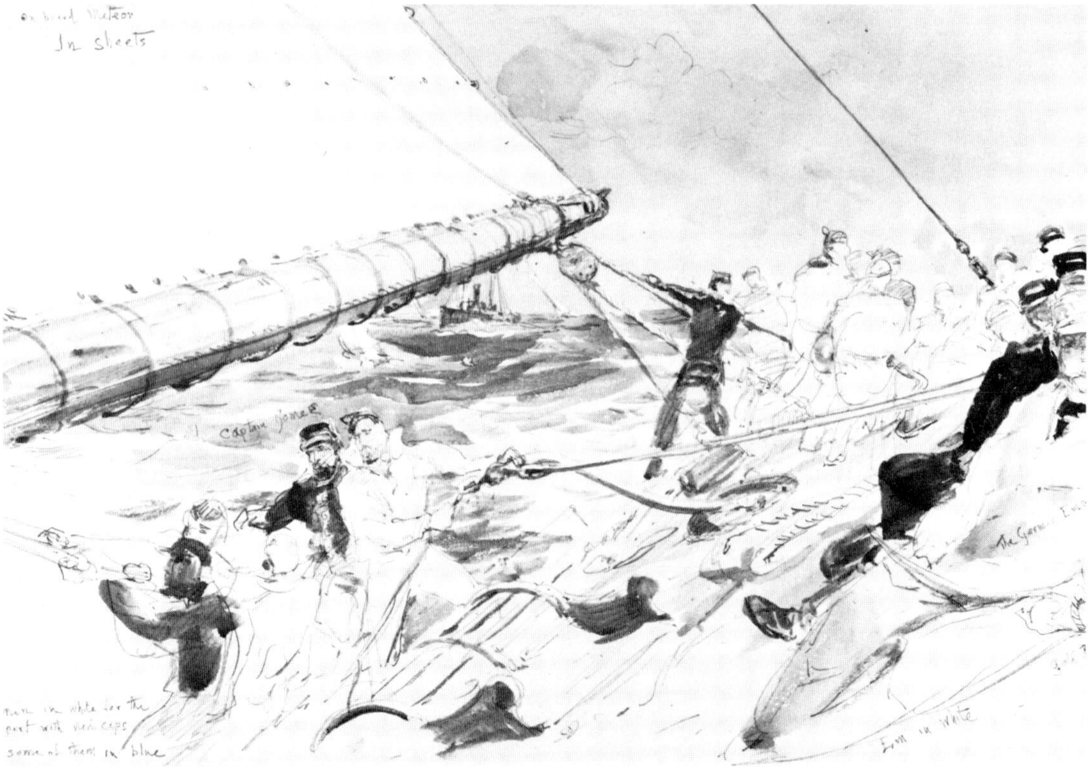

34. On board the German Emperor's yacht *Meteor*
pencil and grey wash, $8\frac{15}{16} \times 12\frac{9}{16}$ (227 × 325)
National Maritime Museum, London
This study, with colour and other notes, shows the German Emperor himself

magazines. At first Wyllie's drawings were reproduced on wood blocks (Plate 27) but this technique later gave way to a photographic process enabling illustrations such as Plate 29 to be photographically reproduced.

To this task, essentially hack work, Wyllie brought to bear all his best skills of draughtsmanship and design. Throughout his career as an illustrator he carried out his work with unusual freshness and inventiveness, even when portraying scenes he had not himself witnessed. Many of the illustrations made for the *Graphic* stand in their own right as the very best of Wyllie's art. In the drawings for such illustrations he used Indian ink, lampblack and Chinese white, with enormous skill and sensitivity, satisfying the requirement for accurate depiction of the event, but allowing scope for delicate and subtle effects. Such work encouraged Wyllie to build up a large repertoire of subjects, ranging from the pageantry of royal visits and naval reviews to the exploits of the Royal Navy in distant corners of the Empire or fashionable society racing their yachts (Plates 29–34), developing in him an astute awareness of detail which he was rarely able to put aside.

Not only did Wyllie's work as an illustrator lay the foundations of his future career, but it also taught him the discipline of working in monochrome. He contributed to exhibitions such as the one at the St James Gallery, King Street St James in 1885 where 'Mr Mendoza has a "black and white exhibition" in which the term is applied in its widest sense, including oil paintings. Of these Mr Webb, Mr Waller and Mr Wyllie contribute the most important'.[22] Thus when in 1883 Wyllie took up etching, he was fully equipped to work within the limitations of black and white.

The medium of the etching suited Wyllie admirably. During a career of nearly fifty years as a printmaker, he was characteristically prolific, producing in the region of three hundred etchings and drypoints. In subject-matter the etchings eventually reflected Wyllie's entire range, extending from Thames and London views, Mediterranean and other topographical subjects, to yachting, the Navy, and the First World War. Many of the early plates, including a number based on exhibited Thames pictures, are deeply bitten, giving the print an almost embossed quality. Following his sailing trip from Hoo to the Netherlands Wyllie exhibited watercolours and etchings at Dunthorne's in 1888. The *Magazine of Art* found the drawings 'too matter of fact', preferring the etchings for their 'poetical feeling':

> Mr W. L. Wyllie's etching of 'Bruinisse' (Dunthorne) is very characteristic of the artist, and shows how the greatest amount of effect can be extracted from the least amount of labour. The picturesque little Dutch village as seen from the broad waters of the Scheldt is represented with great simplicity and breadth, and impresses the spectator with its 'local truth' and its poetical charm.[23]

If Wyllie could be 'poetical' in the Bruinisse plate, he was equally able to be dramatic as in the large plate depicting the escape of HMS *Calliope* from Appia harbour, Samoa, during the hurricane of 16 March 1889 (Plate 35).

Despite a certain carelessness with the use of acid, with the result that Wyllie often lost patience and abandoned plates, his approach to the production of etchings was methodical. Little was left to chance. His wife recalls: 'For the many etchings . . . every drawing was made from nature first, using nothing but black – not body colour, the lights just picked out. He was a rapid worker, and very accurate.'[24] In later years Wyllie turned to drypoint which seems to have suited him better, being 'cleaner'.

Robert Dunthorne first published Wyllie's etchings, and later the Fine Art Society and the Art Union published editions. After the death of Dunthorne publication was continued by his son, and in later years William Howell published them, including the sets of six. Editions of the etchings were printed first by Goulding and later by Welch.

Moving to the area of the Medway in the mid-1880s brought Wyllie into even closer contact with the subjects he loved, in a much freer environment than London. It is also significant that, settling near the Naval Dockyard at Chatham, contact with the Navy both socially and artistically was inevitable.[25]

'Heave Away', Barges upward bound, shooting Rochester Bridge (Plate 37) was the first large picture to derive from Wyllie's contact with the Rochester River, and it was shown in the Royal Academy Spring Exhibition of 1884. Thames sailing barges bound either up or down the Medway had to pass through Rochester Bridge, the green iron bridge in the background of the picture. Their very high masts had to be lowered in order to pass under the bridge, relying on the tide and sweeps (oars) for propulsion. To lower the mast the bargee used the windlass (in the bows) on the stay fall block. This is what has happened in the picture, the bridge having been successfully negotiated. This painting clearly demonstrates Wyllie's intimate knowledge of the craft and the finer points of navigation, and is typical of his time spent on the Medway when sailing was as important an aspect of life for him as painting.

It was from the Boulogne-built yawl *Ladybird* that Wyllie made his preliminary studies for '*Heave Away*', and a number of these are to be found in the Wyllie Collection at Greenwich. They are clear evidence of the way in which Wyllie 'built' his pictures, carefully constructing from separate carefully observed details. In composing he relied to a large extent upon carefully worked out perspective. Having chosen the required elements from sketches he would work out with great precision their correct relationships according to the rules he later set out in *Nature's Laws and the Making of Pictures* (1903). Two of the drawings are studies for each side of the bridge (one of which is shown in Plate 38), while the other drawings work out the position of the figures on the barge (Plates 39 and 40). Wyllie used his wife to model the bargewoman, as was quite often the case when a female figure was required.

The *Magazine of Art* sent Harry Barnett to Hoo Lodge to interview Wyllie, and he was enthusiastic:

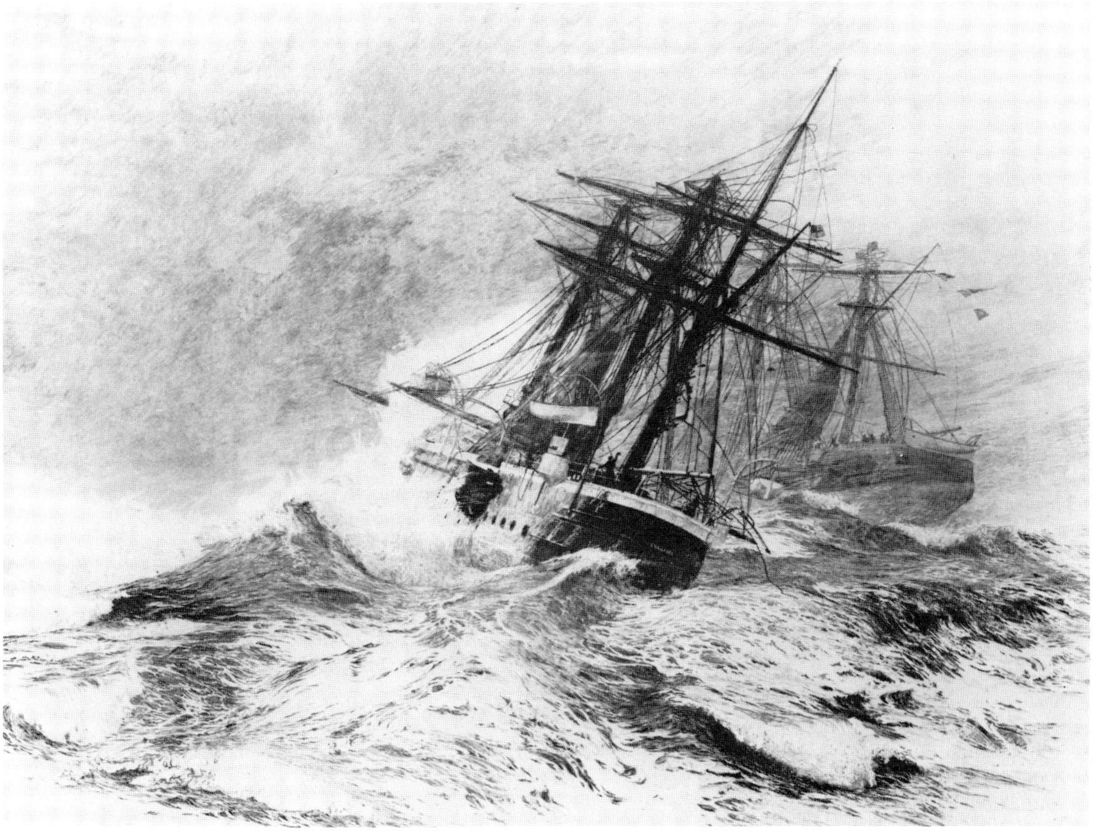

35. The Escape of HMS *Calliope* from Apia Harbour, Samoa, during the hurricane on 16 March 1889
etching, $19\frac{5}{8} \times 24\frac{1}{4}$ (500 × 618)
National Maritime Museum, London

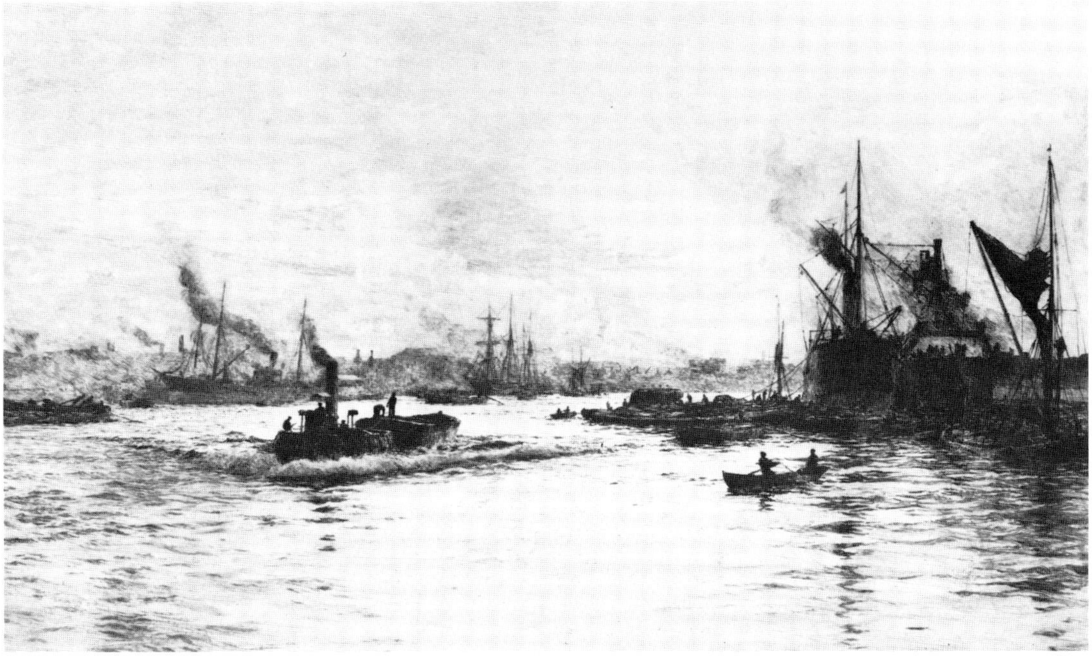

36. The Lower Pool, *c.* 1905
etching, $11\frac{13}{16} \times 19\frac{3}{8}$ (300 × 490)
National Maritime Museum, London

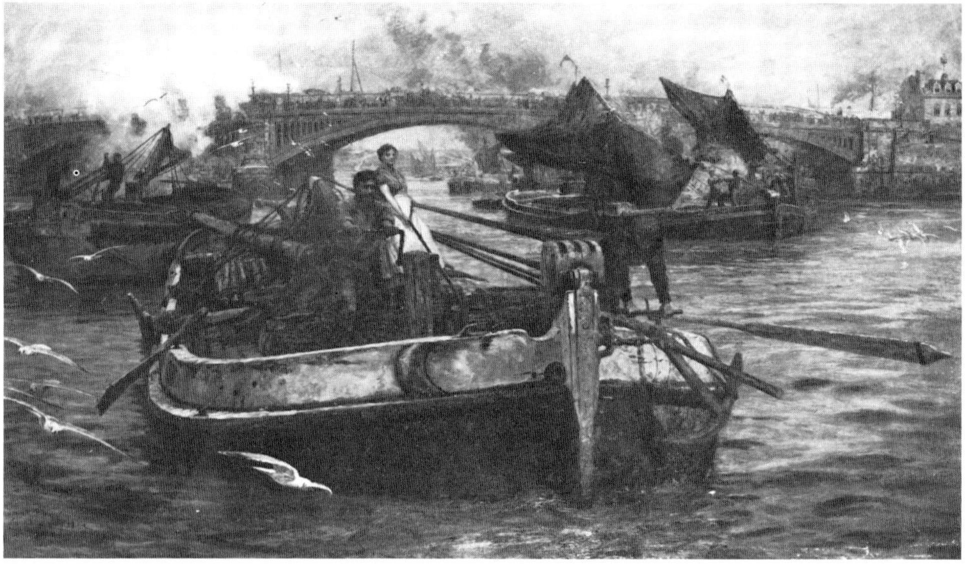

37. 'Heave Away'; barges upward bound, shooting Rochester Bridge, 1883
oil, $35\frac{1}{2} \times 59\frac{1}{2}$ (900 × 1510)
Private collection

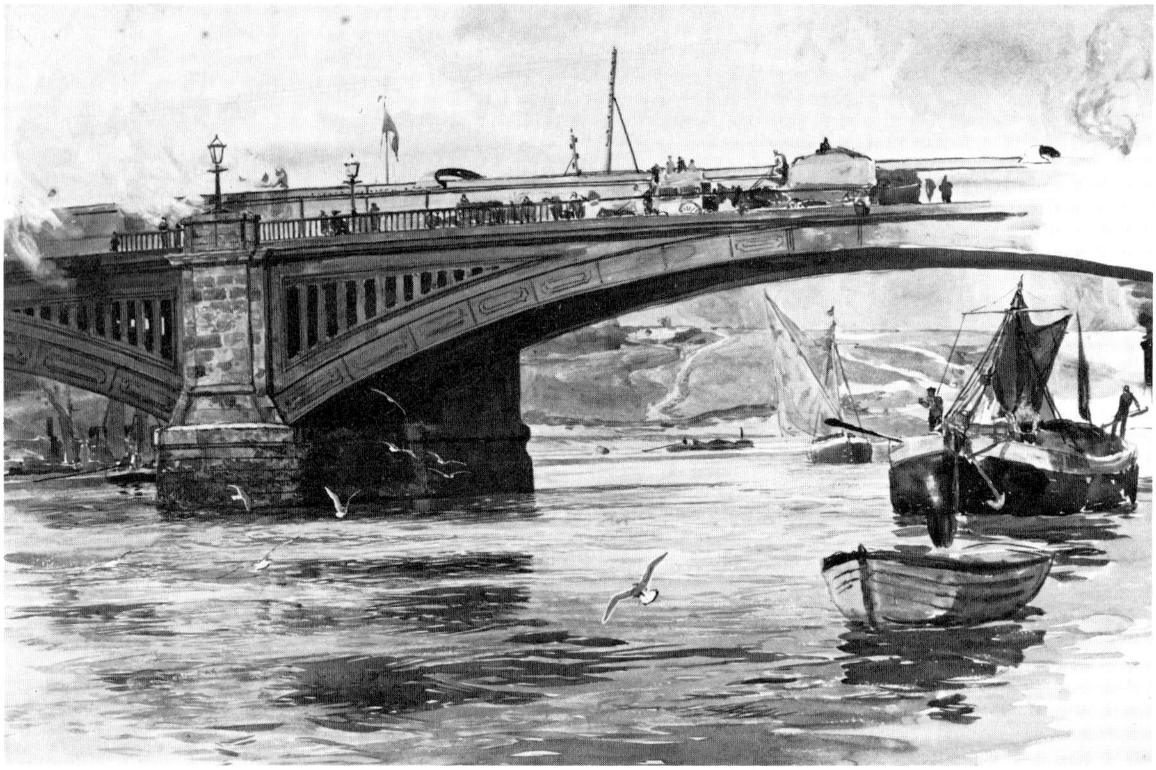

38. Study for 'Heave Away' . . .: Rochester Bridge, *c.* 1883
watercolour, $12\frac{13}{16} \times 19\frac{3}{16}$ (325 × 488)
National Maritime Museum, London

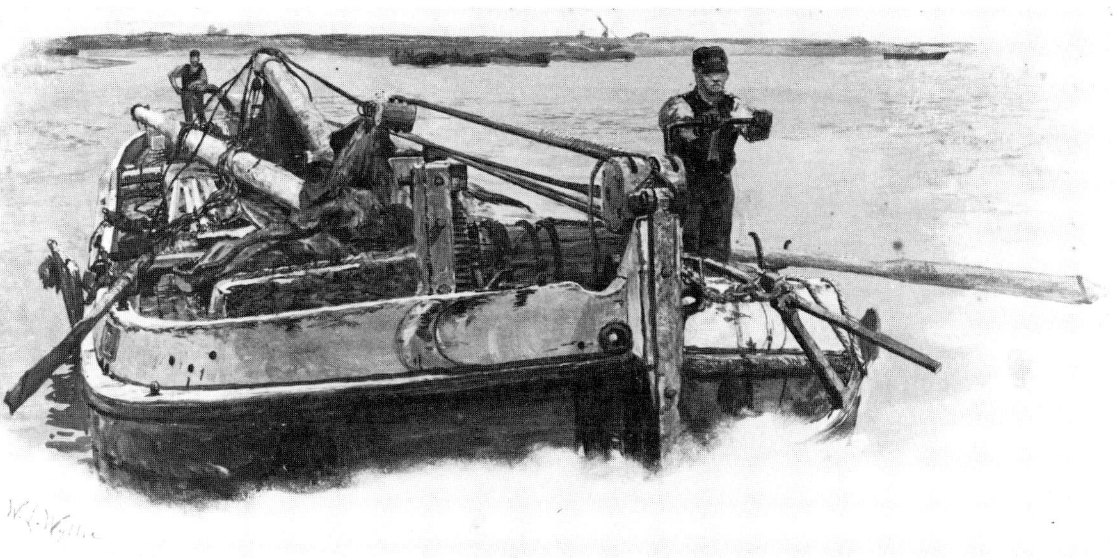

39. Study for 'Heave Away' . . ., *c.* 1883
watercolour, $9\frac{3}{8} \times 19\frac{3}{8}$ (239 × 492)
National Maritime Museum, London

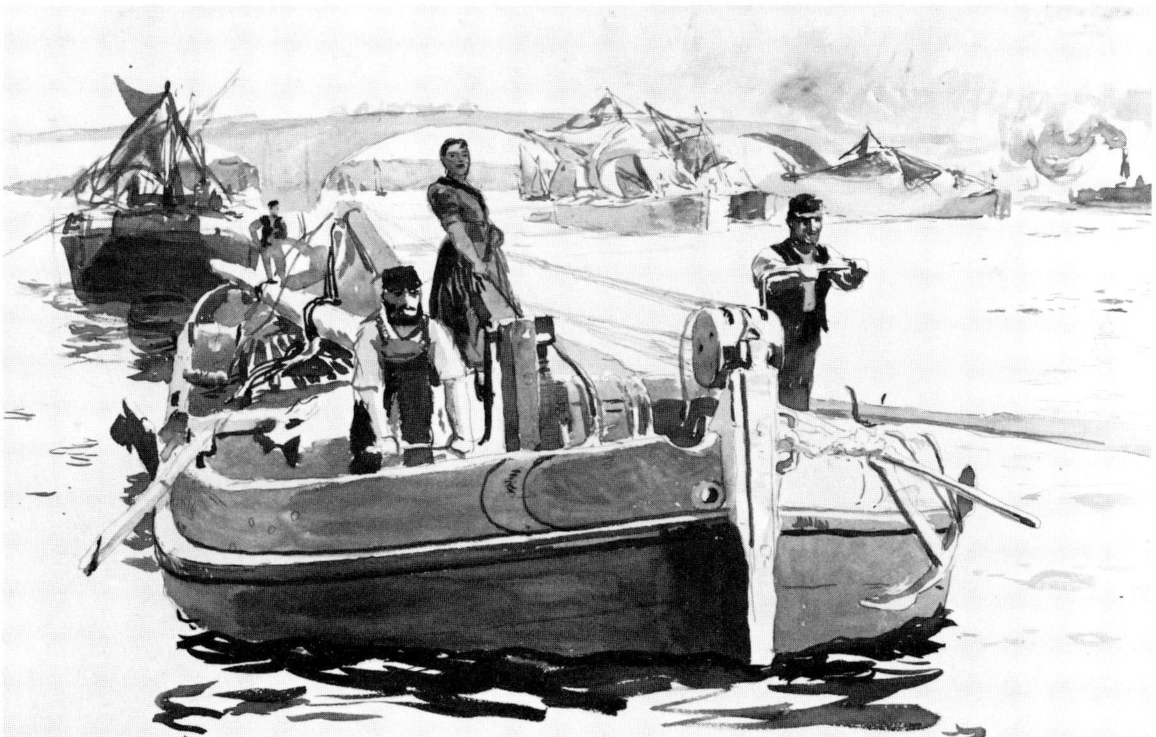

40. Study for 'Heave Away' . . ., *c.* 1883
grey wash, $12\frac{5}{8} \times 18\frac{7}{8}$ (320 × 480)
National Maritime Museum, London

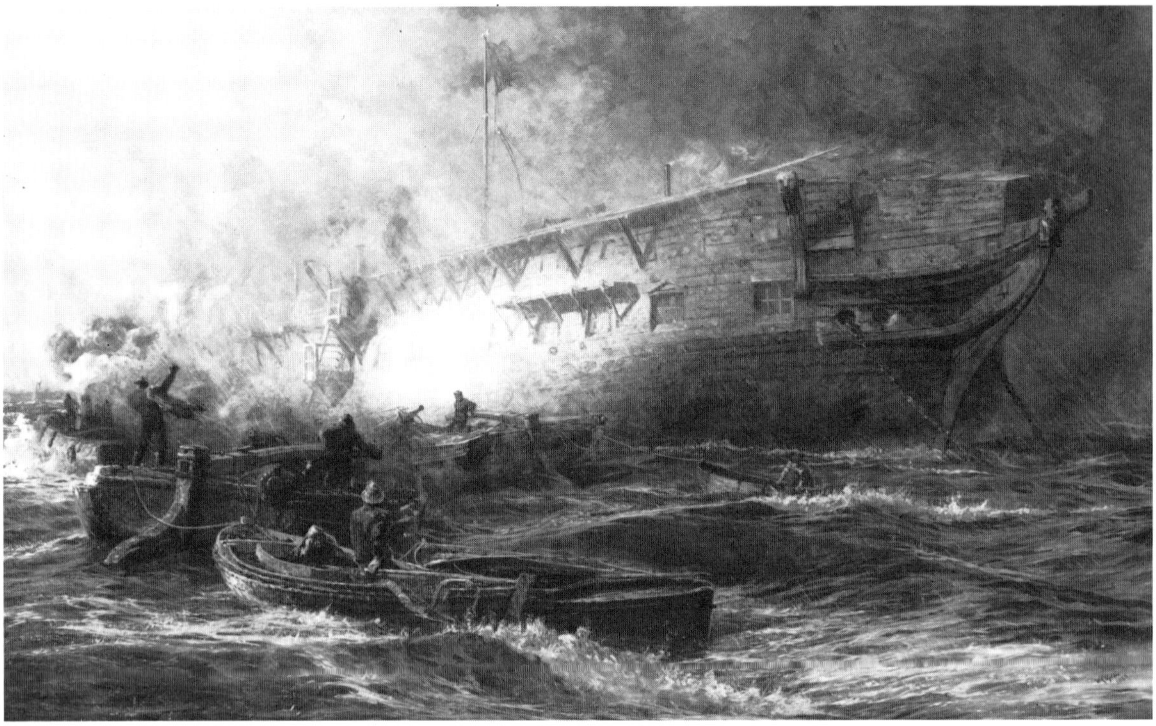

41. Storm and sunshine; a battle with the elements (the *Leonidas* at Upnor), 1885
oil, 42 × 65 (1067 × 1651)
National Maritime Museum, London

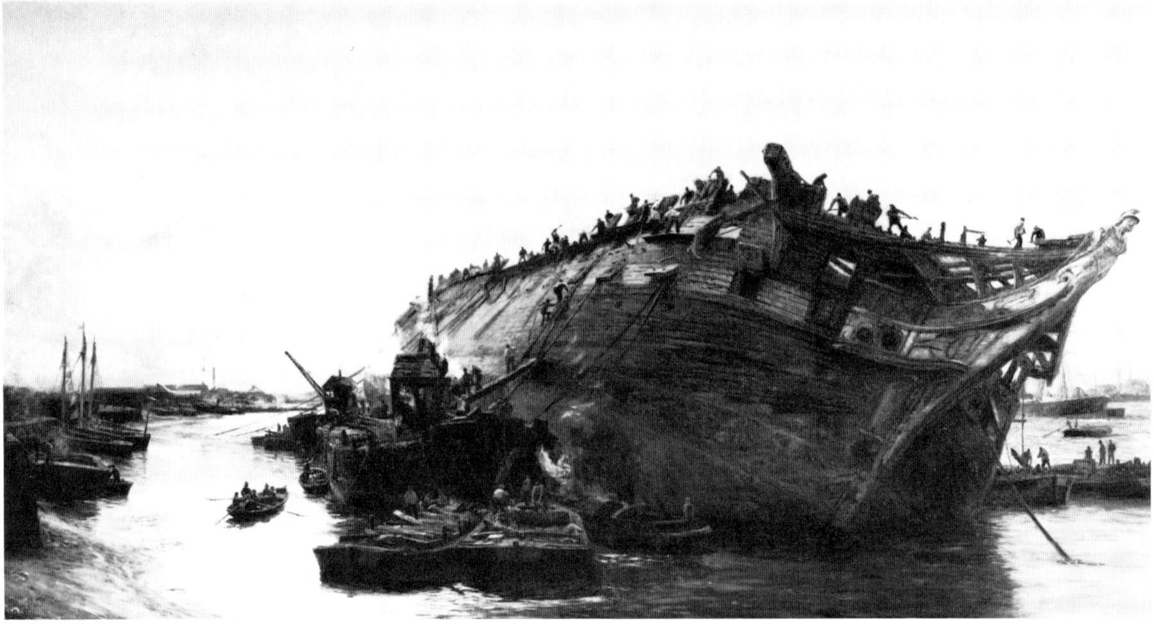

42. Charles Wyllie: A dying giant. 'How are the mighty fallen, and the weapons of war perished', 1885
oil on canvas, 36 × 50 (915 × 1270)
Private collection, on loan to the National Maritime Museum, London

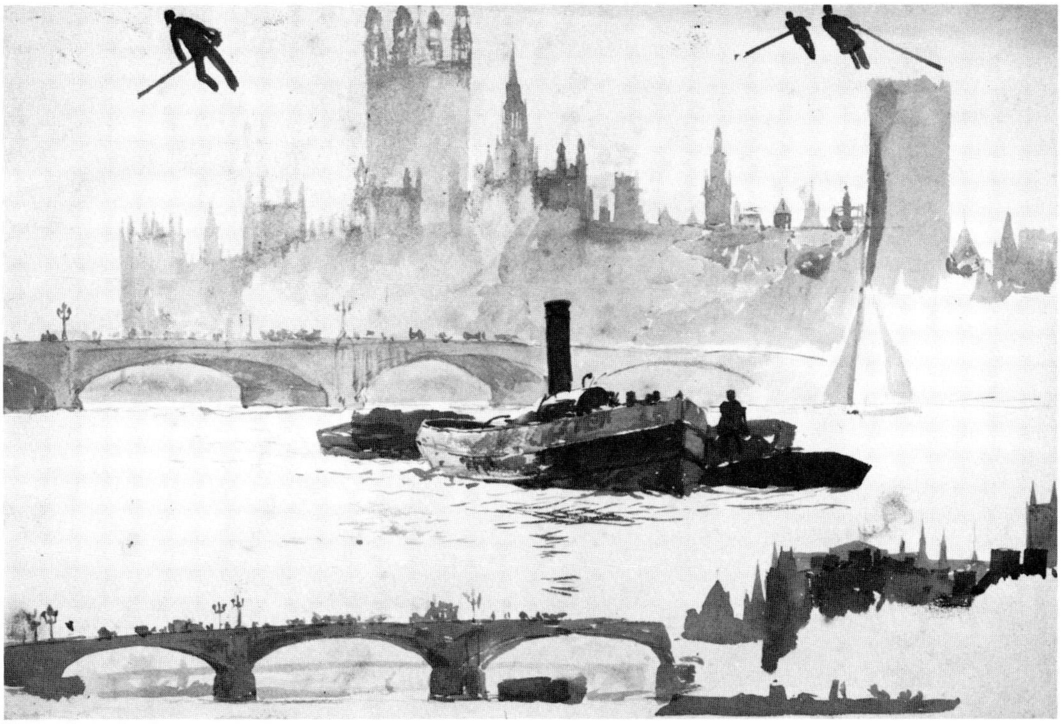

43. Studies made from the Thames at Westminster, *c.* 1880
sepia wash, $8\frac{5}{16} \times 12\frac{1}{4}$ (211 × 312)
National Maritime Museum, London

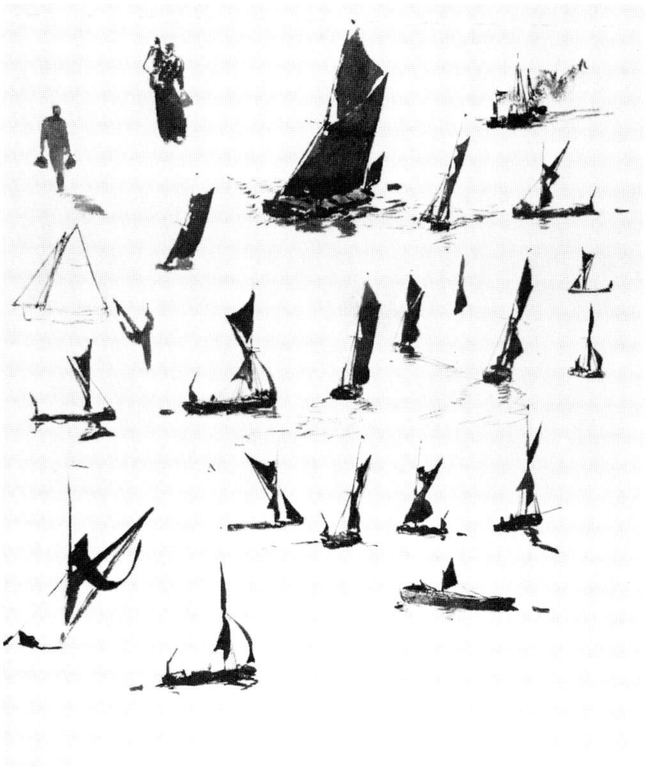

44. Studies of Thames barges, *c.* 1890
sepia wash, $9\frac{11}{16} \times 8\frac{5}{8}$ (256 × 219)
National Maritime Museum, London

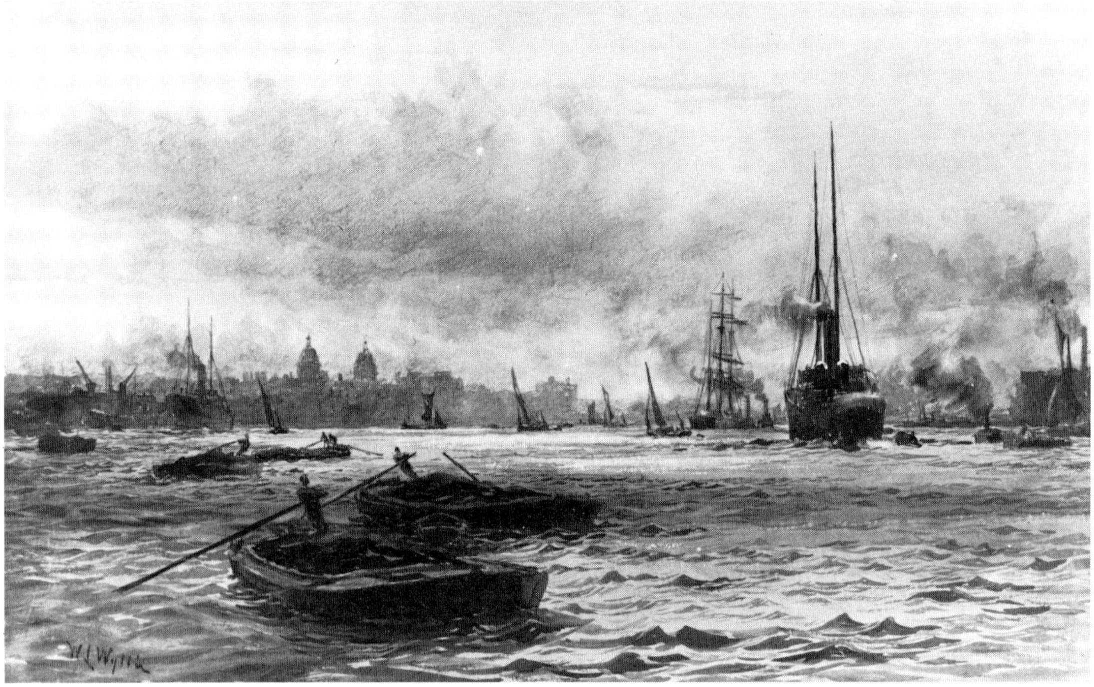

45. Shipping in Greenwich Reach, *c.* 1890
pencil, grey wash and white heightening, $8\frac{7}{8} \times 13\frac{7}{8}$ (224 × 352)
National Maritime Museum, London

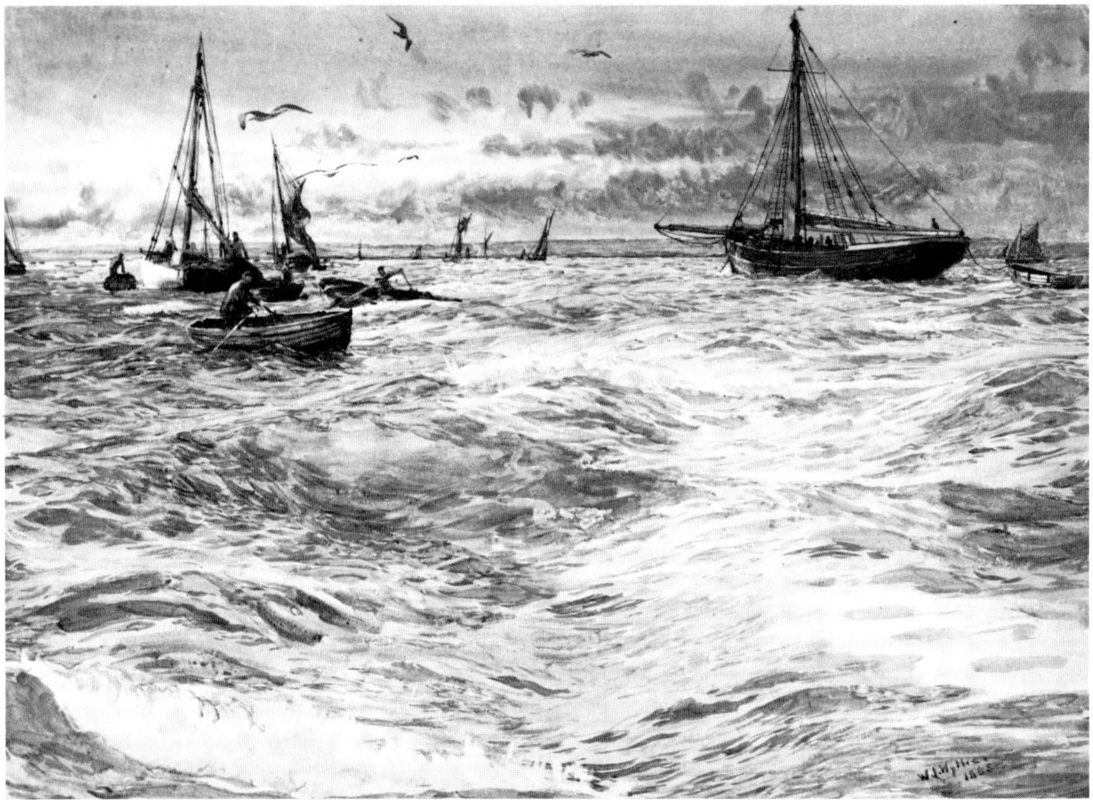

46. On the Banks, 1885
watercolour, $17\frac{1}{8} \times 23\frac{1}{8}$ (435 × 589)
National Maritime Museum, London

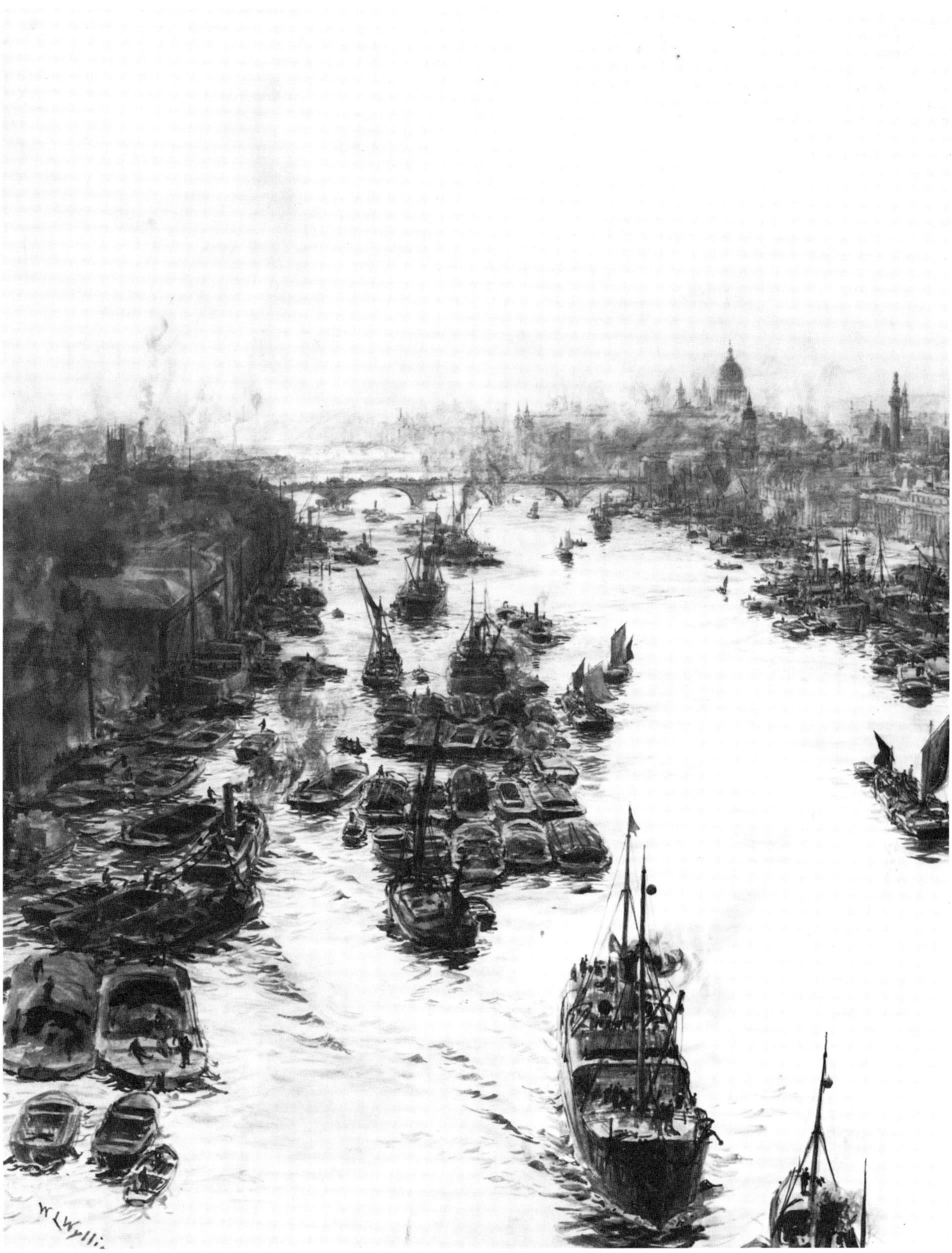

47. The Pool of London, *c.* 1890
black wash, $23\frac{3}{4} \times 18\frac{1}{8}$ (603×460)
National Maritime Museum, London

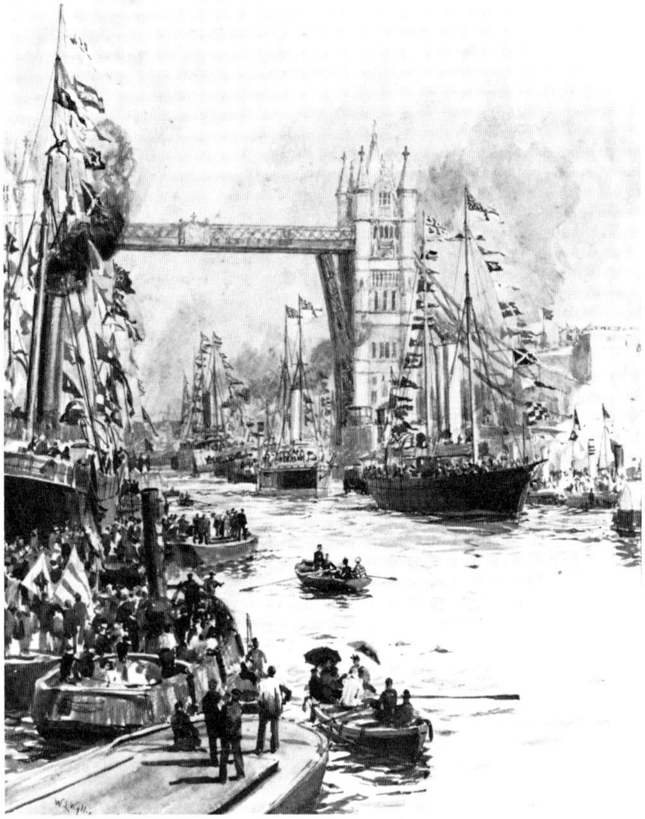

48. The opening of Tower Bridge, 1894
pencil and grey wash, $14\frac{1}{4} \times 10\frac{1}{2}$ (361×266)
National Maritime Museum, London

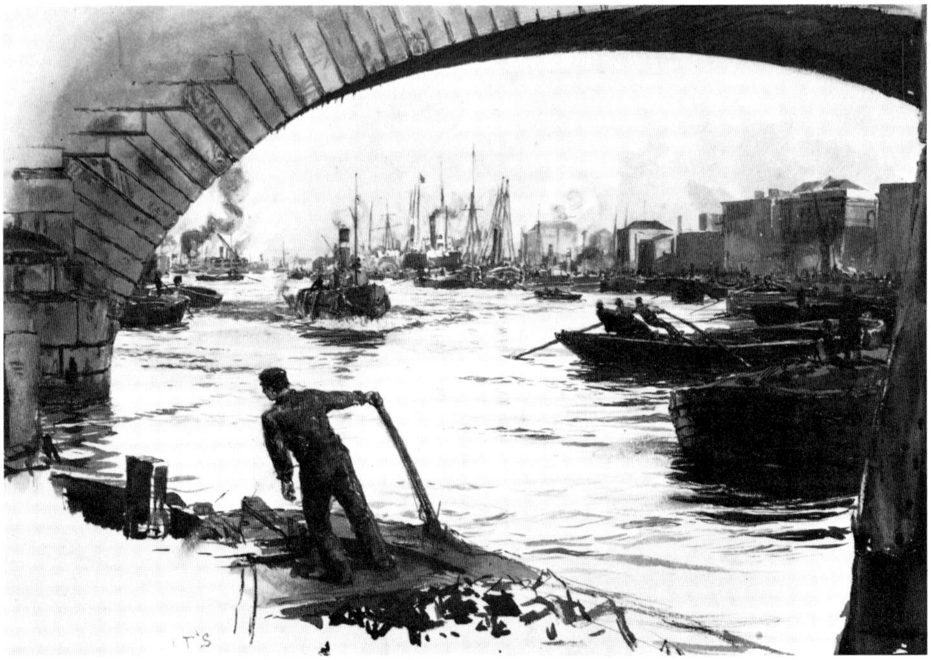

49. Shipping on the Thames seen through an arch of London Bridge, *c.* 1885
grey wash, $9\frac{15}{16} \times 13\frac{15}{16}$ (252×354)
National Maritime Museum, London

> ... the Academy work of this year [1884] is a respectable climax to a Record which, if it is chequered, is on the whole satisfactory, and in places even brilliant. Seldom indeed has a painter come to the front so rapidly, and at the same time so meritoriously. Perhaps that has been said a hundred times before now of a hundred other artists, but never, I think, with equal truth.
>
> It is only fourteen years since he exhibited his first picture; at the present time he is in the front rank of English painters of sky and water, he has scarcely a rival as an exponent of the fact and wonder of our glorious Thames, and as an illustrator in black and white he holds a position in the matter of ships and sea and atmosphere not less eminent than that from which Mr Small dominates the figure draughtsmen.

With relation to Wyllie's treatment of subject-matter, and methodical approach, the critic was particularly perceptive:

> It has been attained partly by a certain originality of view and partly by a manly individuality of method; but chiefly by an unremitting study of nature and a constant application to the manual business of the painter's art.[26]

But the critic of the *Illustrated London News* was a little less warm in his praise of the 1884 pictures: 'W. L. Wyllie ... has nothing so striking as the Thames picture bought from the Chantrey Bequest last year. ...'[27]

The 1885 Academy picture *Storm and Sunshine: a battle with the elements* is a picture in which atmosphere is exploited to the full, and is painted in Wyllie's 'most vigorous style.'[28] It depicts the *Leonidas* (launched in 1807), which at that time was used for the storage of gun cotton, and moored in the river close to Wyllie's house. A sudden squall has come down while the gun cotton is being unloaded. 'Mr Wyllie's "Storm and Sunshine" strives to reproduce a well nigh impossible effect – a passing ray of sunlight on a ship's side, whilst the rest of the hull and surrounding water is lashed by wind and rain.'[29] It is very likely that Wyllie actually witnessed the scene, for the painting of the large oil sketch (Colour Plate 7) is even more vigorous, and for the finished picture there has been only slight rearrangement. The craft in the foreground of the sketch is a doble, a craft used for smelt-fishing in the Medway.

In 1889 Wyllie showed at the Institute of Painters in Oil Colours exhibition a further Thames subject, and received what may well have been a timely warning from the *Magazine of Art*:

> 'Highway of Nations' possesses the merits which characterise all this accomplished artist's drawings of the lower Thames. It seems a pity, however, that, by displaying so little variety either in subject or treatment, he should run the risk of becoming known as a painter of one picture.[30]

There are signs that Wyllie took heed, for he was already expanding his repertoire of subjects. Nevertheless, his output increasingly betrayed a tendency to repetition, which is apparent even in the technically superb engraved work of later years, in which the Thames continued to be a favourite subject.

It was through the patronage of the Fine Art Society that Wyllie produced his first major naval pictures in 1883, two large canvases depicting the recent bombardment of Alexandria. For these and their copyright Wyllie was paid four hundred pounds[31] and the paintings were exhibited at the Fine Art Society in the spring of 1883, along with pictures of the same subject by de Neuville and Woodville.

While the ironclads of the Mediterranean fleet were bombarding the main forts of Alexandria, Captain Lord Charles Beresford, in the gun vessel *Condor*, noticed that they were being annoyed by fire from Fort Marabout, which was somewhat to the east. He therefore took his unarmoured ship in so close to the fort that the guns could scarcely be depressed sufficiently to bear. When she was recalled, Admiral Sir Frederick Seymour sent her the signal 'Well done, *Condor*', the title of the smaller of the two pictures (Colour Plate 8).

Wyllie visited Egypt for the specific purpose of making drawings and was away for six weeks. Some of those he returned with are vivid evocations of Mediterranean sea and light, which may well account for the unusually brilliant colour in the painting.

Wyllie's first direct experience of the Royal Navy was in 1889, when, as press representative for the *Graphic* during naval manoeuvres, he was invited aboard the *Black Prince* in Lough Swilly in Ireland. During this period he made many drawings, and on his return was invited to exhibit at the Fine Art Society, where he showed sixty-nine watercolours in an exhibition entitled *The Queen's Navy*. Plates 50 and 51 show studies made on board the *Black Prince*. According to Mrs Wyllie, it was through this exhibition, with support for Wyllie rallied amongst Royal Academicians by his friend James Clarke Hook (1819–1907), that Wyllie was elected an Associate of the Royal Academy in 1889.

During the late 1880s Wyllie had increasing contact with shipping companies, both as an artist and later as a passenger. He was commissioned not only to paint ship portraits, but also to design various kinds of pictorial material for reproduction. For these commissions he evolved a formula, based on the tradition of the mass-produced nineteenth-century ship portraits, which were intended to provide accurate, or at least recognizable depictions of individual ships. The convention was to show the vessel from the side, in profile and beam view. Wyllie's usual solution was to show the vessel 'port bow' view as in the picture of RMS *Teutonic* (Plate 56). In this kind of painting Wyllie excelled, for he was faultless in draughtsmanship and detail, but it must be remembered that these pictures were for him means of earning a living, such as he himself referred to as 'pot boilers'.

Wyllie's mastery of the watercolour reached its peak in the last decade of the nineteenth century. By this time he had developed a technique which allowed directness as well as precision when necessary. Wyllie's handling of the medium had always been 'skilful', but his art, so dependent on a methodical approach, was prevented from attaining any real degree of fluency until he was completely confident in his draughtsmanship, and in the medium itself, and this did not occur until the late 1890s.

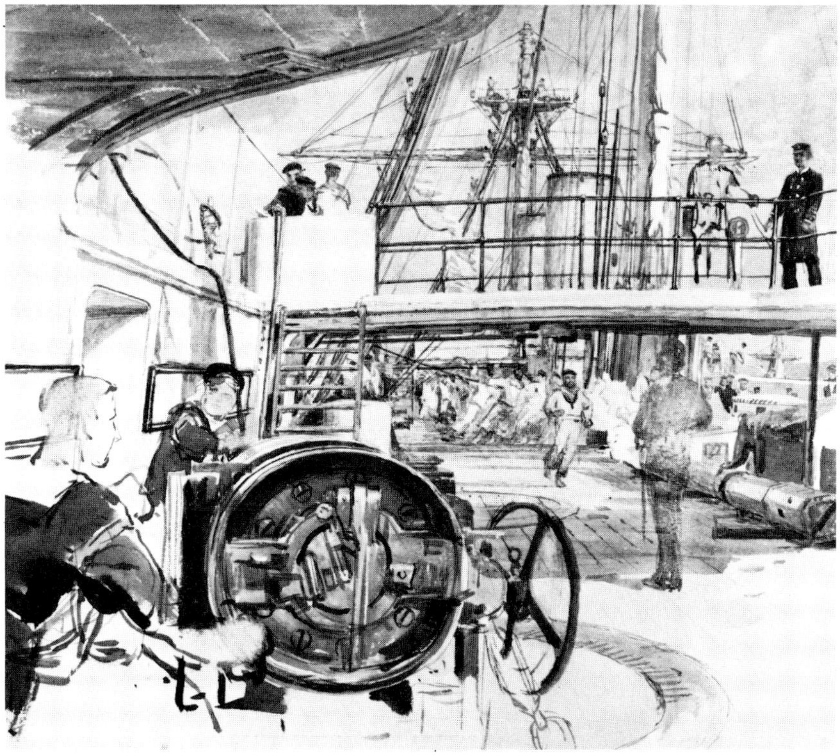

50. On board HMS *Black Prince*, 1889
pencil and watercolour, $10\frac{1}{4} \times 11\frac{1}{2}$ (261 × 292)
National Maritime Museum, London

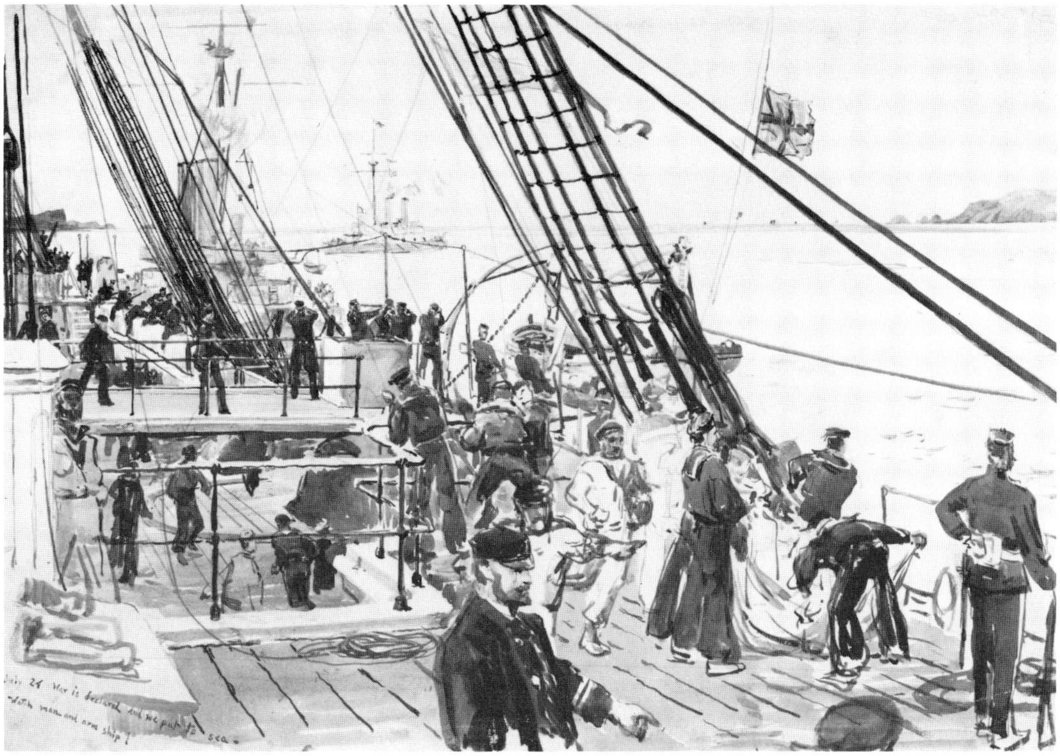

51. Manoeuvre aboard HMS *Black Prince*, 1889
pencil and grey wash, $9\frac{15}{16} \times 13\frac{15}{16}$ (252 × 354)
National Maritime Museum, London

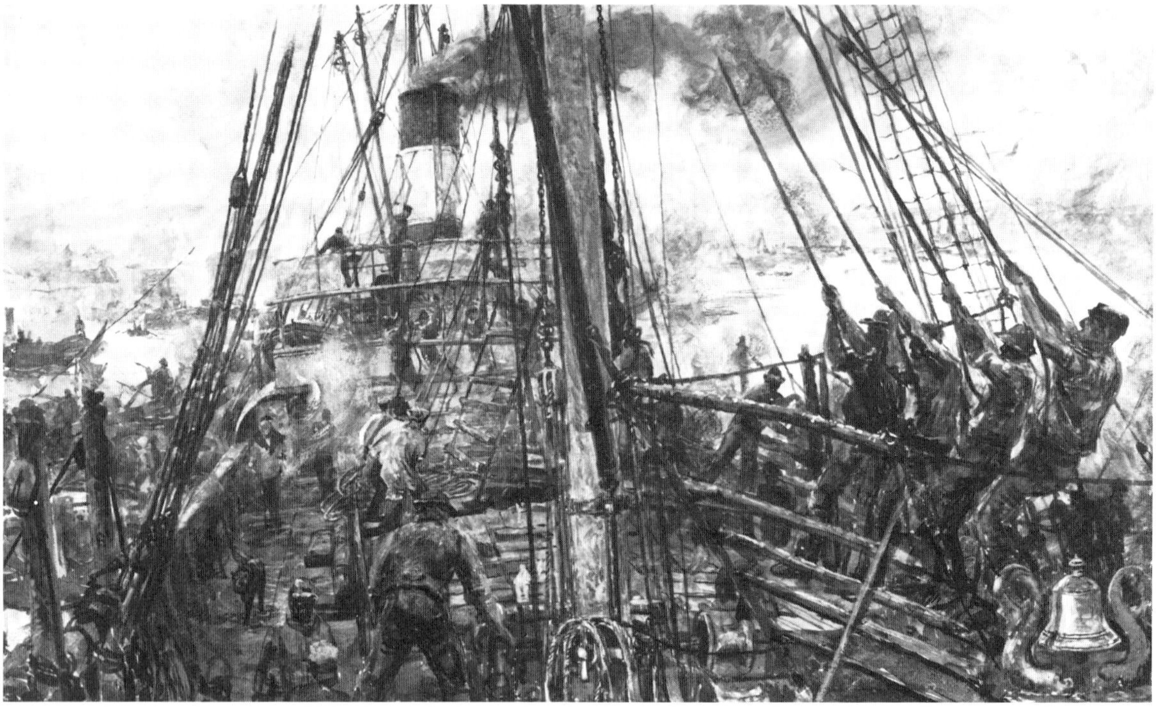

52. Discharging a collier, *c.* 1887
watercolour, $12\frac{3}{8} \times 10\frac{1}{4}$ (314 × 464)
National Maritime Museum, London

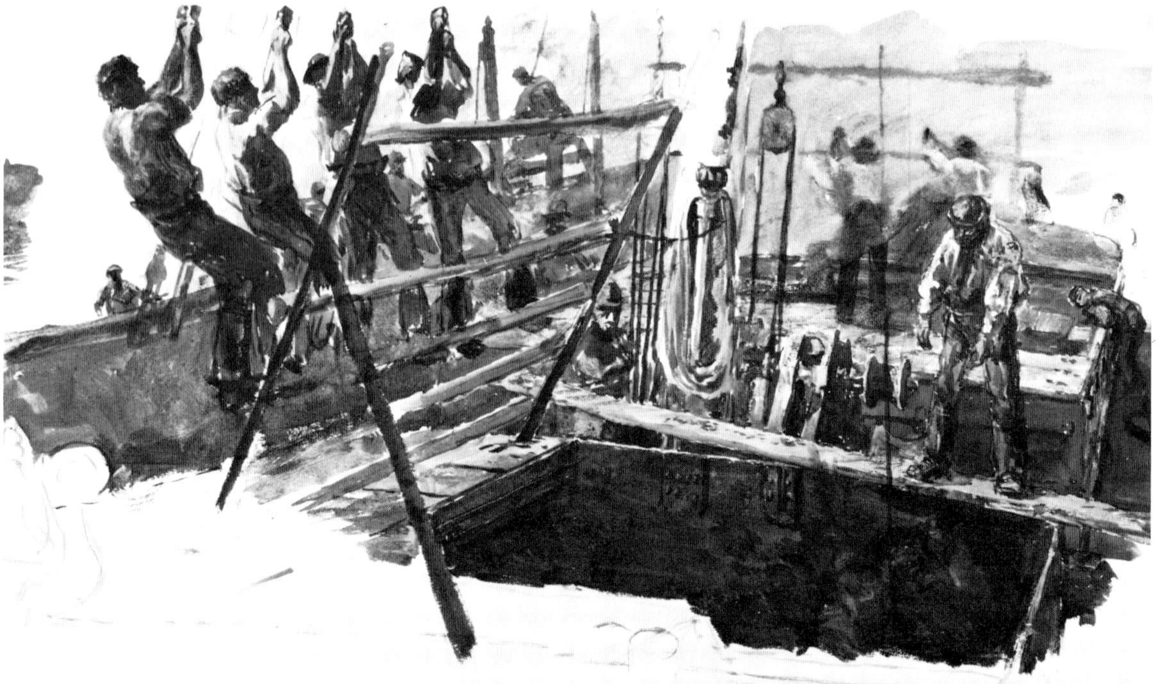

53. Coal whipping, *c.* 1887
watercolour, $12\frac{13}{16} \times 18$ (325 × 457)
National Maritime Museum, London
Men discharging a coastal collier by means of a single block and tackle

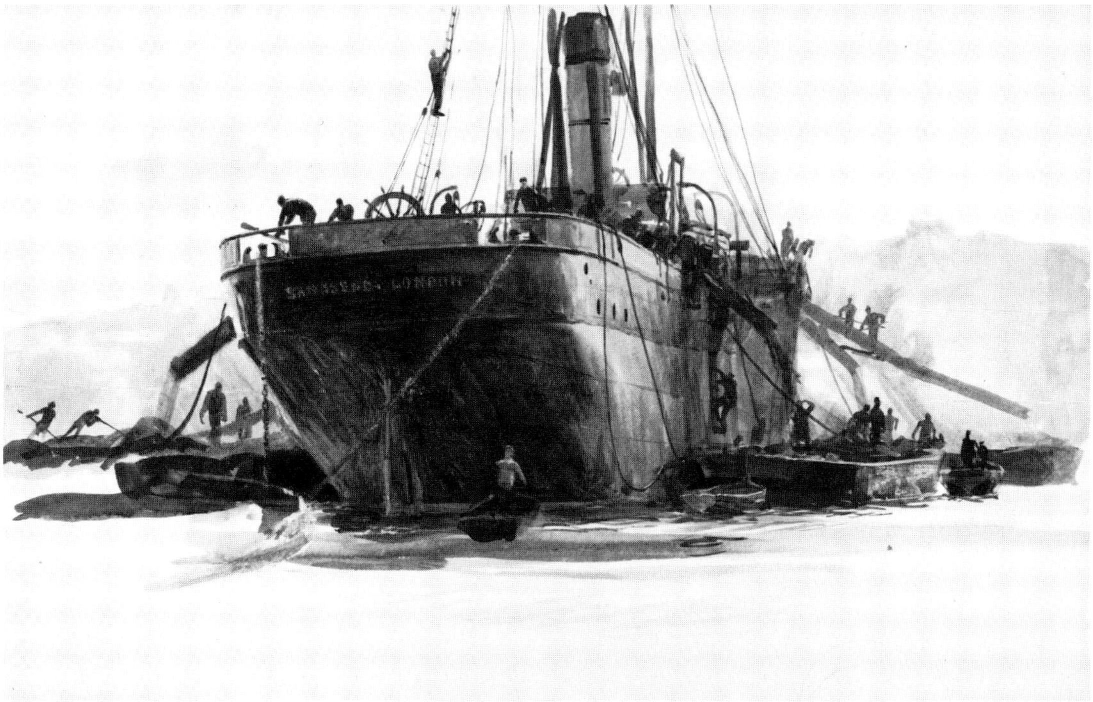

54. *Sandsend* of London discharging coal, late 1880s
watercolour, $15 \times 21\frac{13}{16}$ (382×554)
National Maritime Museum, London

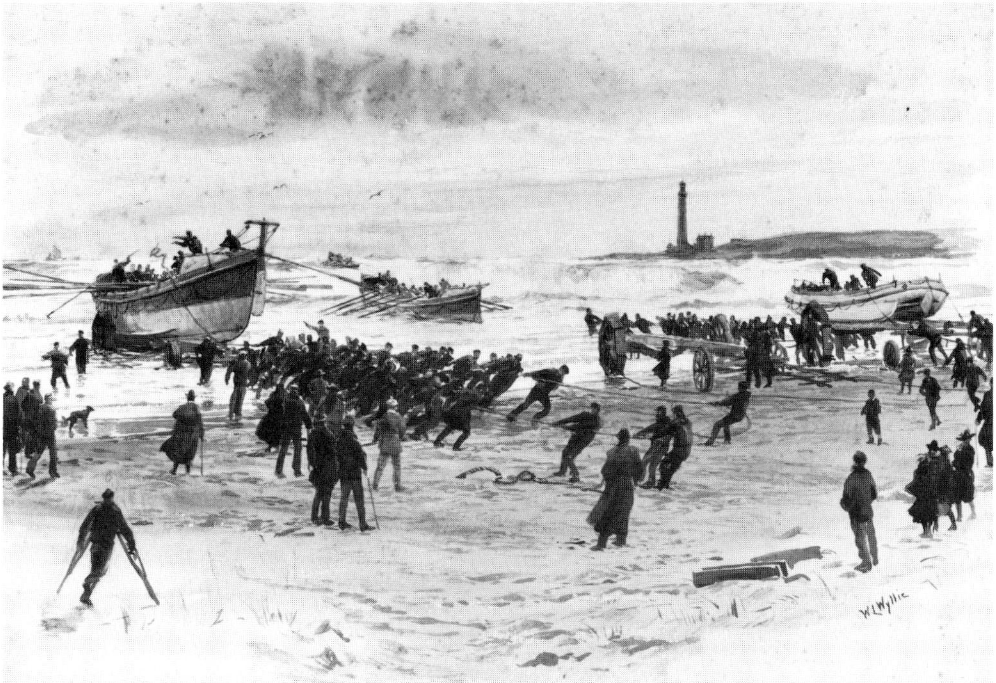

55. Lifeboat trials at Montrose
pencil, grey wash and white heightening, $10 \times 13\frac{13}{16}$ (254×354)
National Maritime Museum, London
This study was made when Wyllie visited Montrose to draw the Lifeboat trials for the *Graphic*. The composition of the 1893 Royal Academy 'Robert and Susan to the Rescue' is based on that of this study

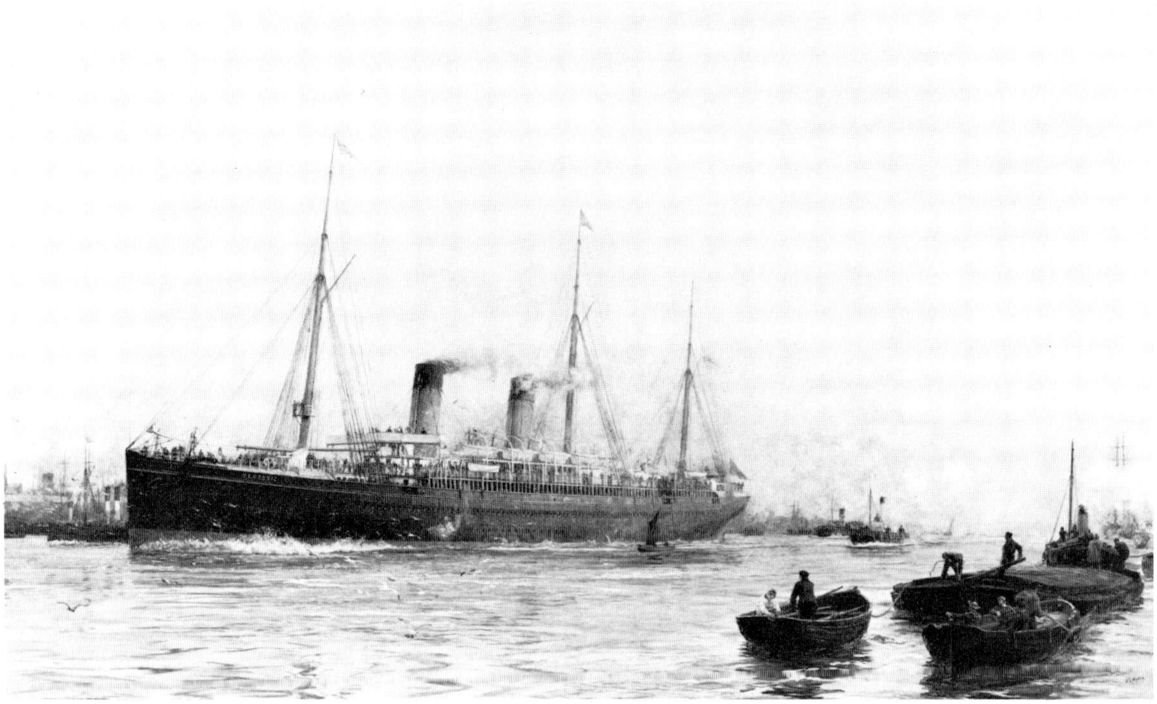

56. RMS *Teutonic* leaving Liverpool in 1889
oil, 36 × 60 (914 × 1525)
National Maritime Museum, London

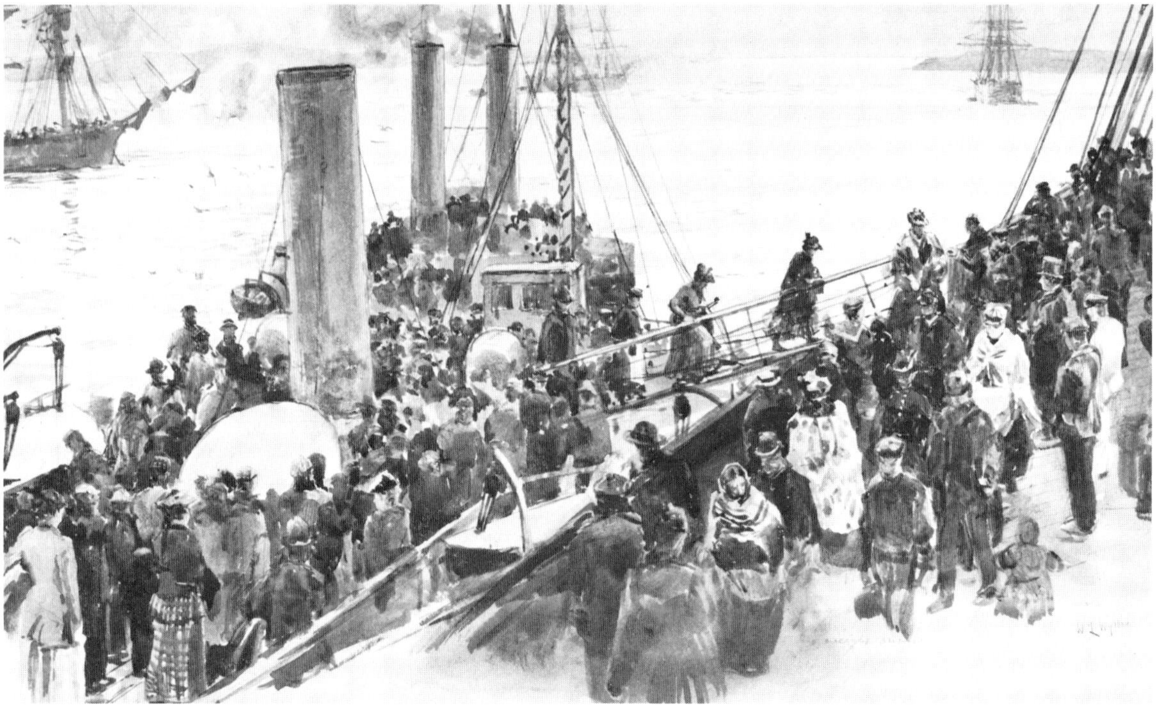

57. Passengers embarking, *c.* 1890
sepia wash, $9\frac{7}{8} \times 13\frac{3}{4}$ (251 × 350)
National Maritime Museum, London

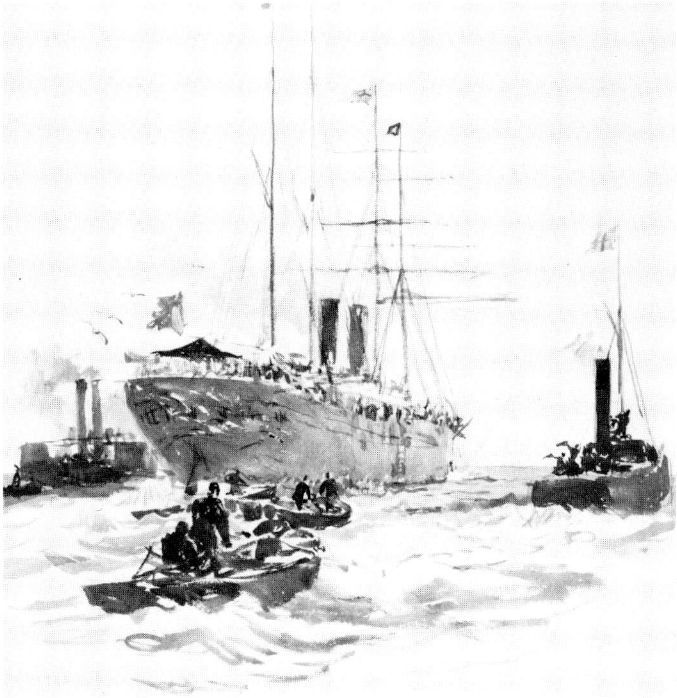

58. A White Star liner, *c.* 1900
grey wash, $14\frac{5}{8} \times 12\frac{7}{8}$ (372×327)
National Maritime Museum, London

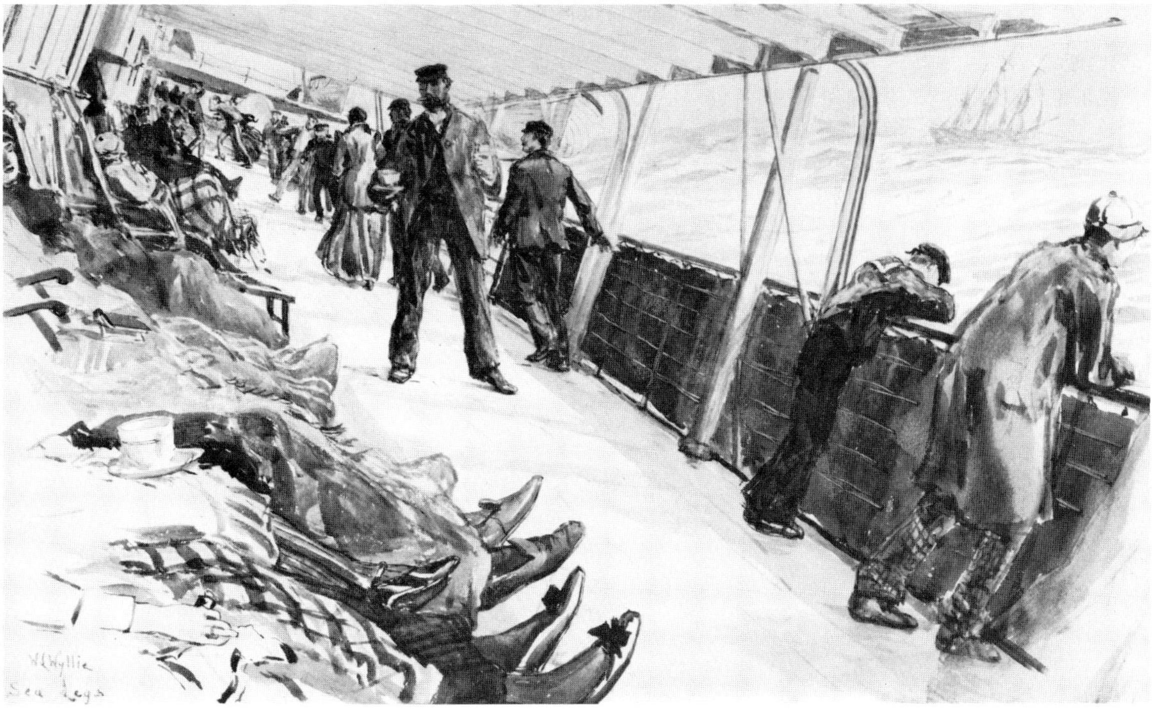

59. Sea Legs, *c.* 1890
sepia wash, $9\frac{7}{8} \times 13\frac{3}{4}$ (252×350)
National Maritime Museum, London

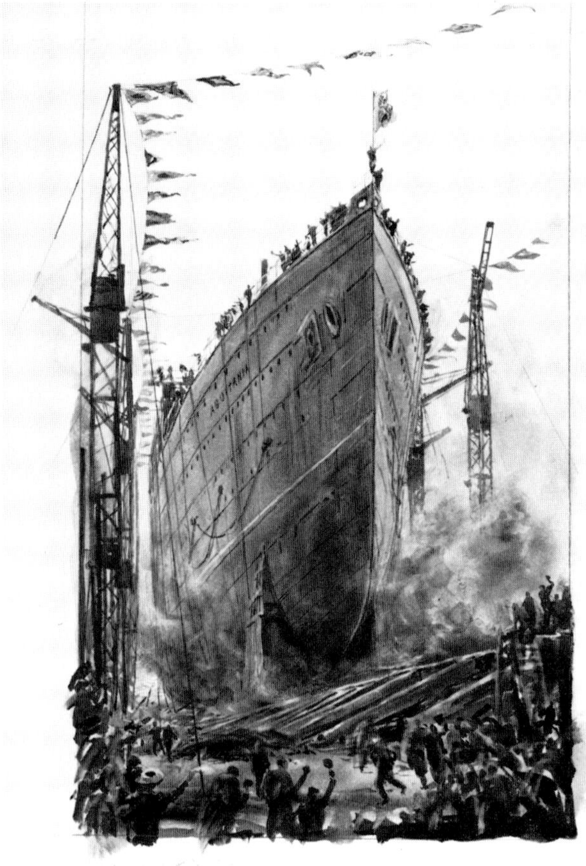

60. Launch of the *Aquitania*, 1915
pencil and grey wash, $12\frac{11}{16} \times 8\frac{3}{8}$ (322 × 212) (subject)
National Maritime Museum, London

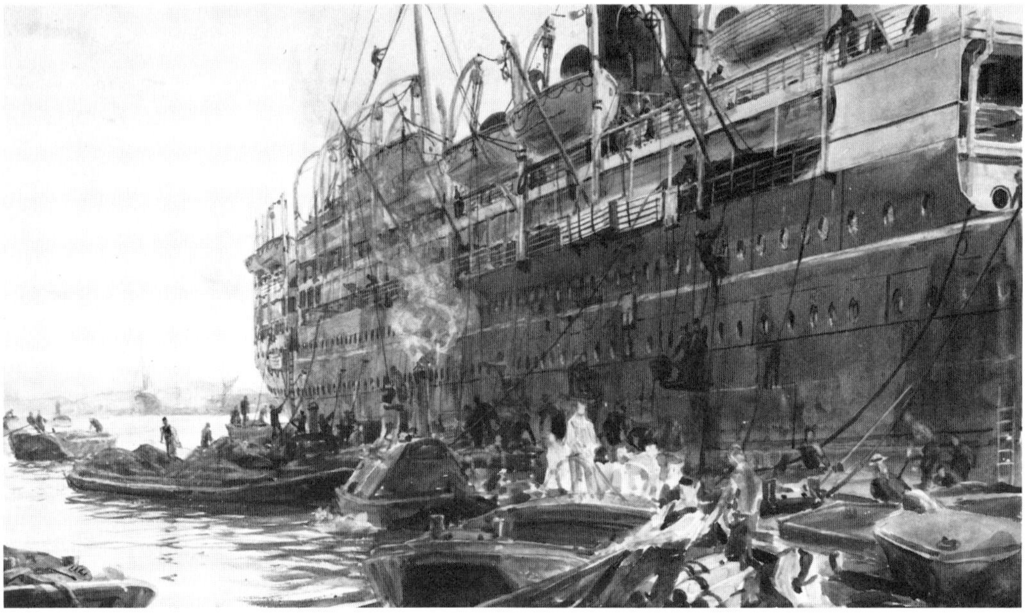

61. P and O liner coaling, *c.* 1905
watercolour, $12\frac{3}{4} \times 18\frac{1}{4}$ (324 × 464)
National Maritime Museum, London

A study of Wyllie's watercolours is hampered because they are rarely dated, although the majority are signed. It is nevertheless broadly possible to trace the stylistic development of his work in this medium.

Although in the late 1860s Wyllie produced some broadly painted experimental watercolours to portray natural effects such as sunset skies, more frequently his watercolours of this period are meticulous and delicate. They are often small in scale and extremely finely painted; landscape, sea, but particularly sky are superbly observed and rendered. This meticulous approach was one which he made use of up to the 1890s alongside more ambitious sophisticated work in the medium. Wyllie referred to these small watercolours as his 'guinea arts' which he sold to friends. They ideally suited the marine artist for whom precision and accuracy were of great importance. They have a cool detached quality, are informative like a map or chart, and are painted with the precision of a miniature (Plate 67).

The watercolours which Wyllie retained for his albums are mainly small coloured notations of views of shipping and coastal views. Some are extremely slight, informative studies produced with a cautious hand. Others are more experimental, such as sunsets, making use of the lurid colours which Wyllie favoured in the early 1900s, or loose, ethereal compositions, with a subtle Whistlerian sense of composition and atmosphere. In these sketches Wyllie could afford to be a great deal more daring, making use of wet paper, blots, and merging colours.

It took thirty years, between approximately 1870 and 1900, for Wyllie's watercolour technique to mature, and the work produced between those years demonstrates a transition from what was essentially a 'dry' technique to a 'wet' one.

The early watercolours rely upon such traditional conventions as scraped highlights, or light areas reserved out of dry paper, which might be used to suggest the lights or foam upon breakers (Plate 46). Wyllie's methodical approach extended to his use of watercolour, and he therefore tended to work over the paper surface in a deliberate piecemeal fashion, filling one area after another, rather as if he were placing together the pieces of a jig-saw puzzle. This method had its pitfalls, evidence of which are the abandoned watercolours with their large areas of untouched white paper.

During the 1880s, in the watercolours of 'sea and sky', Wyllie modelled his seas with small touches of watercolour on dry paper, applying first one tone, then another, until a satisfactory effect was achieved. These pictures show a close affinity with the work of his friend and contemporary Henry Moore (1831–95), then regarded as one of England's most important artists. He is known to have participated in Wyllie's sketching parties down the Thames, along with other Royal Academicians. Indeed, the brilliantly coloured sea and sky pictures of *c.* 1890, with their intense blues, may well have been stimulated by paintings by Moore such as *The Clearness after Rain* exhibited in the Royal Academy in 1887, and in Paris at the Exposition Universelle in 1889 where it won Moore one of the only two *Médailles d'honneur*.[32] Wyllie also exhibited in Paris in 1889, along with his brother Charles.

Wyllie's contribution amounted to seven entries including oil paintings, watercolours, drawings, and the etching *Highway of the Nations*. He won the second class medal in painting and engraving, and the first class medal in watercolour along with Charles Keane, Alfred East and E. J. Gregory.[33]

The watercolours produced by Wyllie on a holiday at Berck-sur-Mer in 1891 are amongst his most sophisticated. These were exhibited along with some drawings made in Italy at the Fine Art Society in 1892, and received with delight by both the *Magazine of Art* and the *Athenaeum*. The catalogue to the exhibition entitled *Holiday Drawings in France and Italy* was prefaced with a narrative of the exhibition by the artist's wife, as a catalogue to the French drawings.

The *Athenaeum* remarked upon Wyllie's use of perspective:

> The Fine Art Society has never offered its visitors greater pleasure than Mr W. L. Wyllie's 'Collection of Holiday Drawings in France and Italy.' There are nearly a hundred of them, sixty-one being derived from that sandy paradise Berck-sur-Mer, in Picardy; the rest are from the Riviera and Italy. Of Mr Wyllie's work it goes without saying that he gives new and brilliant impressions of whatever it pleases him to illustrate, and that there is nothing mannered or conventional about any of his drawings. . . .
>
> Mr Wyllie's felicitous touch puts in their right relationship and proper aerial perspective numerous groups or minute figures, whether in the foreground or background, adjusts the scale of each, and increases the distances of air and sand between each.[34]

The *Magazine of Art* recorded the more atmospheric aspects of the watercolours, recalling the

> long, level foreshores of warm fawn tint, dotted with picturesque figures moving dark against the light about their daily fishing business, quaint craft riding out in deeper water, and grey skies full of wind and weather, melting to a very distant horizon . . . Mr Wyllie's shores have a delicious quality of oily wetness about them; and he is true to the sea, to the ships that sail thereon, and the men and women who live by it, in form and detail, and in feeling and spirit.[35]

The watercolours of bathers (Colour Plate 4) are particularly charming, and like the 1875 oil sketch of figures on a terrace (Colour Plate 3) already discussed, are reminiscent of the work of Boudin, although they lack his breadth of vision and handling. The most impressive aspect of these pictures is the subtlety of their spatial effects achieved with apparent ease. Yet despite their style and outdoor feel, they result from carefully worked out perspective and precise drawings, executed with great delicacy. Diagrams of similar beach scenes appear in Wyllie's treatise on perspective for the amateur, *Nature's Laws and the Making of Pictures* (1903; Plate 71).

It was during the 1890s that Wyllie adopted the 'wet' watercolour technique which was to allow him much fuller and freer expression. As M. A. Wyllie recalls:

> With regard to his watercolours, they really were *watercolours*. He would take his pin board and sheet of paper to a basin or bath, soaking his paper at the back in the water, lay it on a pin board, the frame that fits on the top open, and walk back to his easel followed by a little trickle of water. While the board was still open he laid on the wash for the sky and sea, much darker than it would look when dry, holding the board upright so that the wash should run in the right direction while wet.

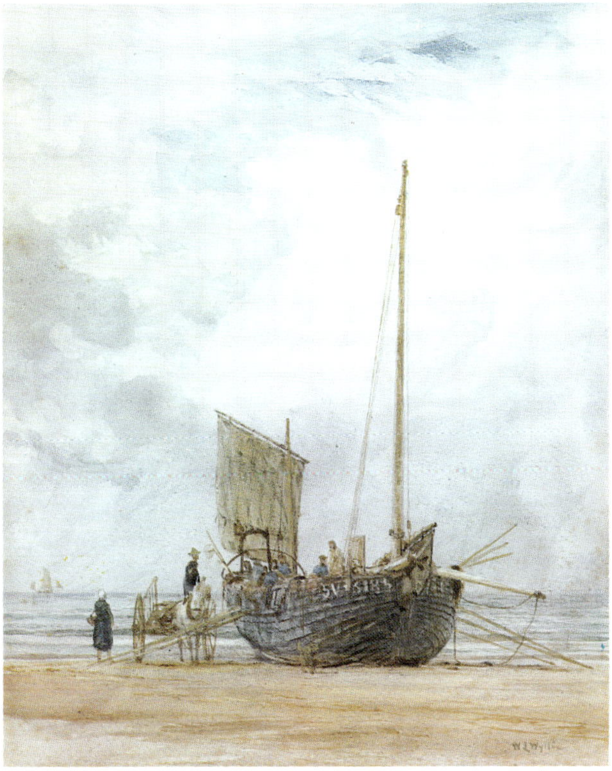

1. A fishing boat from St Valéry-sur-Somme unloading her catch, c.1875
watercolour, 12 × 9$\frac{7}{16}$ (305 × 240)
National Maritime Museum, London

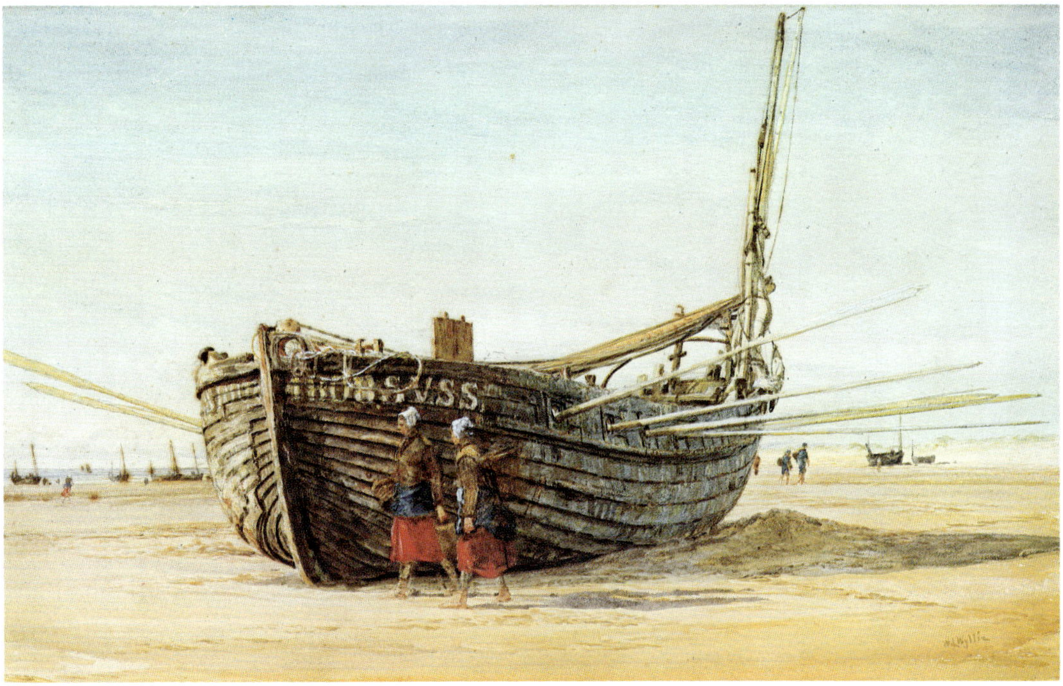

2. Fishing boat from St Valéry-sur-Somme, c.1875
watercolour, 10$\frac{5}{8}$ × 16$\frac{3}{4}$ (271 × 424)
National Maritime Museum, London

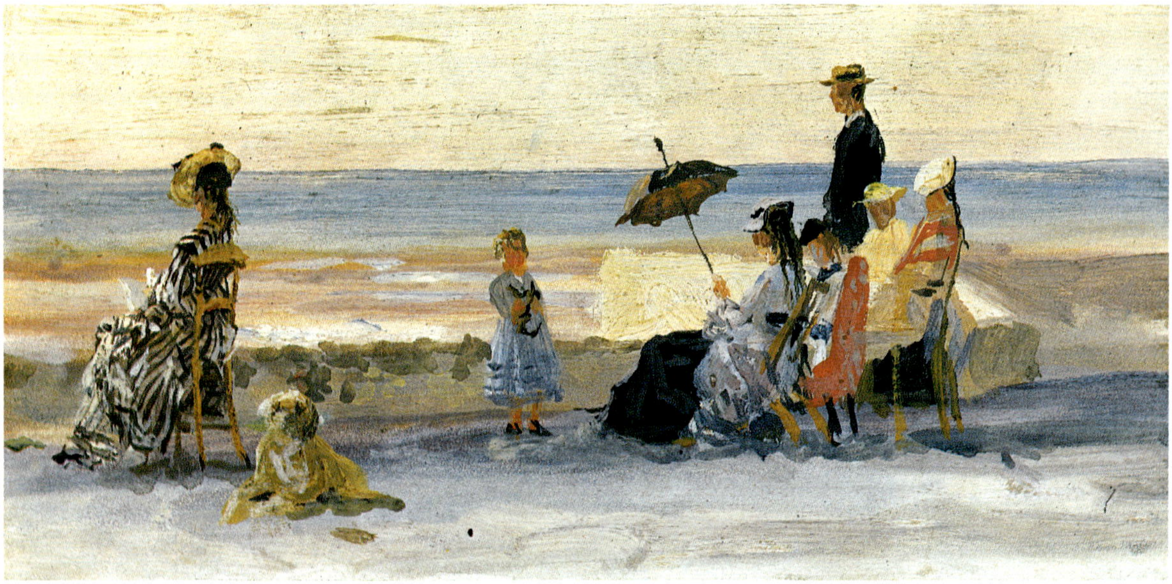

3. Figures on a terrace, c.1875
oil on paper, $3\frac{1}{8} \times 6\frac{1}{8}$ (79×156)
Miss A. D. Wyllie

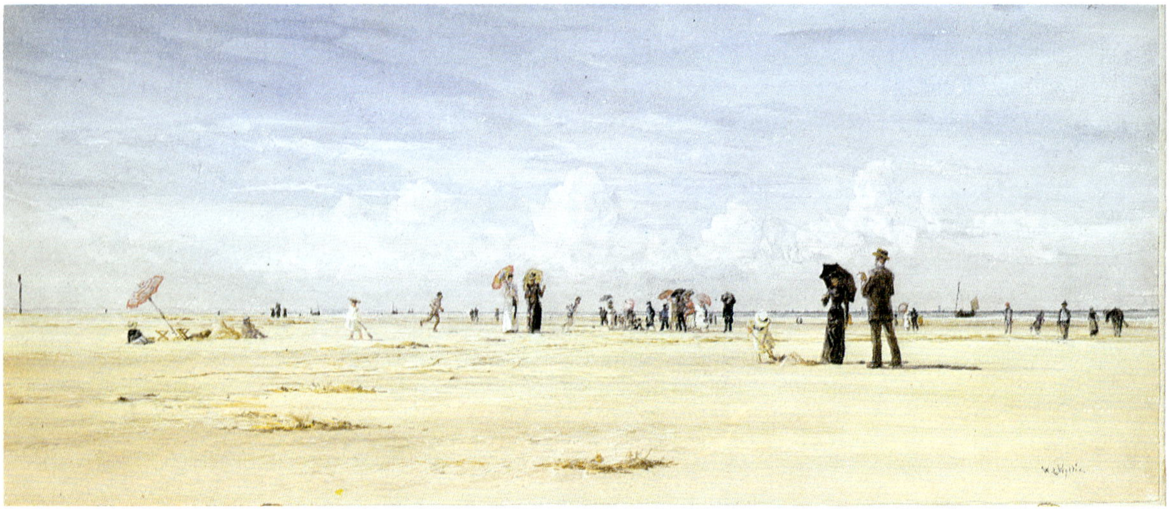

4. Figures on the beach at Berck-sur-Mer, 1891
watercolour, $7\frac{5}{16} \times 16\frac{9}{16}$ (185×422)
National Maritime Museum, London

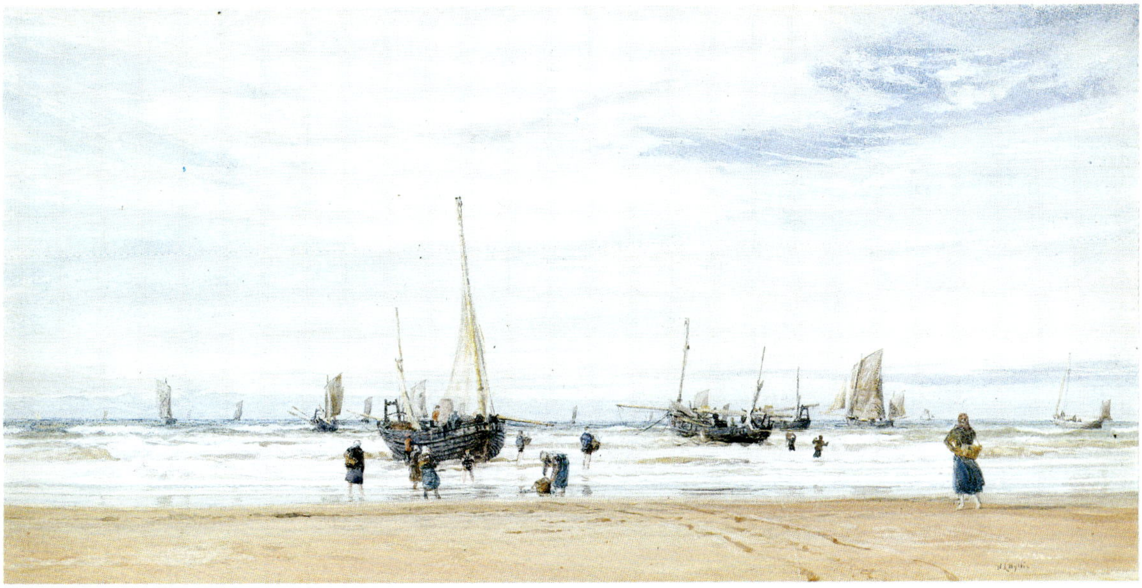

5. Landing the catch, Northern France, c.1875
watercolour, $10\frac{1}{2} \times 16\frac{3}{4}$ (267 × 426)
National Maritime Museum, London

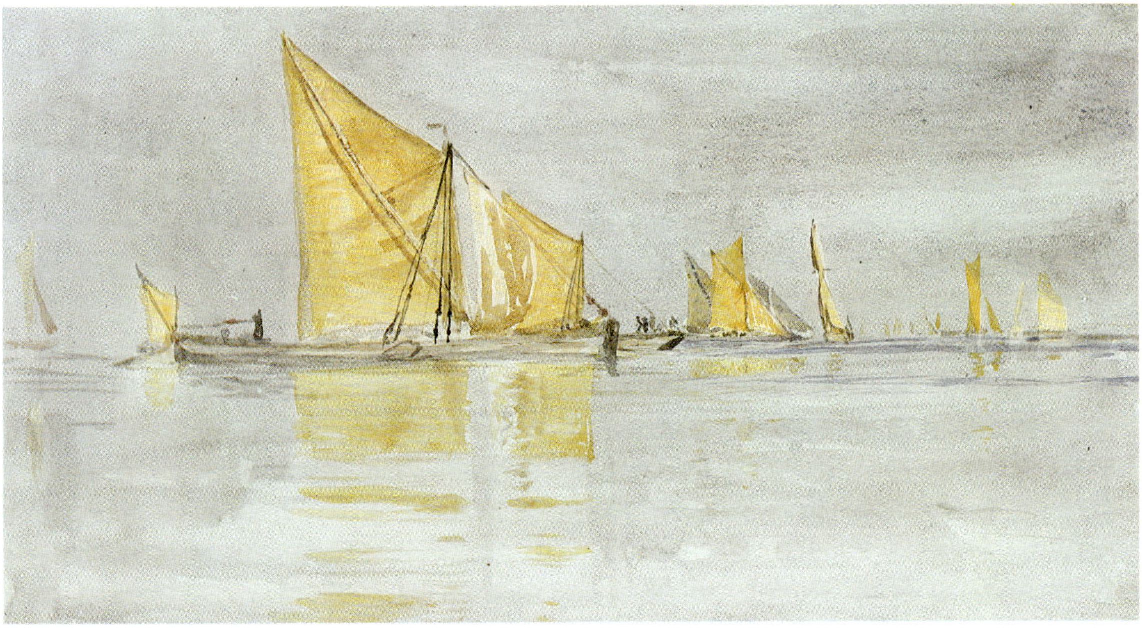

6. Thames sailing barges, c.1875
watercolour, $7\frac{9}{16} \times 13\frac{1}{8}$ (191 × 347)
National Maritime Museum, London

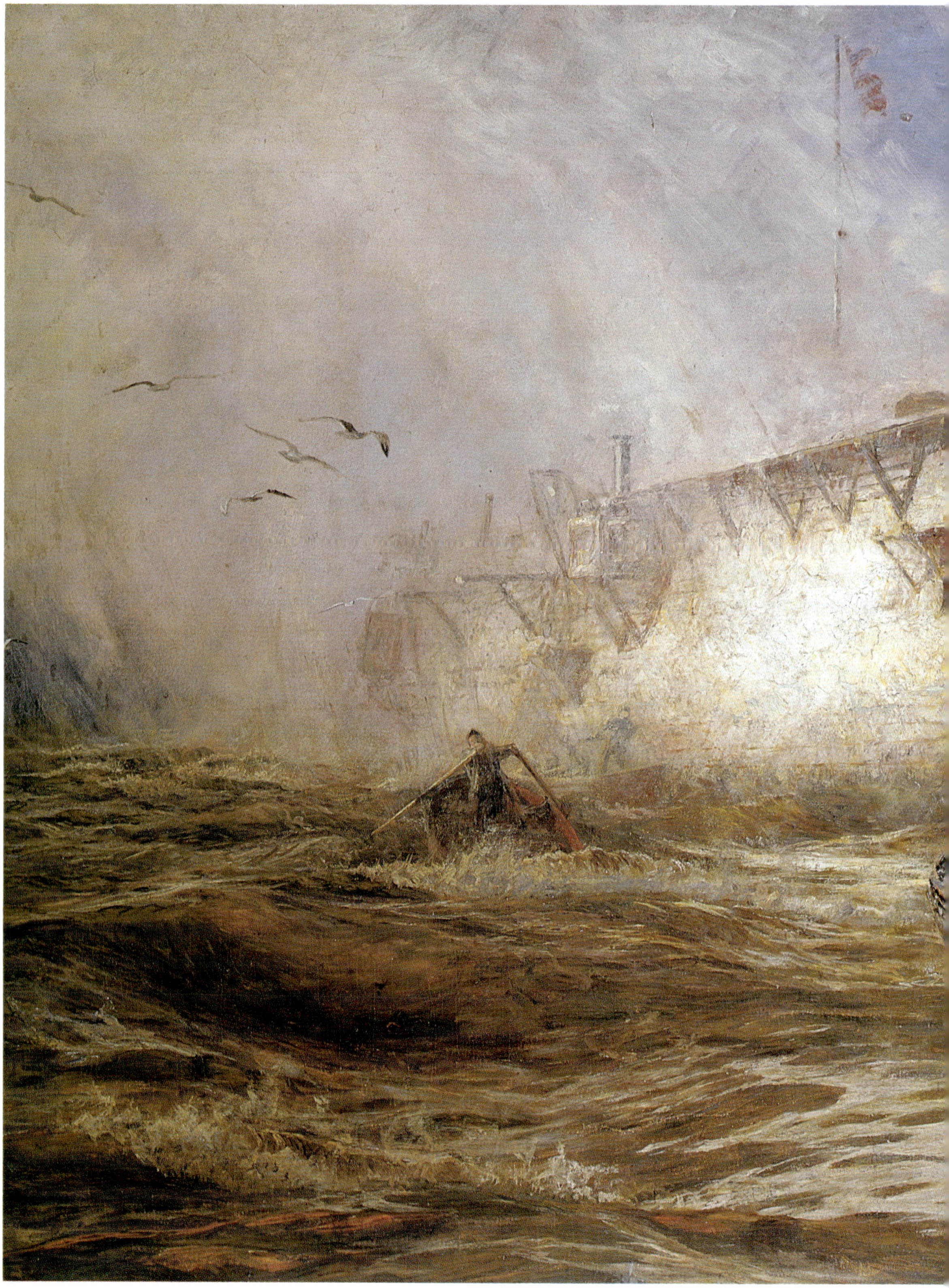

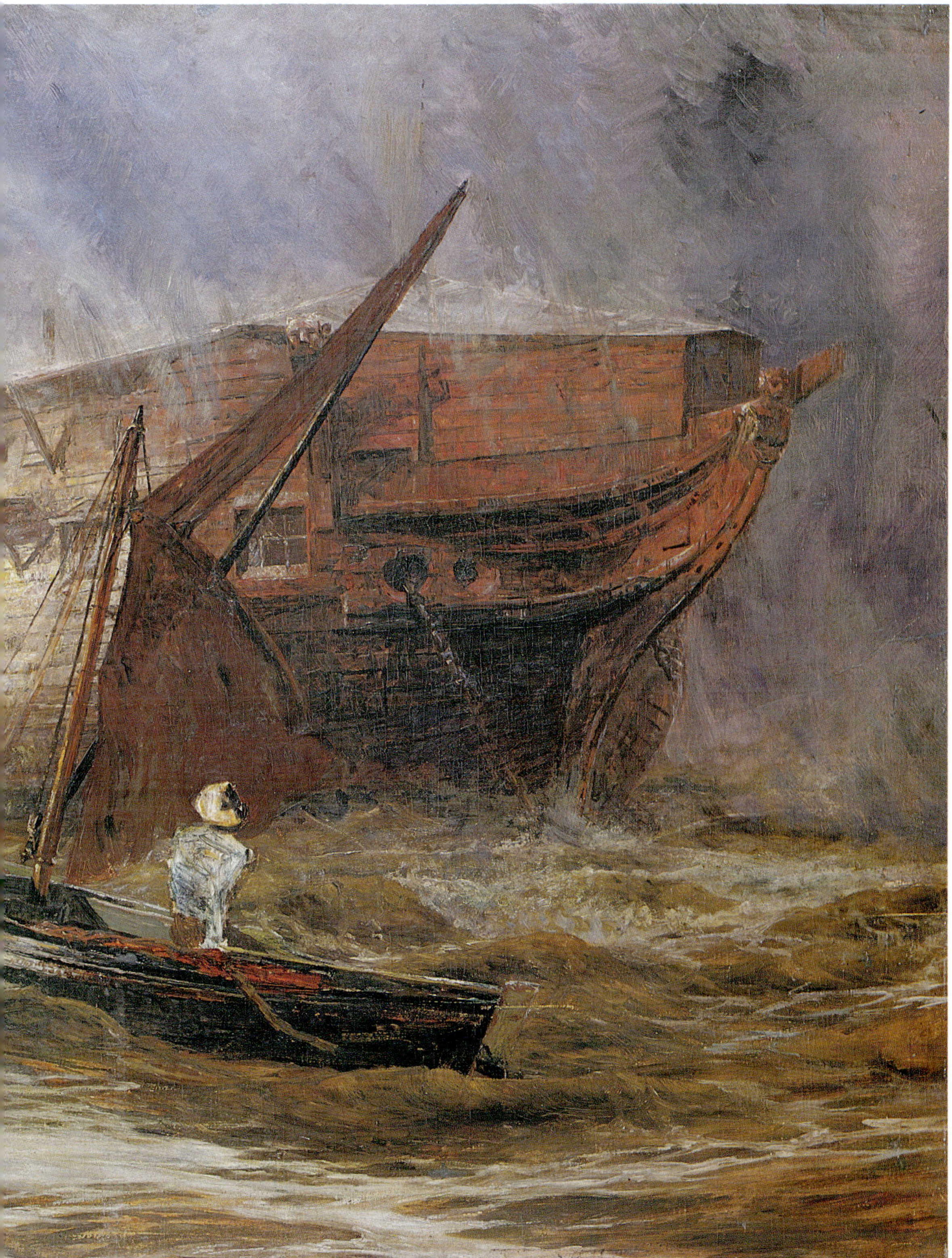

7. *Leonidas*, powder hulk, 1885
oil, 41 × 65 (1042 × 1651)
National Maritime Museum, London

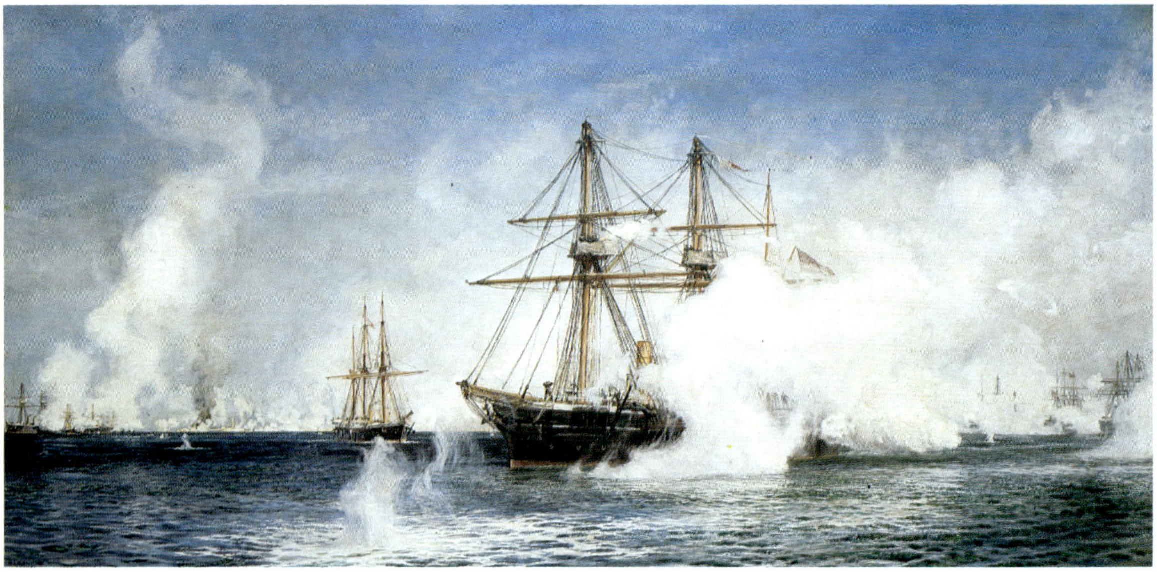

8. 'Well done, *Condor*': the Bombardment of Alexandria, 11 July 1882
oil, 36 × 60 (914 × 1525)
National Maritime Museum, London

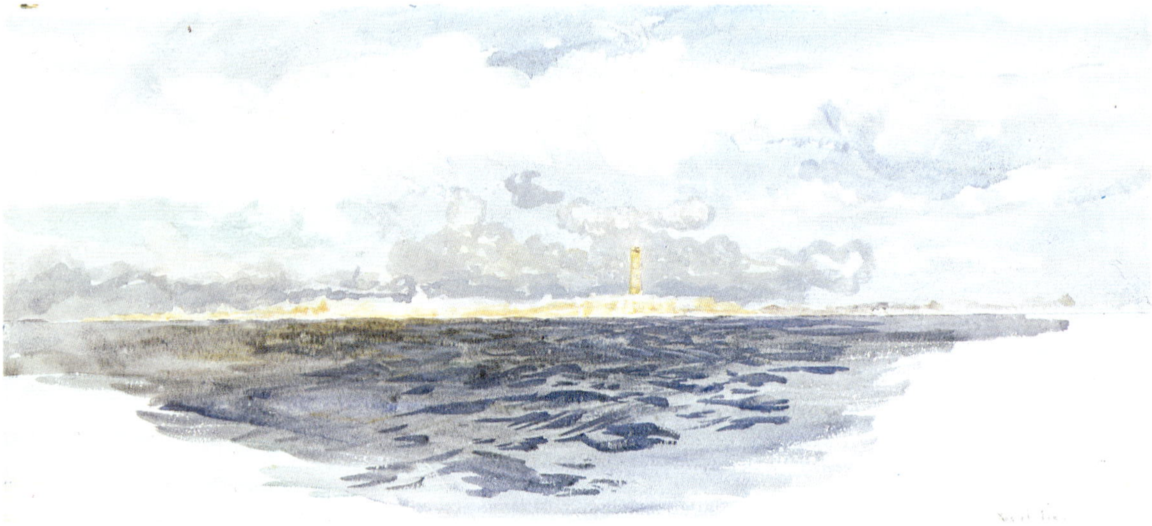

9. Alexandria from the sea, c.1883
watercolour, $9\frac{7}{16}$ × $20\frac{7}{8}$ (240 × 530)
National Maritime Museum, London

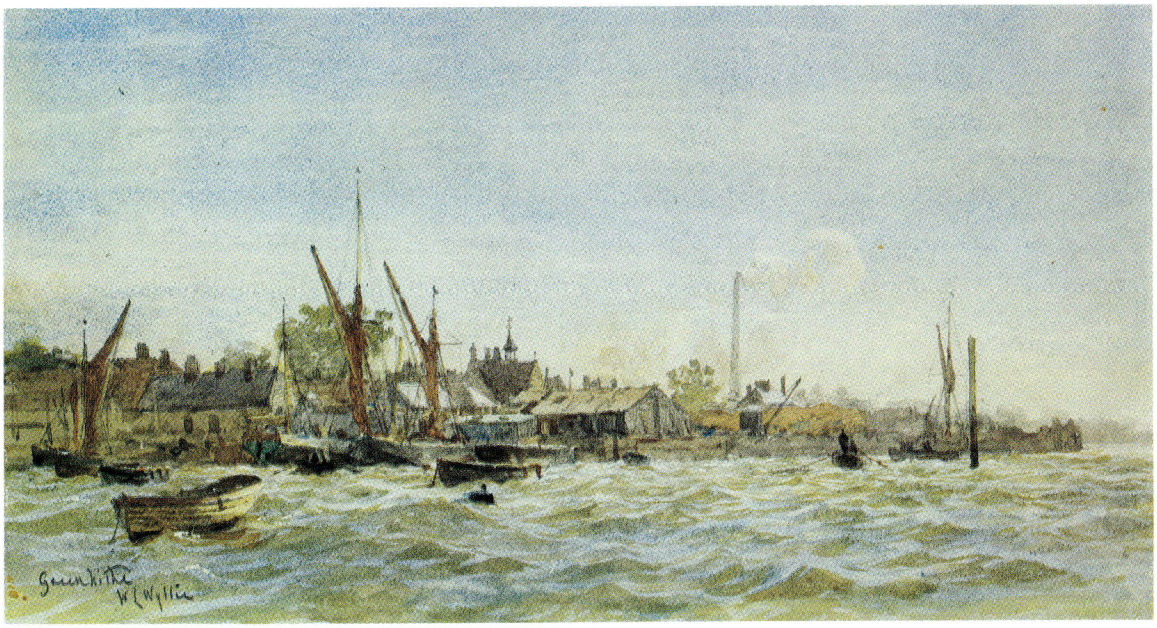

10. Greenhithe: Brisk East Wind, c.1905
pencil and watercolour, $17\frac{1}{8} \times 13\frac{1}{4}$ (180 × 335)
National Maritime Museum, London

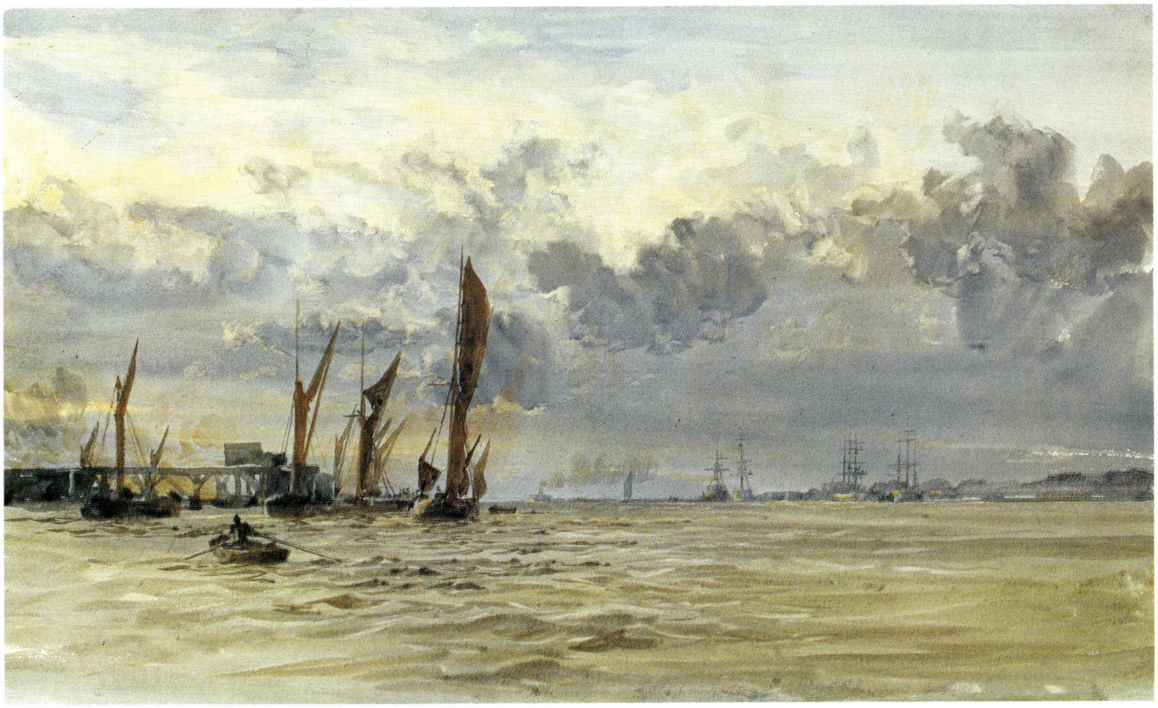

11. Thames barges in the Medway, c.1900
watercolour, $11\frac{1}{4} \times 18\frac{1}{8}$ (285 × 464)
National Maritime Museum, London

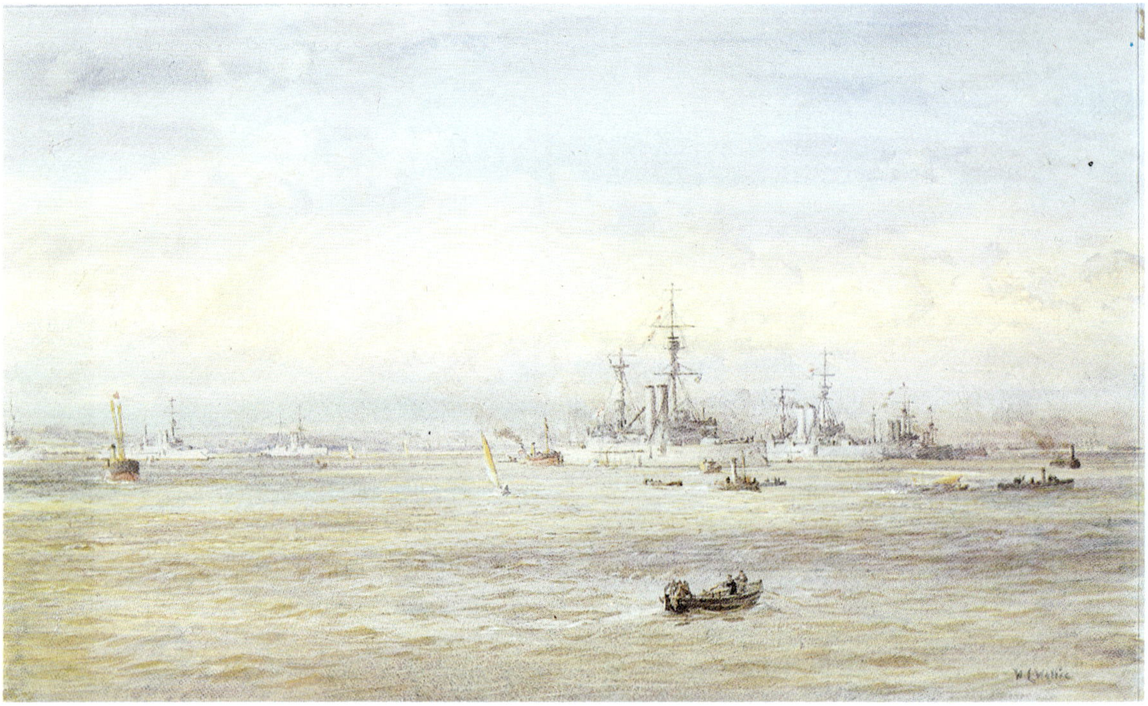

12. The Third Battle Squadron off Southend, 1915
watercolour, $11\frac{1}{8} \times 17\frac{11}{16}$ (282 × 449)
National Maritime Museum, London

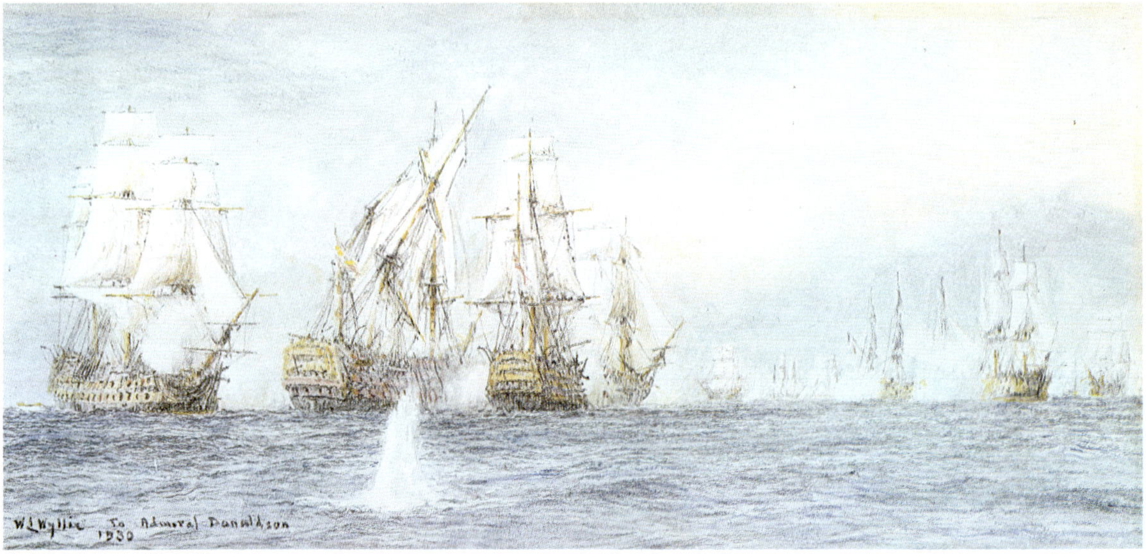

13. The Battle of Trafalgar, 21 October 1805:
Santissima Trinidad and *Neptune*, 1930
hand-coloured etching, $6\frac{15}{16} \times 14\frac{5}{16}$ (177 × 363)
inscribed to Admiral Donaldson
National Maritime Museum, London

'The largest ship afloat in 1805 was the four-decker *Santissima Trinidad*, the flagship of Hidalgo Cisneros. She is here seen surrounded by British ships. *Leviathan* is about to rake her astern. The 90 gun ship *Neptune* engages to leeward and the *Africa* pours in her broadside close ahead. The main and mizzen masts of the hapless four-decker are coming down with a crash, and her sides are much battered.'

All his lights, such as clouds, waves, etc. were picked out at this moment with a big soft brush that he *sucked* into a hard, broad point. It is usual to tell a child 'You must not suck your brush,' but in Bill's case he would never have got the wonderful delicacy of his watercolours without it.[36]

Such a technique provided, in the best examples, a freedom from a tendency to too much detail. Ships, barges, fishing boats, set amidst sea, sky and clouds exist for the interest of their shape and form alone rather than for the details of their build. In the best of the watercolours produced around 1900, hand and eye work in perfect balance, with bold calligraphic brushwork (Colour Plate 11).

Wyllie's two manuals on the painting of watercolours, *Marine Painting in Watercolour* (1901) and the *Sketchbook* (1908), provide a clear insight into his working methods in the first decade of the century. Each coloured plate is accompanied by instructions describing how particular effects were achieved. Wyllie's limited palette is described in the *Sketchbook:*

Mr Wyllie does not use many colours. This is his palette:—

Yellow Oker (*sic*)	Raw Sienna	Aureolin	Rose Madder
Venetian Red	Cobalt	Indigo	French Ultra-marine
Ceruleum	Burnt Sienna	Vandyke Brown	

But for local touches of colour he has occasional resort to

Veronese Green (Green Oxide of Chromium)	Lemon Yellow	Sepia
Cobalt Green	Cadmium	Lamp Black
Chrome Yellow	Vermillion[37]	

The deterioration of Wyllie's art in the years around 1905, symptoms of which were a flatness, a coarsening of brushwork, and the adoption of lurid colouring, may well have arisen from an over-confidence in his technical abilities, although Mrs Wyllie attributed it to his continued use of the telescope. In the landscapes of this period Wyllie had an unfortunate inclination to use quantities of undiluted acid greens with an apparent insensitivity to their effects. The watercolours he now produced for reproduction as colour plates to the books he illustrated – *Norway and its Fjords* (1909), for example – often had an unusually harsh quality of colour which may well have infected watercolours not intended for reproduction. Aside from the influence of Turner upon his use of colour (to be discussed further in the next chapter), it is possible that in later years travel itself affected Wyllie's palette, inclining him sometimes to bright 'technicolour' effects with vivid blues and greens. Whatever the reasons, the results were clearly evident to the critic of the *Athenaeum* in 1907:

These records, at the Fine Art Society's rooms, of P and O cruises 'from Spitsbergen to the Golden Horn' show Mr Wyllie with all his accomplishments, but also with the want of high cultivation on the side of colour that tends in an increased degree to modify our admiration of his work. By an unfortunate irony of circumstance, certain subject-matters that he has been latterly much addicted to – the gay colours of bunting, for example, or the bravery of painted hulls or smoke-stacks – are of a sort that emphasise this defect, as do also subjects of Southern sunlight with impossible blues and the like spendour of sub-tropical effects.

These splendours become rather crude and disjointed in the hands of a painter accustomed, apparently, rather to 'match' individual colours than to examine the whole scheme of colour as a living structure, in which parts are as closely related as the wonderful web of fine perspective drawing which he flings so lightly upon paper.[38]

Nevertheless, Wyllie's sale of watercolours to fellow passengers on cruises often, it is said, paid for his passage. Throughout his life, but particularly in the latter part, he produced many delightfully atmospheric 'sea and sky' studies of foreign coastlines (Plate 81). These are very much in the tradition of the naval officer's 'coastal profile', drawn and used as a navigational aid, but in Wyllie's case they were drawn for pleasure during cruises when his compulsion to paint continued unabated.

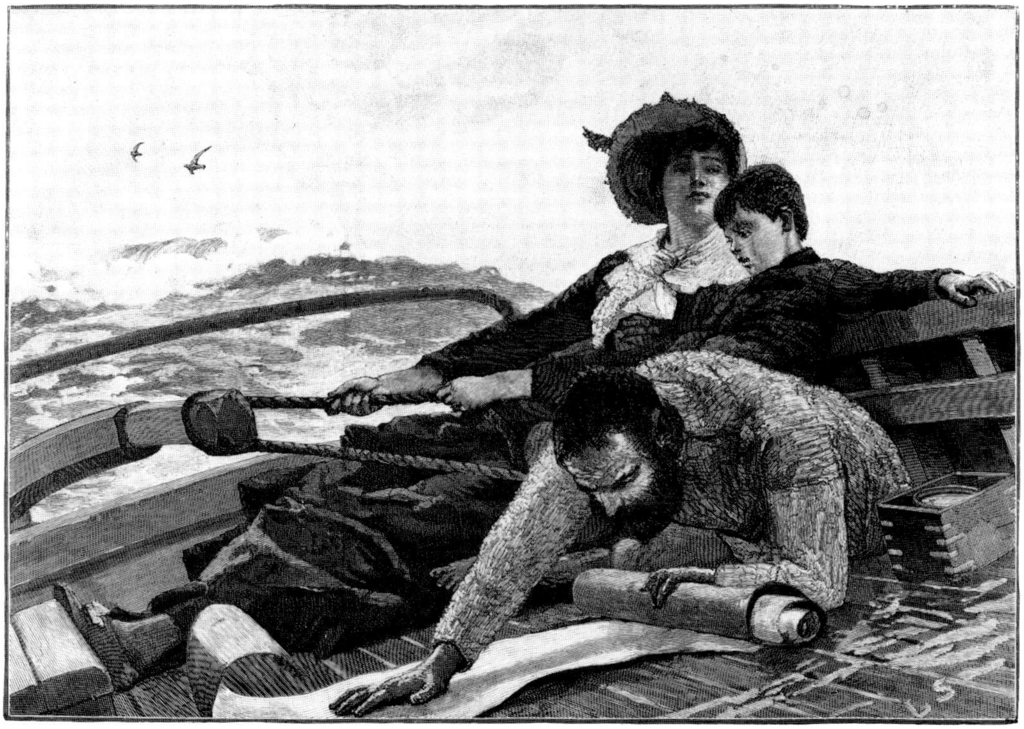

62. On the way to Holland
wood engraving after a drawing by Lionel Smythe,
Illustrated London News, 4 May 1889

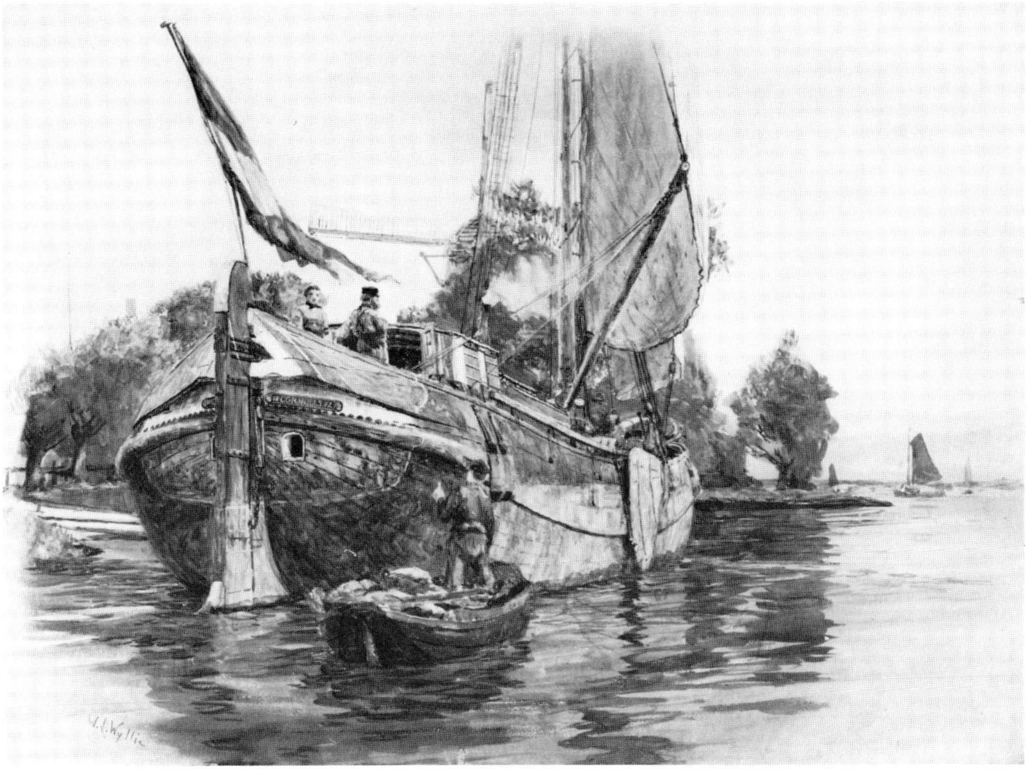

63. A Dutch barge, *c.* 1888
watercolour, $17\frac{1}{2} \times 23\frac{1}{2}$ (443×597)
National Maritime Museum, London

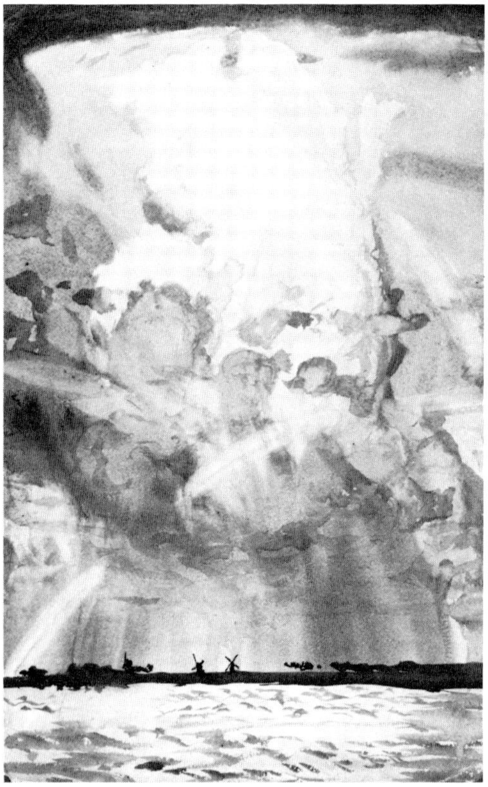

64. Study in Holland, *c.* 1886
watercolour, $9\frac{3}{4} \times 15\frac{13}{16}$ (248×389)
National Maritime Museum, London

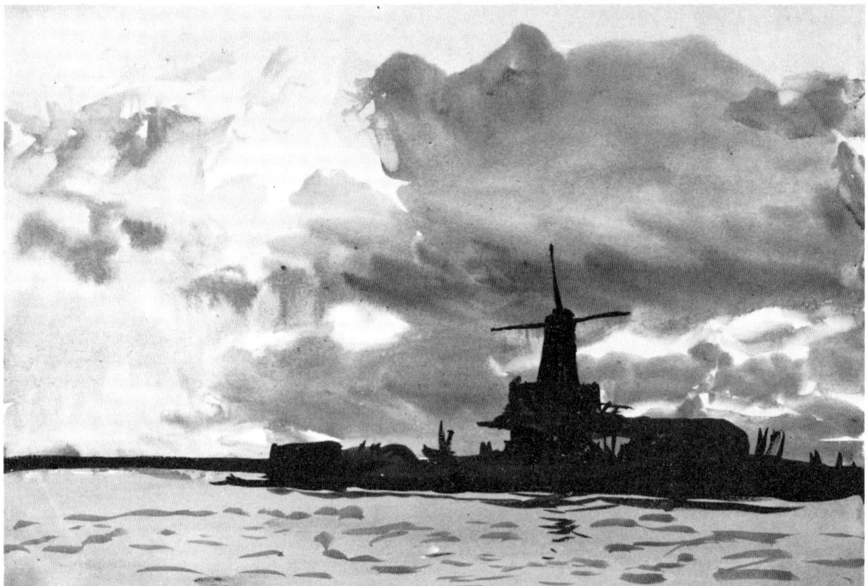

65. Windmill at Zandam, *c.* 1900
watercolour, $9\frac{7}{8} \times 13\frac{15}{16}$ (252×354)
National Maritime Museum, London

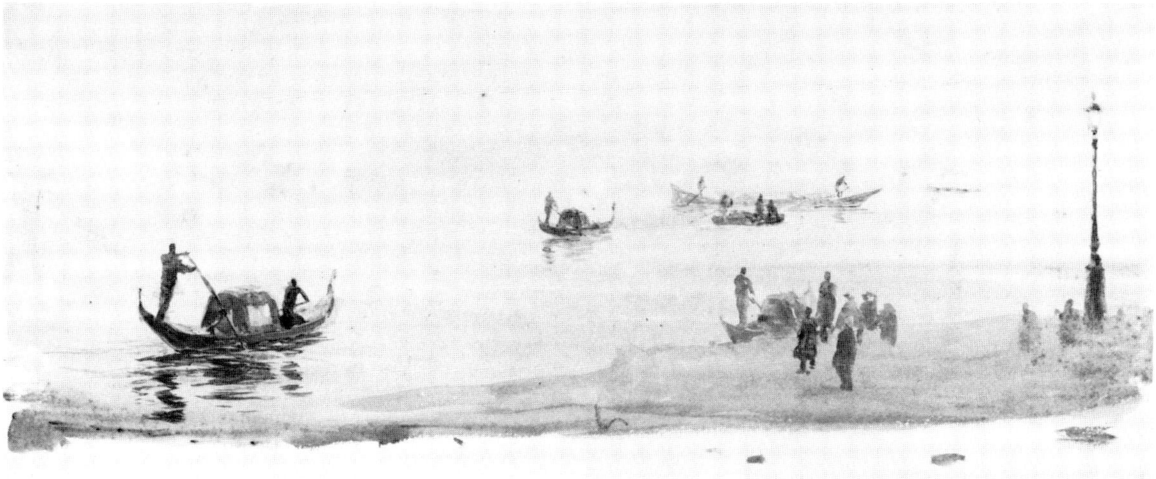

66. Gondolas, Venice, *c.* 1896
watercolour, $7\frac{3}{16} \times 18\frac{1}{4}$ (183 × 464) (subject)
National Maritime Museum, London

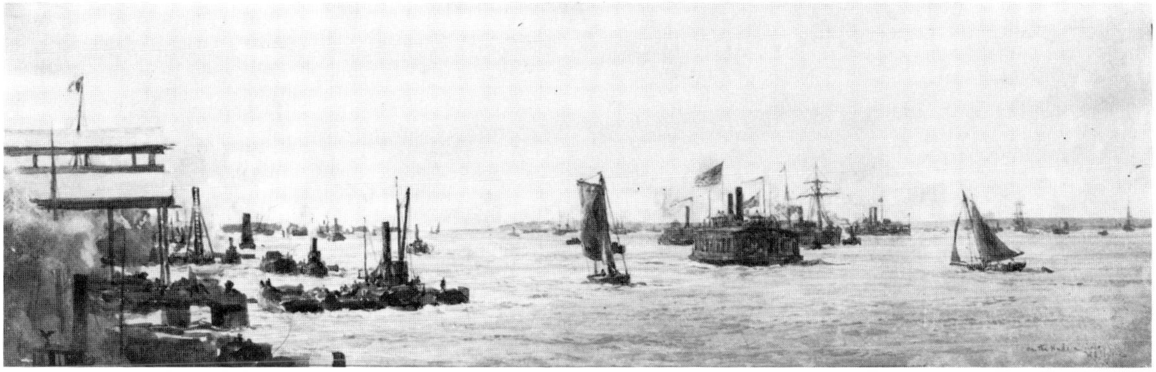

67. On the Hudson, 1891
watercolour, $4\frac{1}{4} \times 13\frac{1}{8}$ (117 × 333)
National Maritime Museum, London

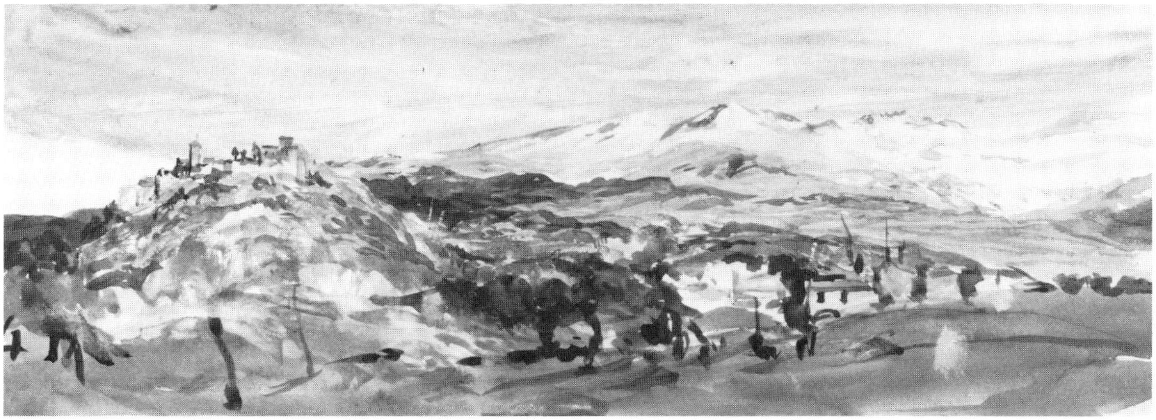

68. Landscape with hill town, *c.* 1890
watercolour, $3\frac{5}{8} \times 10$ (93 × 254)
National Maritime Museum, London

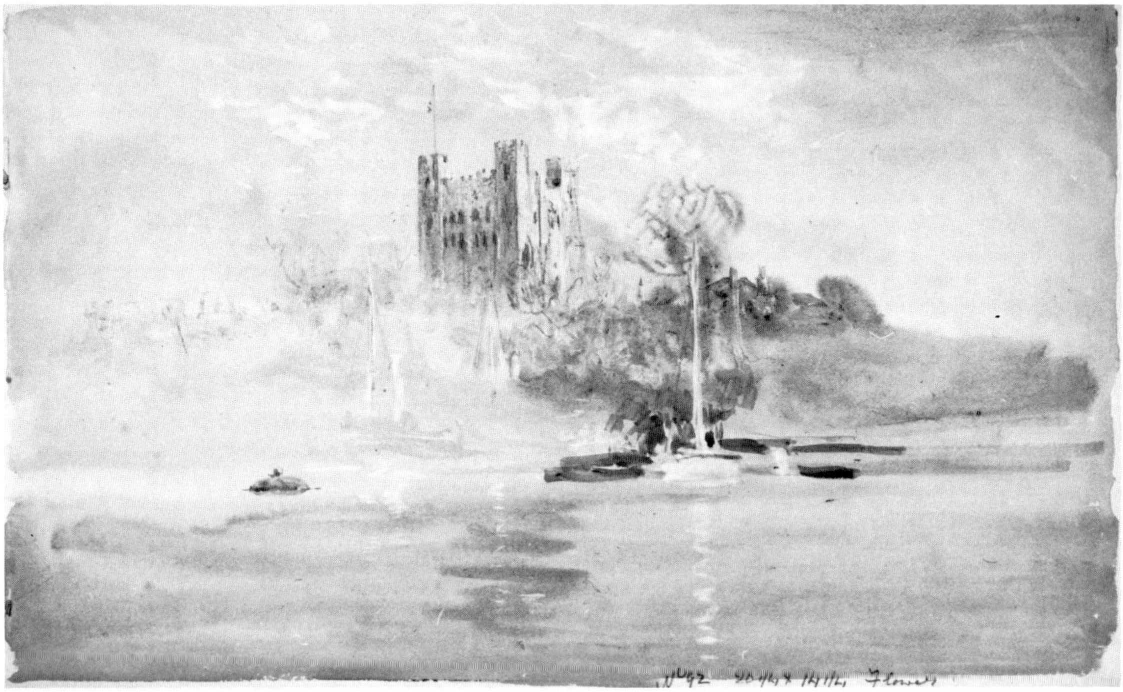

69. Rochester Castle, *c.* 1900
watercolour, $12\frac{7}{8} \times 19\frac{5}{8}$ (327×498)
National Maritime Museum, London

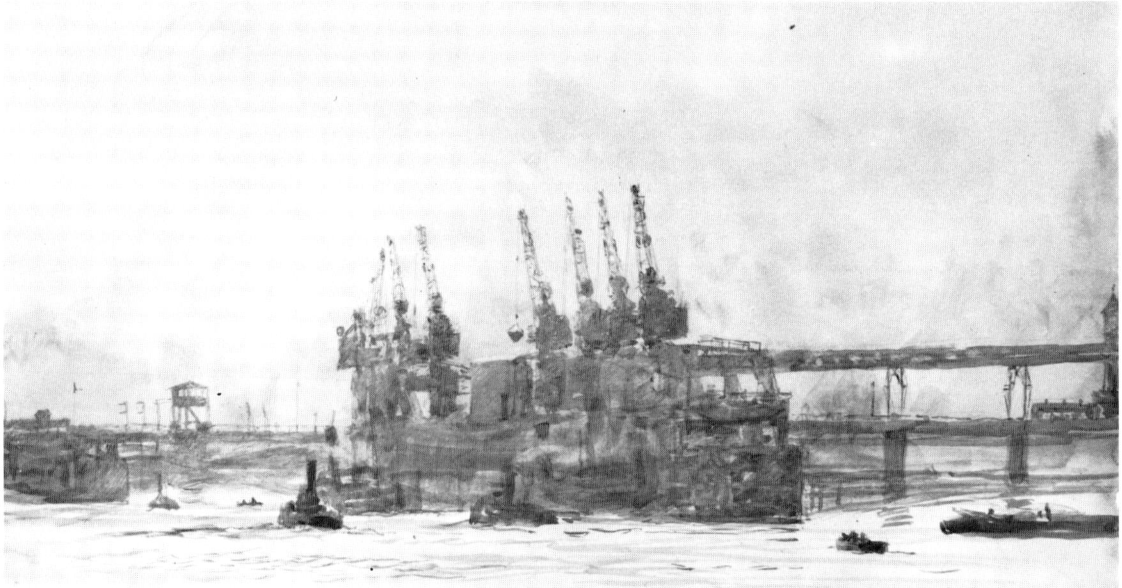

70. Beckton Gas Works, *c.* 1900
watercolour, 14×20 (356×509)
National Maritime Museum, London

30 NATURE'S LAWS AND THE MAKING OF PICTURES

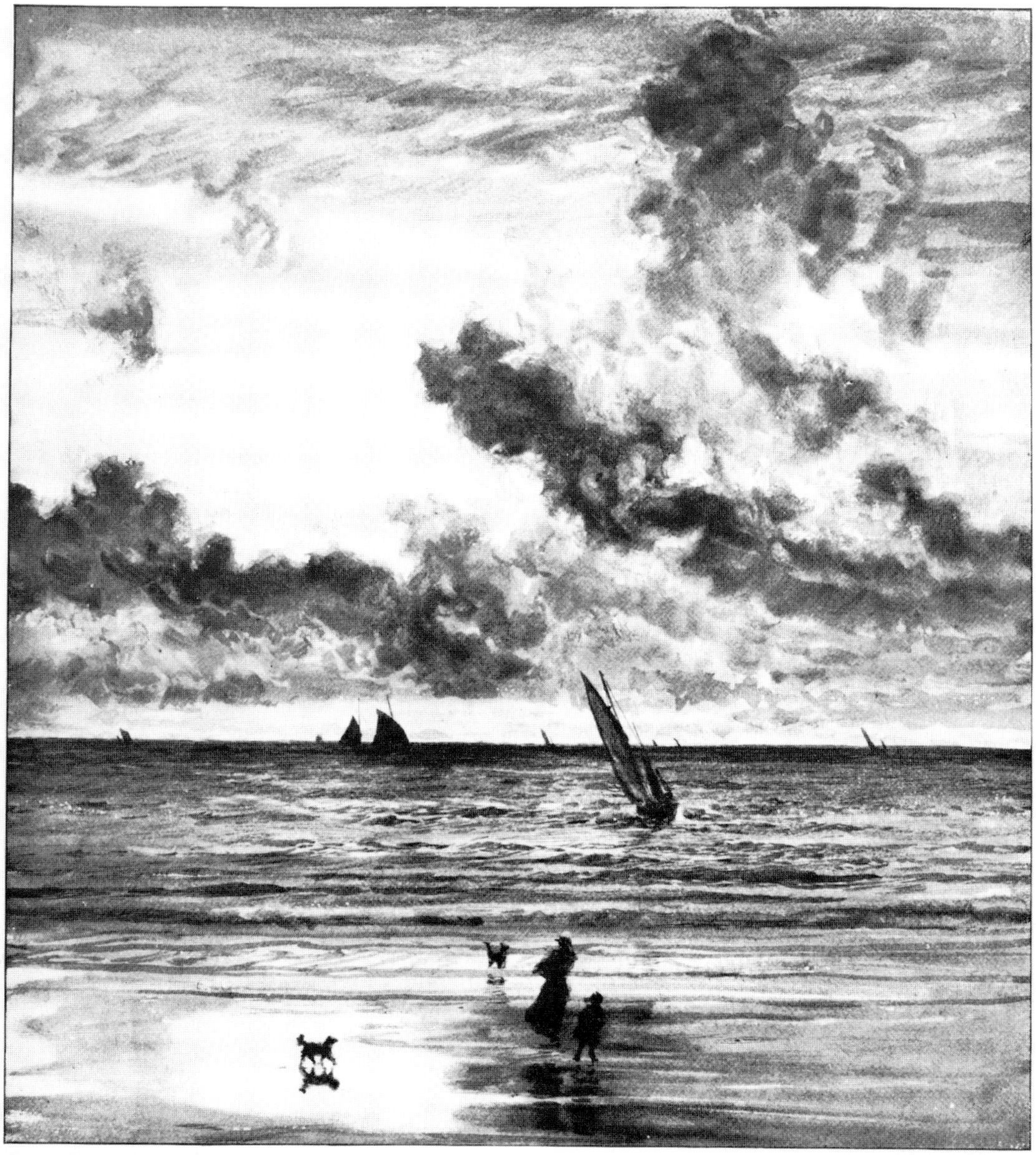

In this illustration I have tried to show two surfaces of cloud, and underneath, first a slope of wet shining sand, and then the rounded surface of the sea. The light upper layer of mottled cirrus shows a gently curving under surface, and the lines of dapple vanish away towards points low down on the far right, and nearer in on the left of the drawing. Under this is a bank of fluffy nimbus of all shapes. You will notice that as these woolly clouds stretch away into the distance they get more and more behind the horizon, peeping up half hidden, and at last disappearing behind the sea altogether. Then take the wet sand: it slopes away towards the sea; its vanishing-line is somewhere about the hull of the nearest boat, for you notice that the sails of the distant craft are reflected in its surface. This would not be the case if the sand were level, for then the reflection would only be the usual length, viz. the length of the mast repeated underneath.

71. Page from Wyllie's book on perspective *Nature's Laws and the Making of Pictures*, 1903

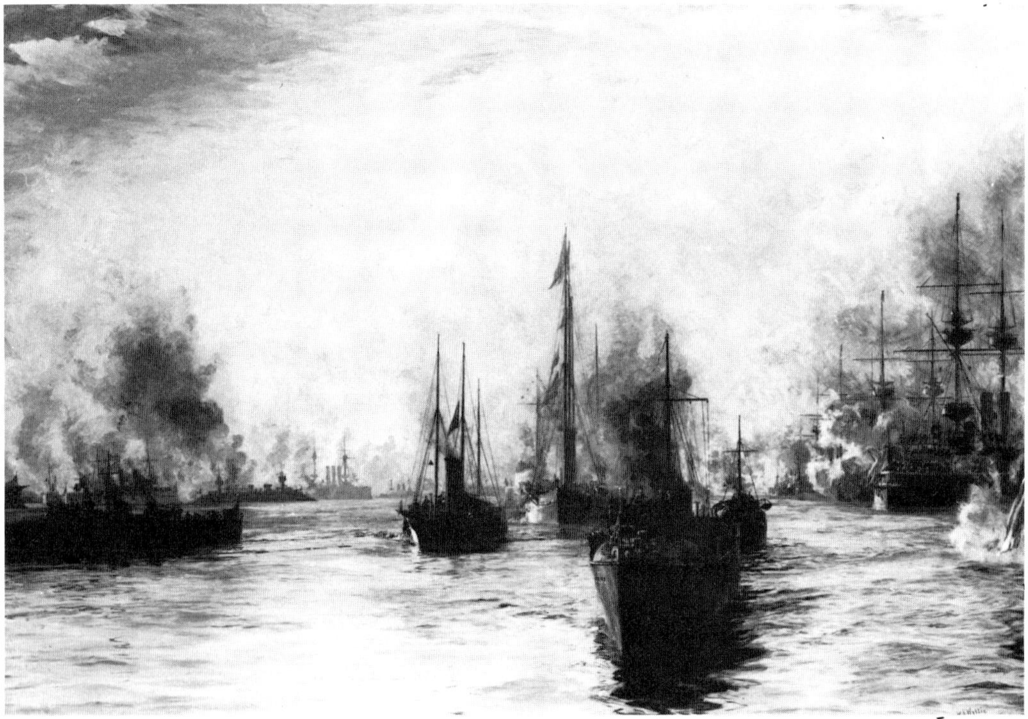

72. The passing of a great Queen, 1901: Queen Victoria's funeral, February 1901
oil, $60\frac{1}{8} \times 83\frac{7}{8}$ (1527 × 2143)
Walker Art Gallery, Liverpool

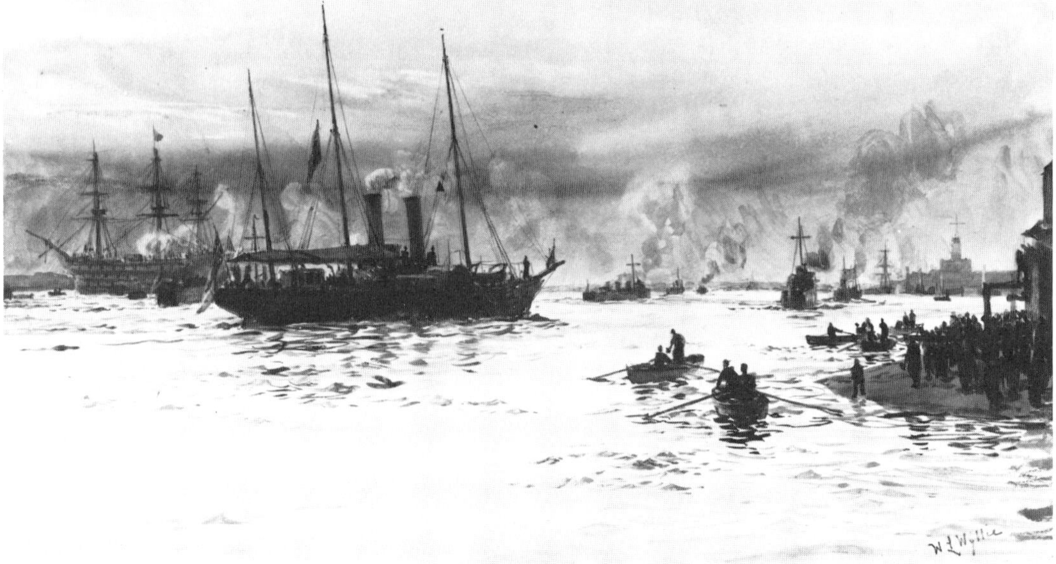

73. Queen Victoria's funeral: HMY *Alberta* entering
Portsmouth Harbour, February 1901
pencil, grey wash and white heightening, $11\frac{1}{4} \times 15\frac{3}{16}$ (285 × 386)
National Maritime Museum, London

3

'The Grand Fleet in its Pride'[39]: 1907-1931

Turner was the one artist above others for whom Wyllie professed a true admiration. This is expressed in his book on the artist which he was invited to write in 1905, and in later years Wyllie is known to have inspected the pictures of the Turner Bequest in the basement of the National Gallery.[40] As Turner died in 1851, the year in which Wyllie was born, some have found it convenient to suggest that the mantle of Turner, as marine painter, descended upon Wyllie. But it would be misleading to suggest that Turner's influence on Wyllie was profound, although as early as 1889 the *Magazine of Art* considered the Royal Academy picture *The Phantom Ship* 'curiously reminiscent in design of Turner's *Fighting Temeraire* and *The Burial of Wilkie*'.[41]

Wyllie's view of Turner will certainly today seem naïve, although there is no doubt that he admired and was affected by Turner's pictures. He identified in a simple way with what he understood as Turner's response to, and assimilation into his art, of the physical world:

> The man who strives to rival Turner must go out and study nature as he did. On the mountainside, in crowded cities, or afloat on the ever changing ocean. He must be able to watch every passing phase, with the power of storing up, and afterwards sifting and winnowing his observations. To these the gifts of imagination, originality and individuality must be added.[42]

But it seems to have been Turner's use of colour which particularly attracted him. In the deterioration in Wyllie's art in the early years of the century, associated with the adoption of a crude colouring and the use of strong pinks, yellows and blues, it seems very likely that Wyllie's renewed interest in Turner's art was an important factor. In 1910 the *Art Journal* commented:

> Many artists have praised Turner's *Bay of Baiae* since it was first exhibited in 1823, but none perhaps more sincerely than Mr W. L. Wyllie, RA, who in his monograph on the artist, relates that when he was a student that was his favourite picture. . . . Ruskin complained that it was crude in colour, but in these days we are so accustomed to such characteristics that the picture does not seem extraordinary in this respect.[43]

In 1904 the *Art Journal* had commented on Wyllie's Royal Academy exhibits: 'Mr Wyllie is not in great force this year and his *Towing past the City* seems almost identical with earlier works.'[44] The *Athenaeum* was almost damning in its criticism of works in the Fine Art Society Exhibition *Pleasure Cruises in a P & O, from Spitsbergen to the Golden Horn* of 1907:

> . . . he who once was a colourist may produce very poor colour indeed. In this show there is a tendency for the bright hues to flash out at once in a thin and unsupported fashion, and the recollection of Mr Wyllie's stronger work threatens to make us unjust to an extraordinarily capable collection. If performing a difficult task with magical ease be genius, here we have it. Exact delineation is accomplished with a facility that almost compels belief in its truthfulness; but if it be truth, it is truth to a world of little charm or beauty.[45]

By the outbreak of the First World War Wyllie's art had recovered, although the breadth of vision and toughness of the last years of Victoria's reign were never again to be equalled. The many fine watercolours of the vessels and actions of the war tend to resort once again to detail. This was partly due to the fact that Wyllie was once again an illustrator, if not for books on the war, then for naval officers who demanded factual exactness in the pictures they commissioned. (Plates 82–92; Colour Plate 12.)

The years around 1900 saw an increase of Wyllie's interest in historical subjects, the subjects which the Van de Veldes, Pocock and Turner had painted. His thorough knowledge of the navy of a previous age was founded upon first-hand experience of some of the vessels themselves. For in the 1860s and 1870s many old wooden sailing warships, no longer of fighting use, were given other rôles, and lay sadly in the rivers and estuaries close to the naval dockyards. The *Leonidas* was such a vessel (Colour Plate 7). From the very earliest Wyllie drew these ships, sometimes in the minute watercolours later collected in his albums (Plate 16) or in more elaborate studies, such as the ones made in the 1920s depicting work on the *Victory* (Plate 79).

The Battle of the Nile was one of the first historical paintings which Wyllie exhibited at the Royal Academy, in 1899, following *Cripped and Unconquered* in 1896. It was painted the previous year as a commemoration of the battle, and was the second of Wyllie's pictures to be purchased by the Chantrey Bequest (Plate 74). Compositionally it follows the formula of the battle pieces painted by the eighteenth-century marine painters, whose work would have been well known to Wyllie from engravings, or from the wealth of naval pictures which hang in the Painted Hall at Greenwich. *The Battle of Trafalgar* (Colour Plate 13), also a commemorative picture, exhibited at the Royal Academy in 1905, follows an almost identical formula, and was etched by Wyllie as a large plate for publication by the Art Union (Plate 75). Considering Wyllie's formidable reputation from this period to the end of his life – together with his son Harold – for detailed knowledge of the navy of the Napoleonic era, it is perhaps surprising that he was to exhibit no more historical paintings until the *Panorama of the Battle of Trafalgar* of 1929/30.

During the last phase of his life in Portsmouth Wyllie continued to develop his printmaking to a superb technical standard. This was at a time of great upsurge,

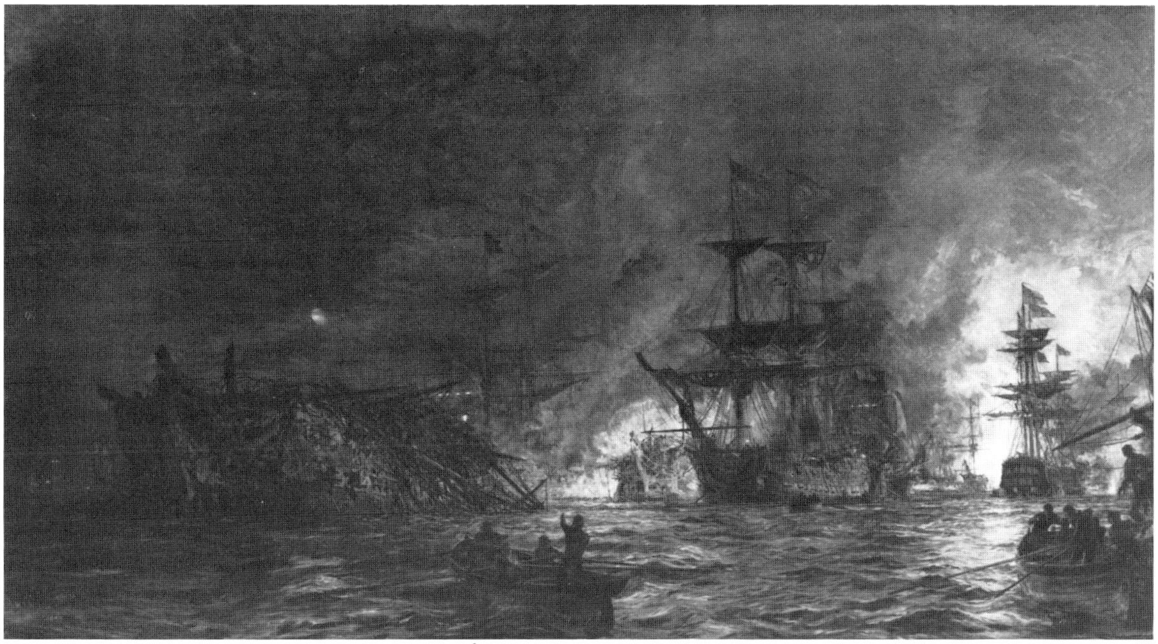

74. The Battle of the Nile, 1 August 1798; 1899
oil, 60 × 108 (1525 × 2745)
Tate Gallery, London

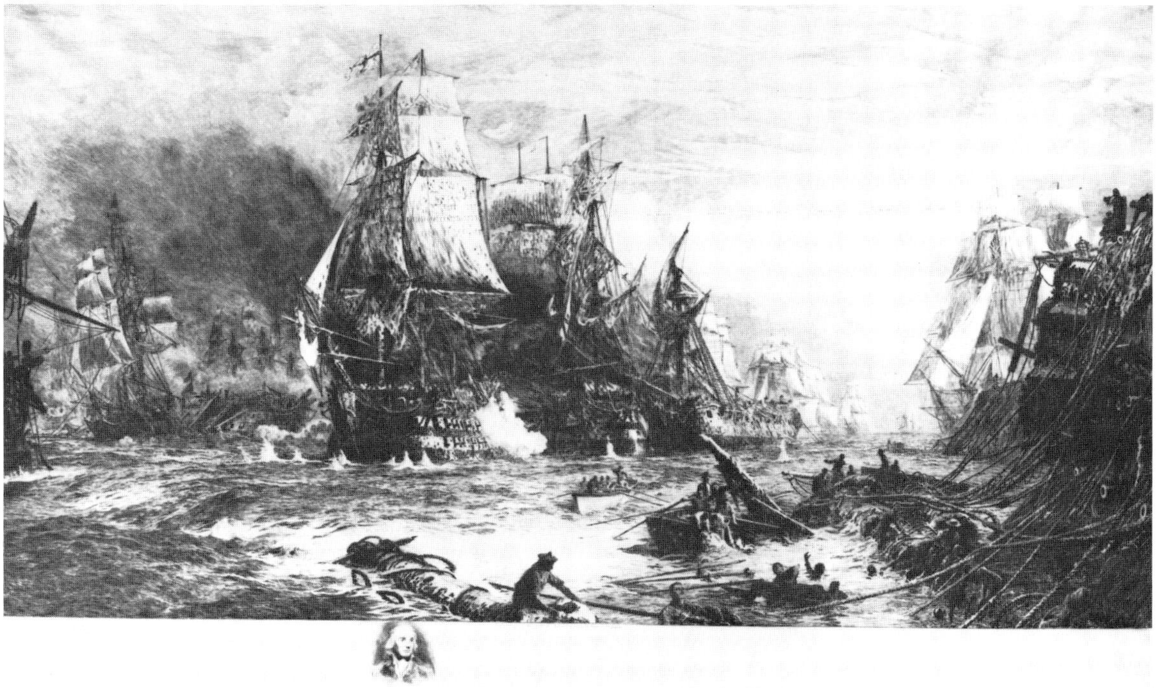

75. The Battle of Trafalgar, 21 October 1805; 1905
etching, $17\frac{1}{2} \times 29\frac{1}{8}$ (446 × 740)
National Maritime Museum, London

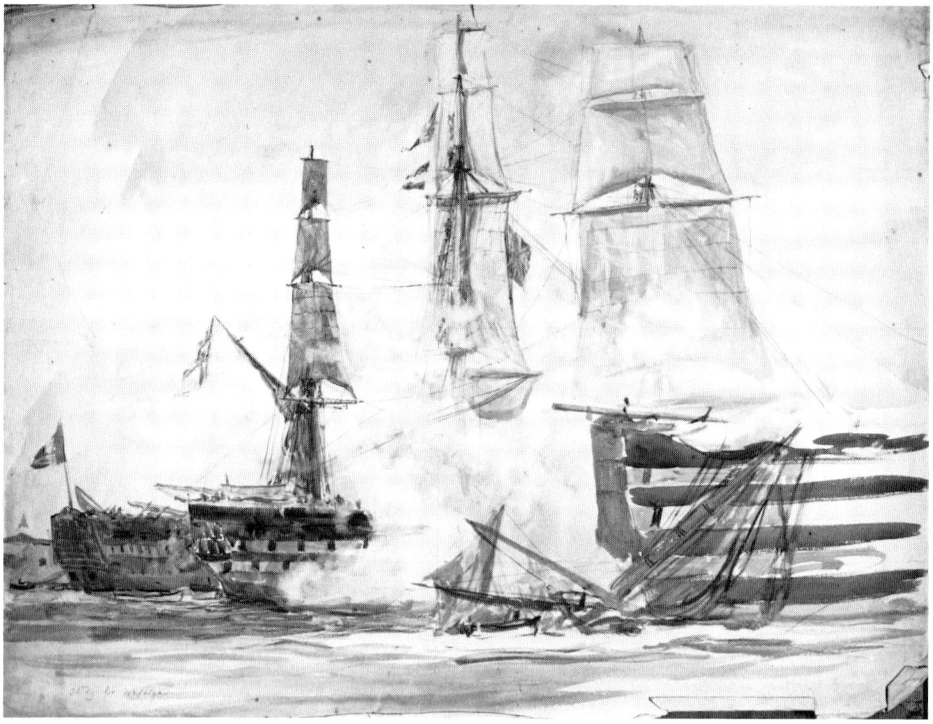

76. Study of the Battle of Trafalgar
pencil and watercolour, $19\frac{11}{16} \times 25\frac{5}{8}$ (500×650)
National Maritime Museum, London

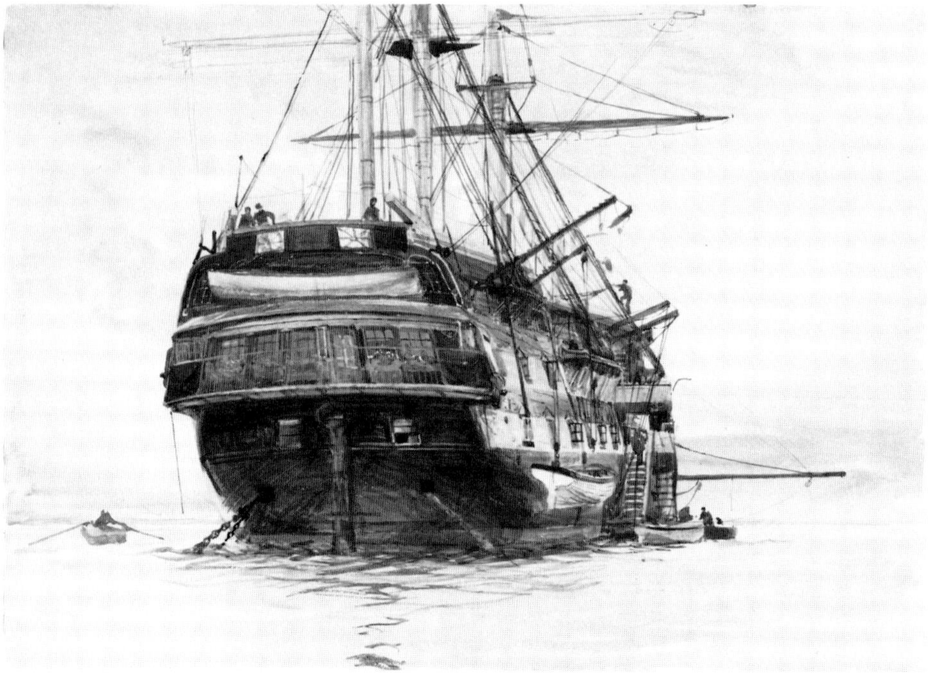

77. HMS *Cornwall*, *c.* 1900
watercolour, $19\frac{11}{16} \times 25\frac{1}{2}$ (500×648)
National Maritime Museum, London
This vessel was built of teak at Bombay and launched in 1815 as the *Wellesley*. In 1868 she was renamed *Cornwall* and became a training ship a Purfleet (Juvenile Reformatory Ship)

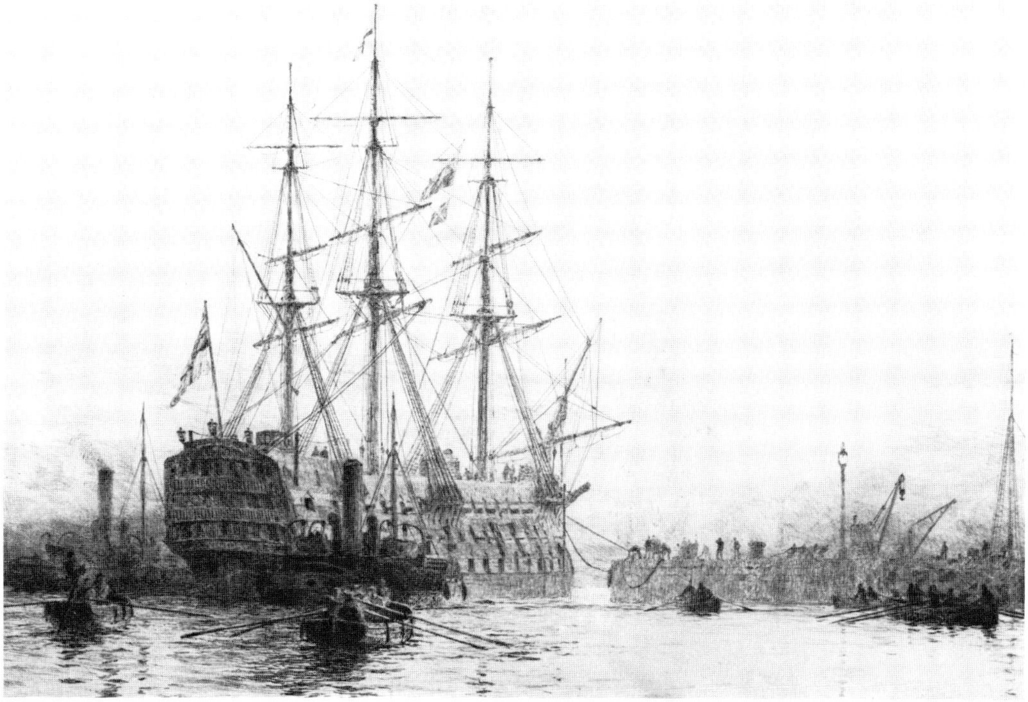

78. The *Victory* in Portsmouth Harbour, *c.* 1920
etching and drypoint with roulette, $8\frac{9}{16} \times 12\frac{3}{8}$ (217×313) (detail)
National Maritime Museum, London

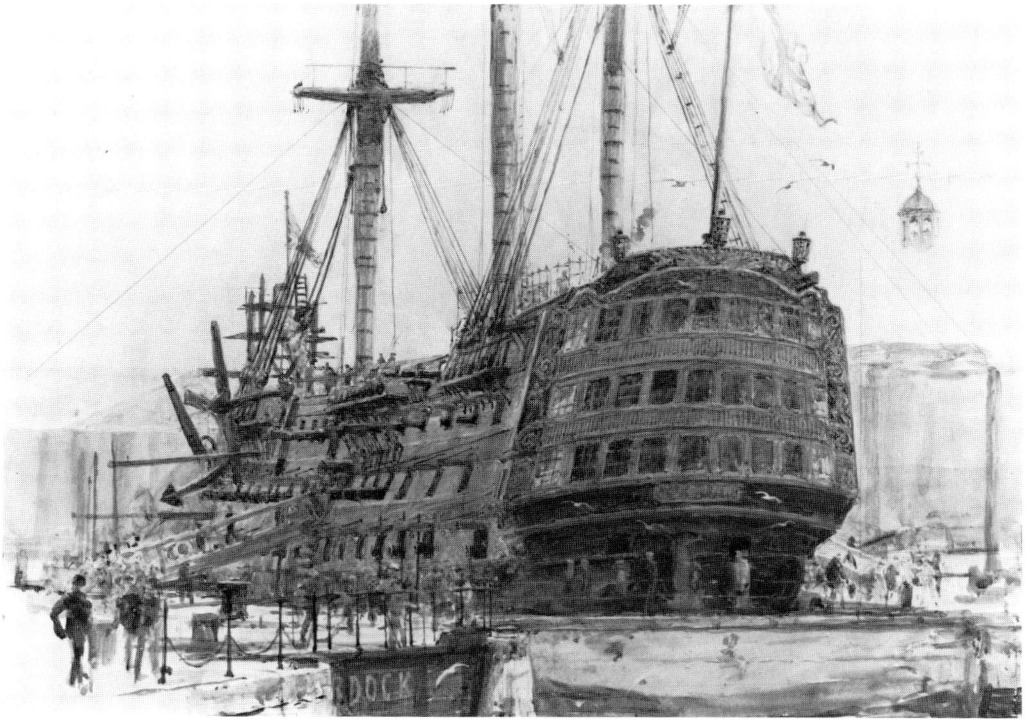

79. HMS *Victory* in dry dock during her restoration, *c.* 1925
watercolour, 18×13 (458×330)
National Maritime Museum, London

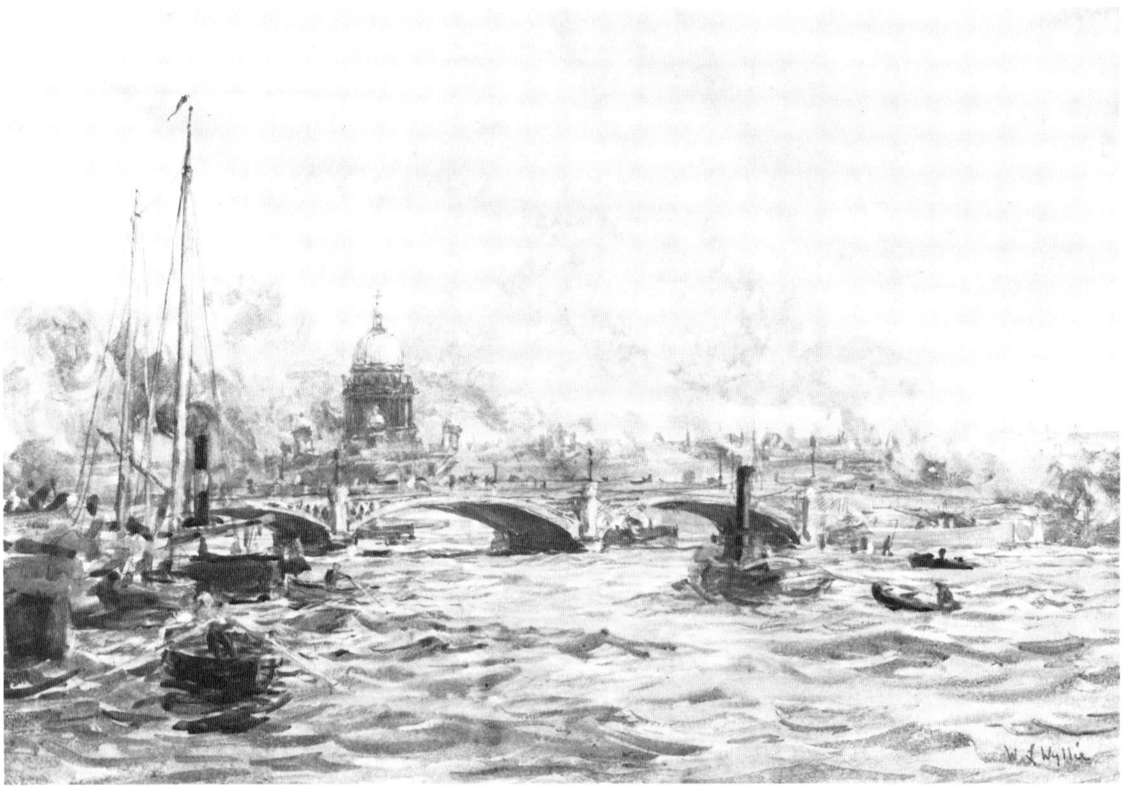

80. St Isaac. The Approach to St Petersburg, 1909
pencil and watercolour, $9 \times 13\frac{1}{16}$ (229×331)
National Maritime Museum, London

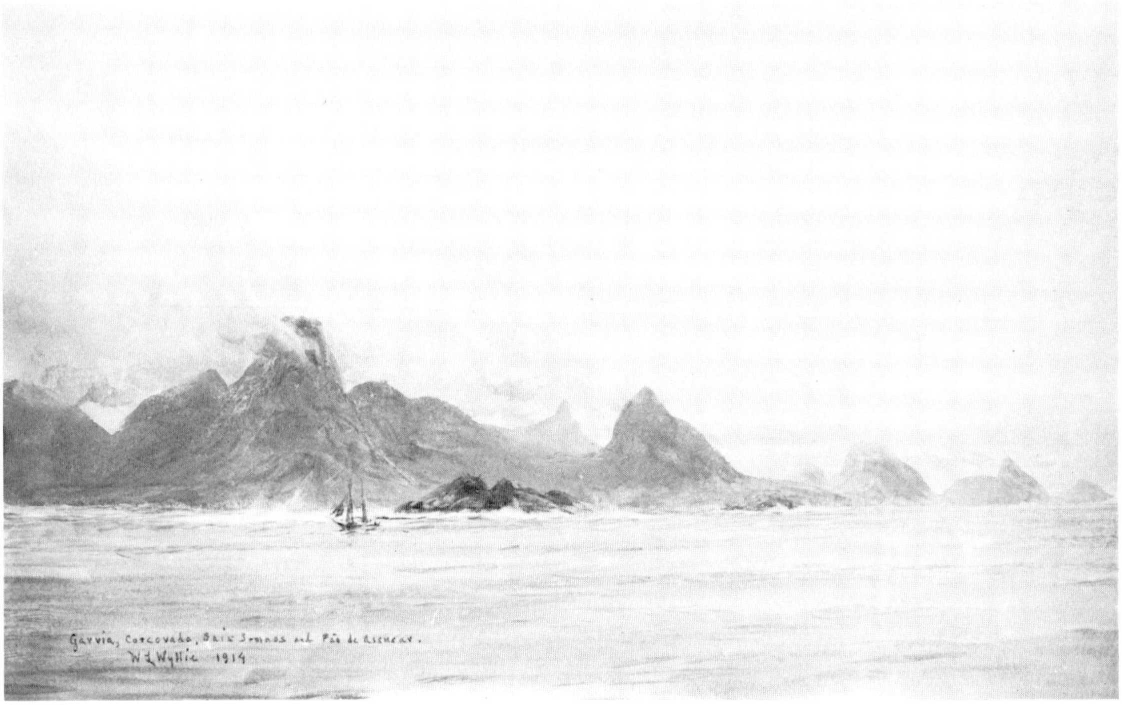

81. The coastline of Rio de Janeiro, 1914
watercolour, $11\frac{9}{16} \times 17\frac{3}{4}$ (294×451)
National Maritime Museum, London

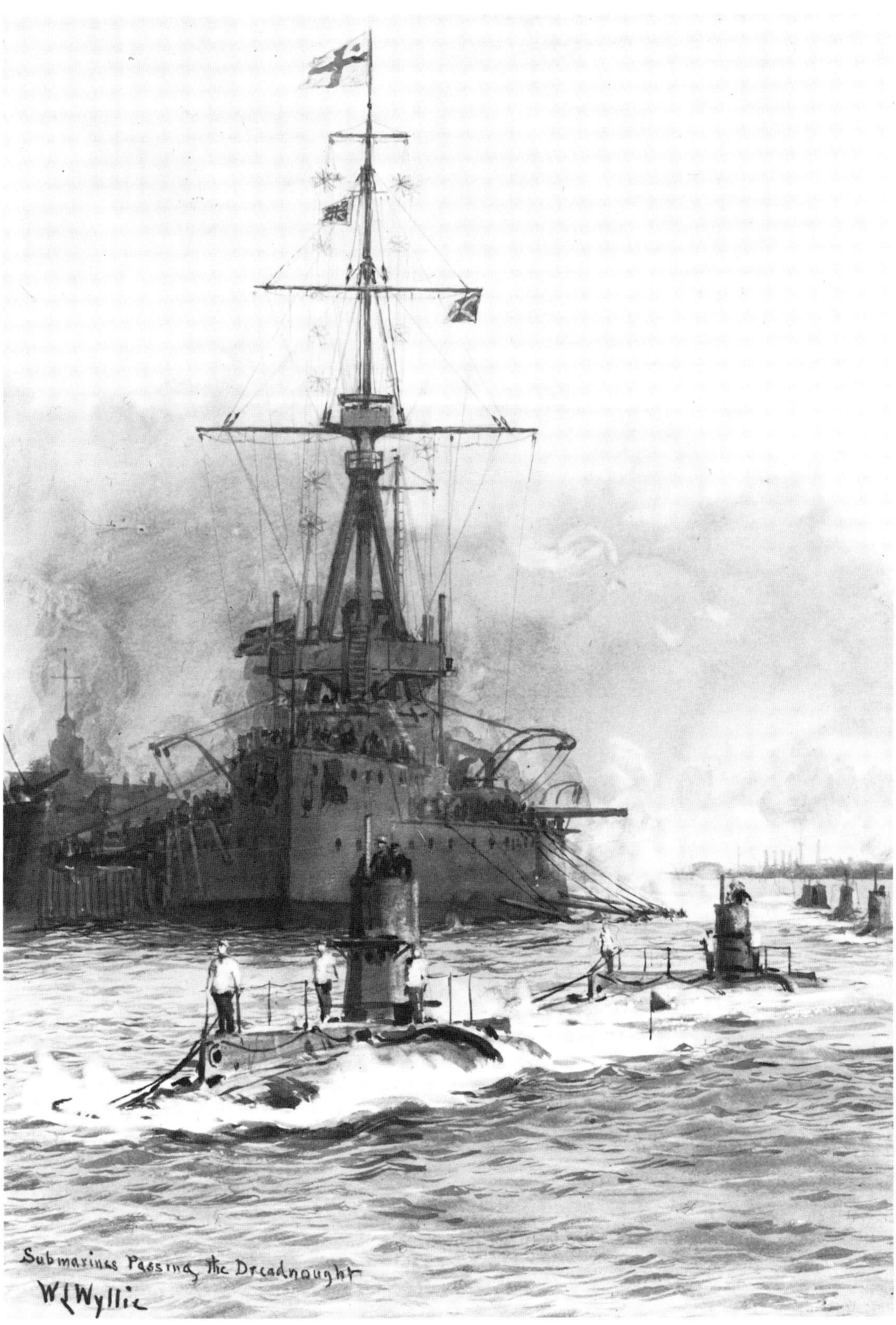

82. Submarines passing the *Dreadnought*, *c.* 1910
grey wash, 10 × 7 (254 × 177)
National Maritime Museum, London

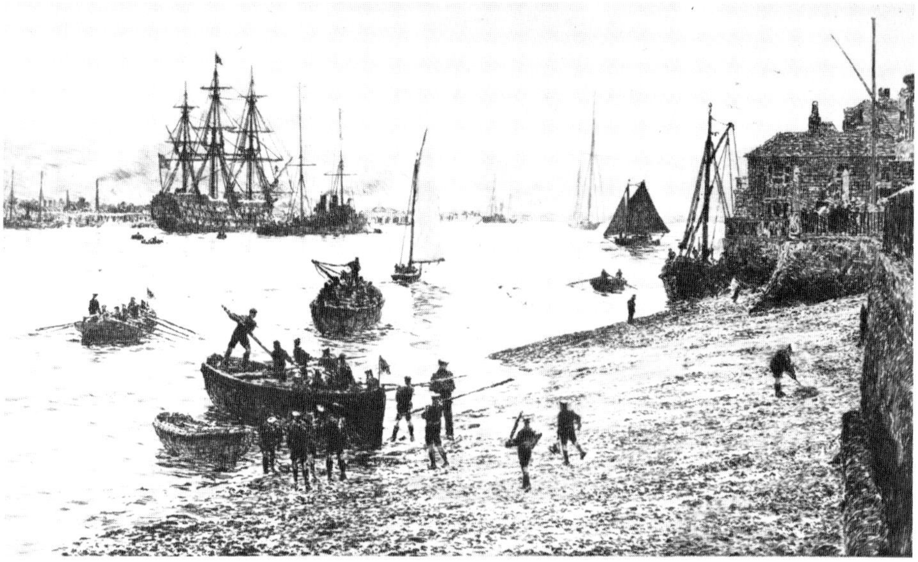

83. HMS *Victory* afloat in Portsmouth Harbour, seascouts in the foreground, 1916
etching with drypoint, $5\frac{7}{8} \times 9\frac{13}{16}$ (150 × 250)
National Maritime Museum, London

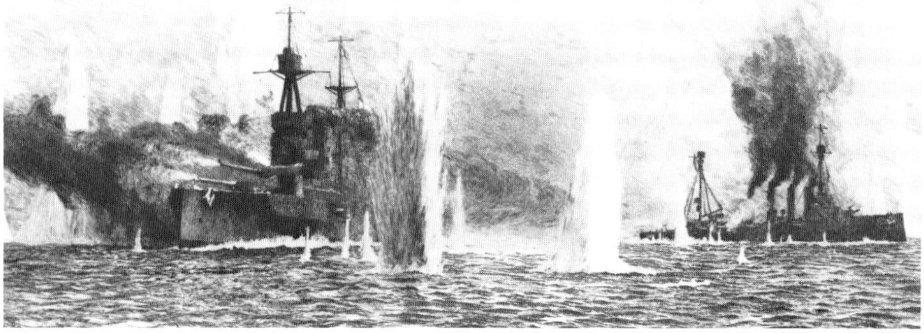

84. *Warspite* and *Warrior* at the Battle of Jutland, 31 May 1916
etching, drypoint and roulette, $8 \times 16\frac{3}{8}$ (203 × 416)
National Maritime Museum, London

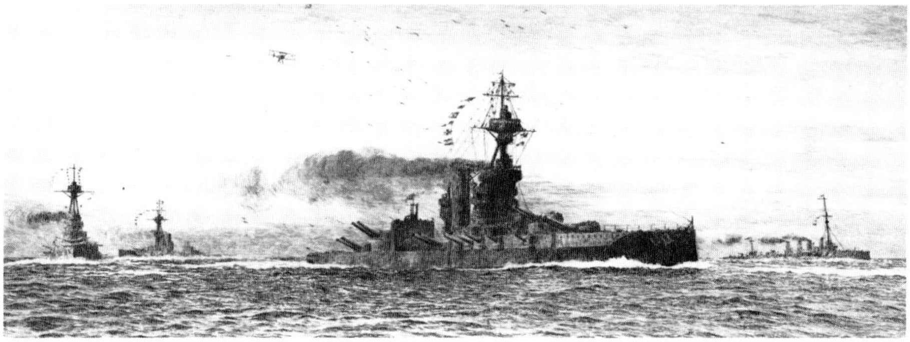

85. Ships of the *Iron Duke* class putting to sea, *c.* 1915
etching with drypoint, $6\frac{13}{16} \times 16\frac{7}{8}$ (174 × 429)
National Maritime Museum, London

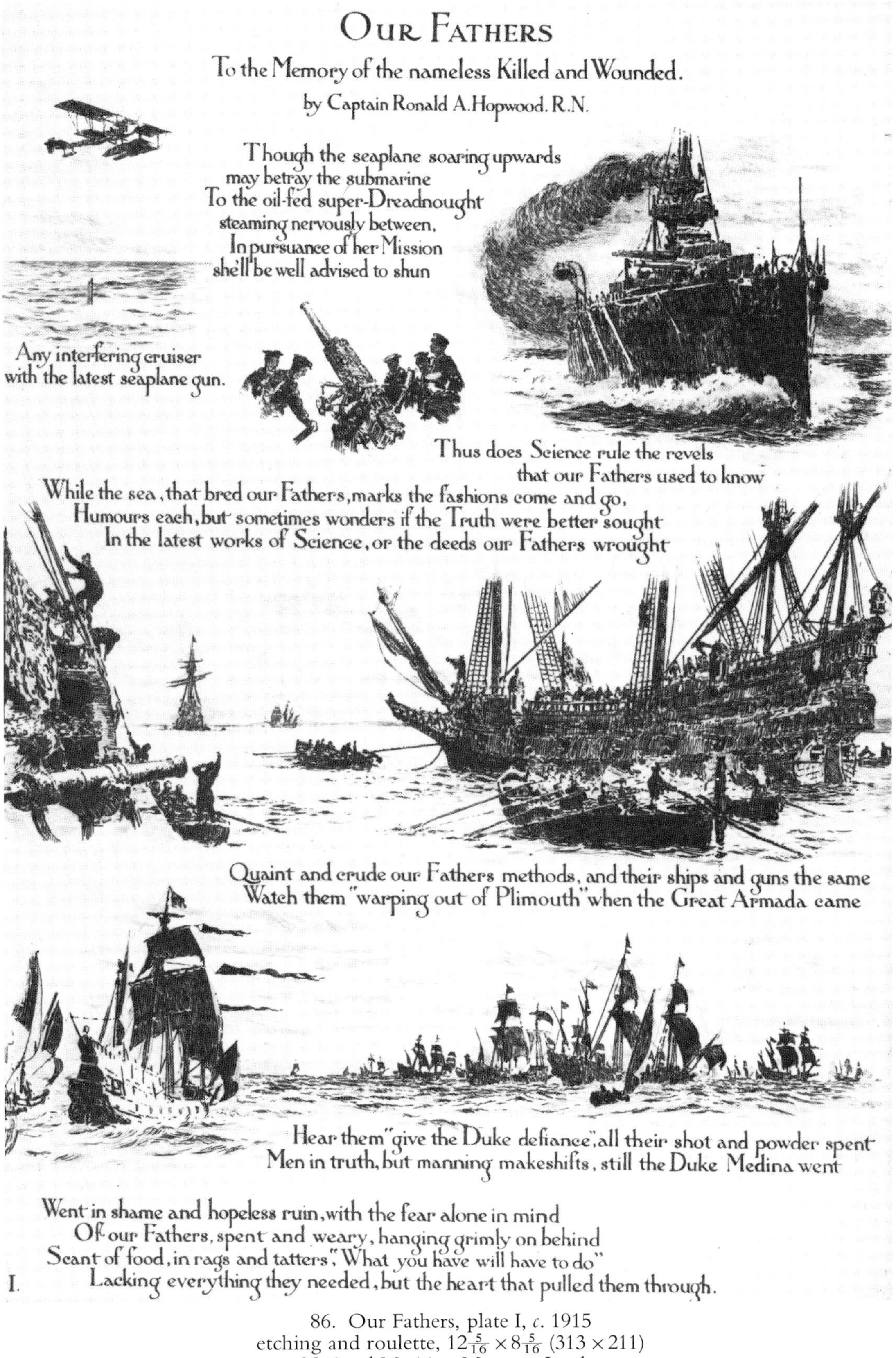

86. Our Fathers, plate I, *c.* 1915
etching and roulette, $12\frac{5}{16} \times 8\frac{5}{16}$ (313 × 211)
National Maritime Museum, London

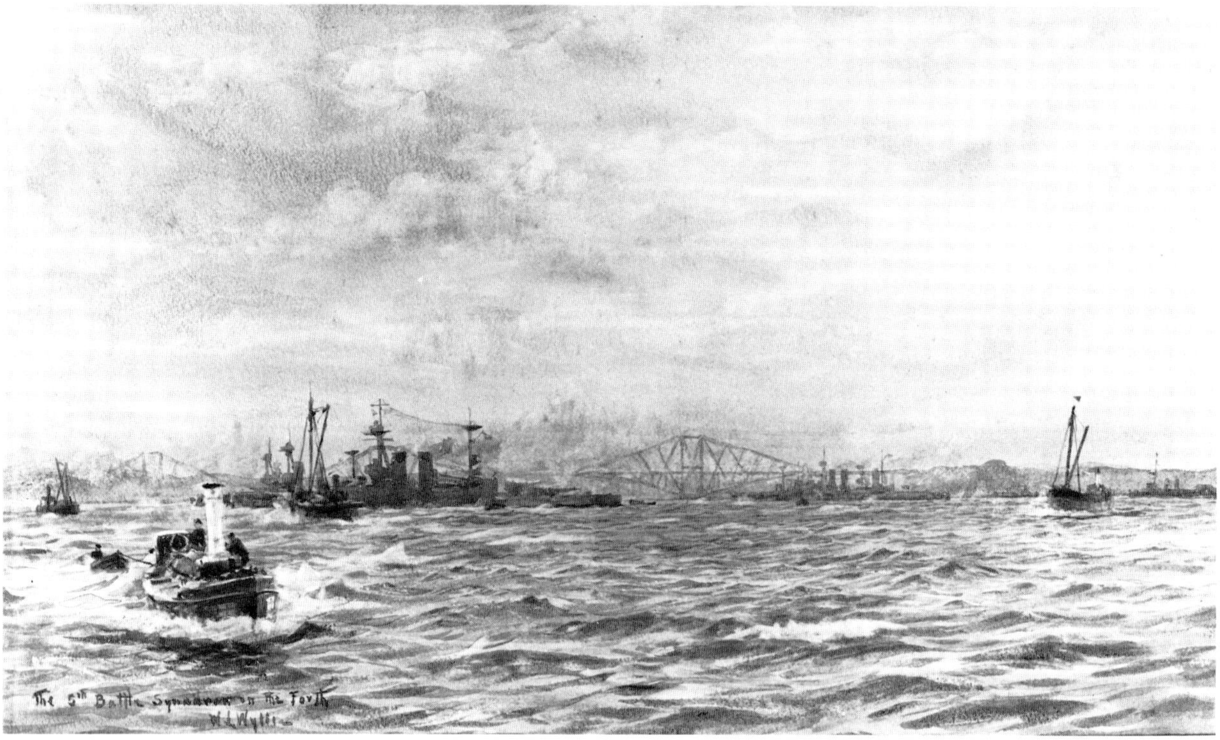

87. The Fifth Battle Squadron in the Forth, *c.* 1918
watercolour, $14 \times 9\frac{1}{2}$ (358×241)
National Maritime Museum, London

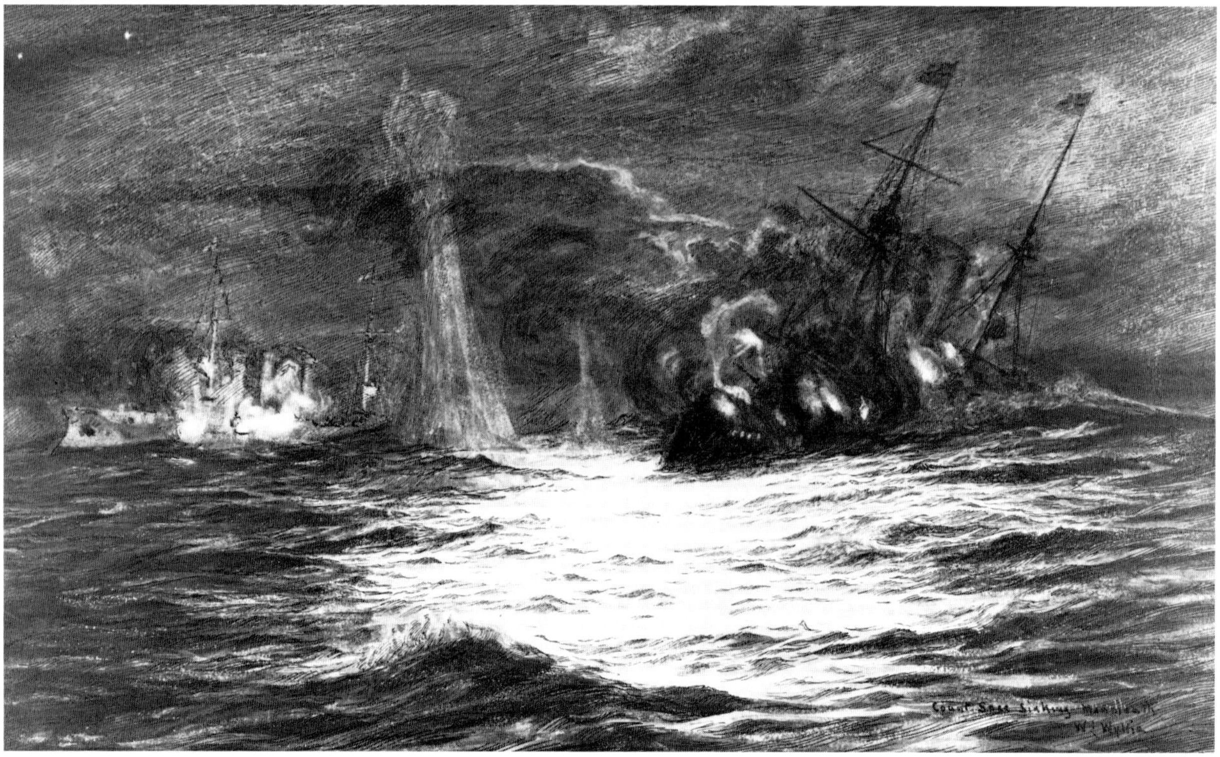

88. *Count Spee* sinking *Monmouth*, 1916
pen, ink and watercolour with scraped highlight, $10\frac{5}{8} \times 16\frac{7}{8}$ (267×428)
National Maritime Museum, London

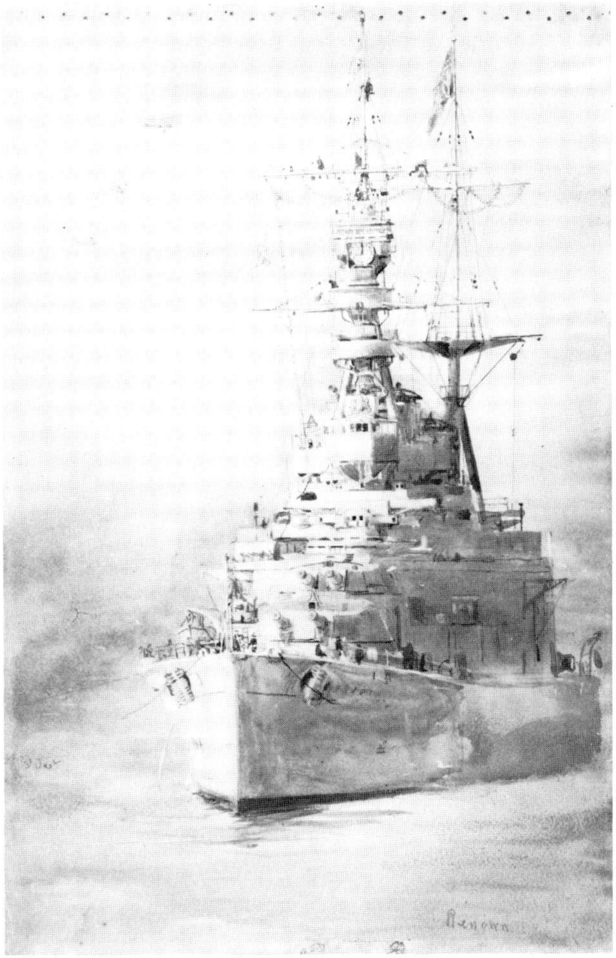

89. HMS *Renown*, *c.* 1916
pencil and watercolour, $17\frac{5}{8} \times 11\frac{1}{8}$ (447×284)
National Maritime Museum, London

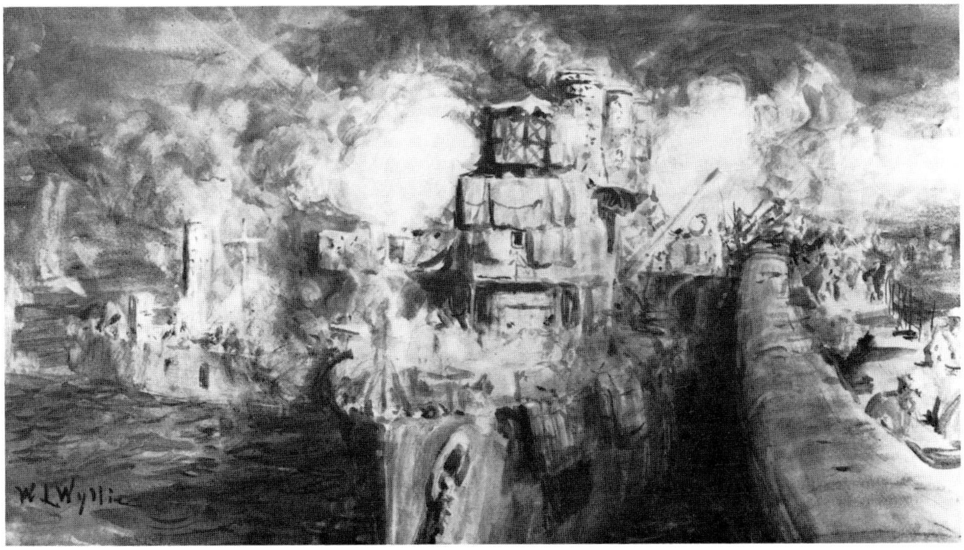

90. HMS *Vindictive* at Zeebrugge, 23 April 1918
pencil and watercolour, $9\frac{15}{16} \times 17\frac{7}{8}$ (253×455)
National Maritime Museum, London

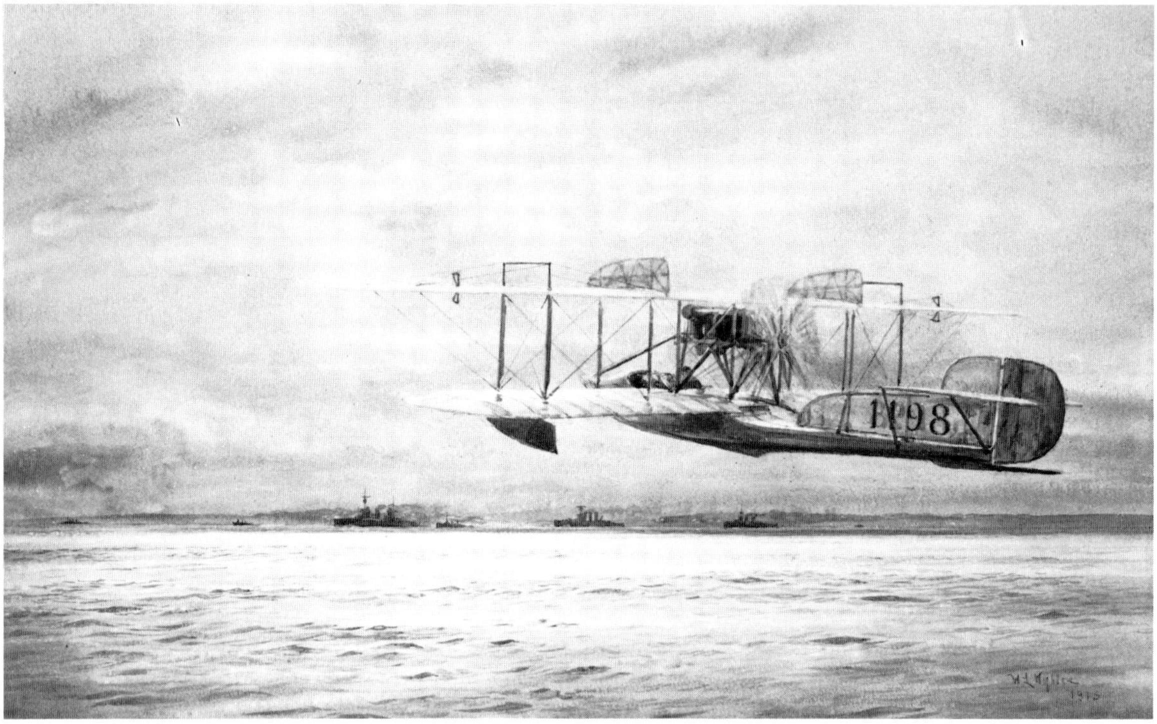

91. A sea-plane, 1916
pencil and watercolour, $11\frac{1}{16} \times 17\frac{9}{16}$ (281×446)
National Maritime Museum, London

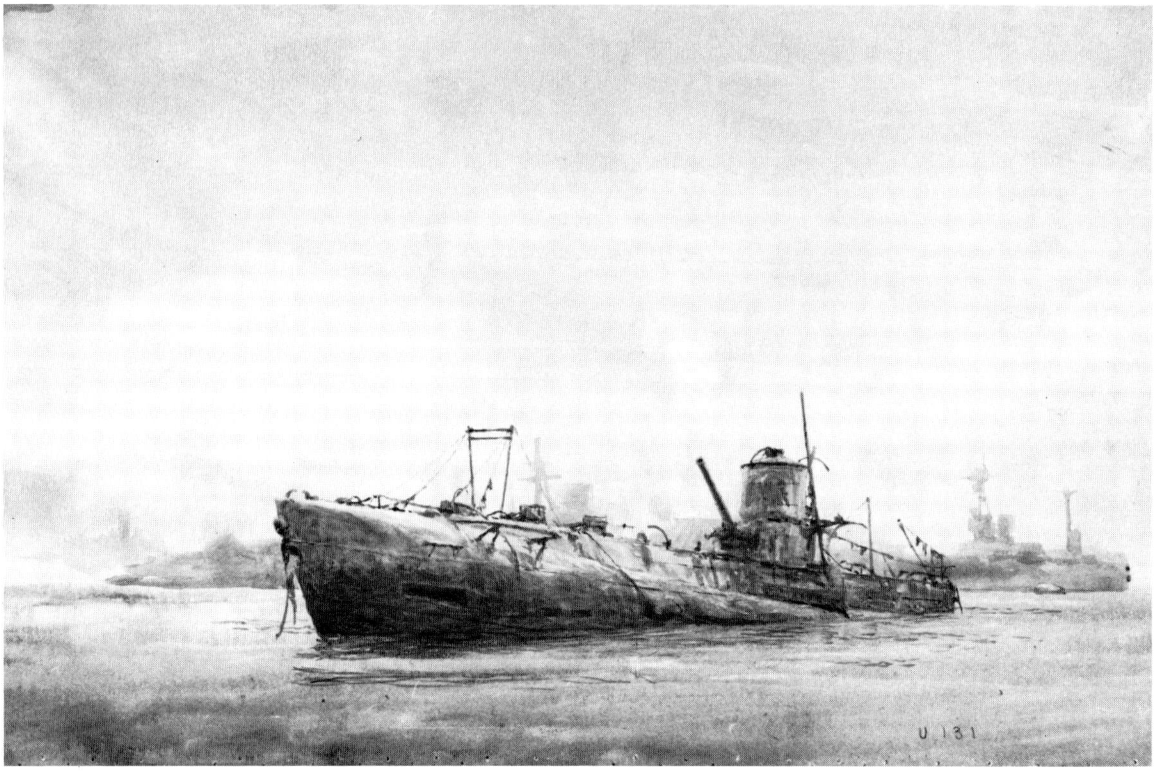

92. German submarine U131, *c.* 1918
watercolour, $12\frac{3}{4} \times 17\frac{5}{8}$ (320×450)
National Maritime Museum, London

throughout the world, in the making and marketing of prints. Wyllie increasingly used drypoint, with extreme skill, in a way which made it almost indistinguishable from etching. Sometimes he added aquatint to his drypoint, perhaps for increased atmospheric effect, and in many plates he made use of the mezzotint rocker.[46] London and Thames subjects occupied him to the end of his life, and in these technically brilliant plates he sometimes achieved remarkable atmospheric effects, akin to those of Whistler's sparse compositions in the same medium. But where Whistler's art was essentially reductive, Wyllie's was, in most cases, quite the opposite. He had long before succumbed to a tendency to 'pile up facts, and nothing but facts, with more or less discrimination', for as early as 1884 the *Magazine of Art* had warned: 'From him we have a right to expect something higher than mere topography however skilful, or than mere pictorial inventories however full.'[47] Nevertheless, the engraved works of Wyllie remain perhaps his most lasting achievement. Like the best of his watercolours they are the fruit of sheer familiarity with subject and process.

When living in Portsmouth Wyllie did not have access to the etching press: '. . . the plate was in Portsmouth & the press in London.' His method

> was to make the study straight from the subject in black paint on very thin paper & then stick the paper reversed on the window in front of him. . . . His etching tools lived in an old leather glove hung on the wall: a burin, a darning needle in an old paint brush handle, a chipped diamond, a burnisher, a little tin of Globe metal polish to rub into the scratches to get a black image.[48]

Wyllie had the family motor car fitted with a mirror so that when a suitable view was encountered, the driver was asked to stop, and with a few adjustments a drawing, already reversed, could be made from the mirror. Sometimes a telescope was also employed. Having worked on a plate to his satisfaction, Wyllie would then visit his printers, Charles and Frank Welch in Hammersmith, where a proof was taken, touched up in watercolour, and the plate worked upon. At this point Dunthorne, or whoever was publishing the plate, would come over to approve it before the edition, usually of 150, was printed.

Next to his etchings the finest works of Wyllie's later years were his watercolours of the British Fleet at the time of the First World War (Plates 87–92; Colour Plate 12). At this time he illustrated in watercolours two commentaries on the war, *Sea Fights of the Great War* (1918) and *More Sea Fights of the Great War* (1919). In such watercolours he was able to include a wealth of detail using a technique which allowed for atmospheric content. 'No one more gracefully recorded the Grand Fleet in its pride', Oliver Warner has written.[49]

On several occasions during the course of the War Wyllie travelled with the fleet by special licence in order to make drawings, many of which still bear the stamp of the Official Censor. A glimpse of one such visit to the fleet is provided by Admiral Sir Charles Madden who, as a boy of thirteen at the time of the Armistice in 1919, was aboard the battleship HMS *Revenge*. The other guest on the *Revenge*, flagship of Admiral Sir Charles Madden senior, was Wyllie, who stayed for a month. During this time he made drawings of the British and German fleets as they steamed up the Firth of Forth, the British ships escorting the German to their internment at Scapa Flow. The young Madden was set to paint with Wyllie, the first time he had thought about painting, and he has since become an accomplished artist in his own right.

The two worked in the Admiral's after cabin of the *Revenge*, sometimes in heavy seas which never deterred Wyllie. Charles Madden recalls that Wyllie's paint box was swimming with water, with large quantities of paint squeezed out, viridian in particular. He was taught Wyllie's practice of using a brush *sucked* dry to draw pigment from the entirely wet paper. If Wyllie happened to discover a blemish on his paper ('Oh damn, there's a scratch on this paper!'), it was ingeniously concealed with a funnel or masts. During this trip Wyllie produced sketches which he later used for at least two oil paintings and etchings, and made numerous studies of the massive arches of the Forth Bridge. He sometimes painted from the stern walk of the *Revenge*, making studies of the picket boats and drifters lying astern.

In the early Twenties Charles Madden visited Wyllie at Portsmouth, where once again he watched him paint in the big studio. At one time he posed for one of the figures in *Zeebrugge, St George's Day, 1918*. Like another young artist, Claude Rogers, who also visited Wyllie's house, he was fascinated by Wyllie's method of setting out the position of the ships in the fleet pictures on the floor of the studio, drawing lines to the picture surface. This method, though it resulted in the ships being seen in correct perspective and positioned correctly, was rather unsatisfactory, as the ships in the background of the picture were usually too small to relate to the composition of the picture as a whole.

It is interesting to note that Charles Madden did not share his father's passion for Wyllie's etchings and drypoints produced during this period. He later discovered, however, the earlier subjects not then generally known, including the Thames views.

The idea of painting a panorama of the Battle of Trafalgar had occurred to Wyllie many years earlier during his youth as a result of seeing a similar one portraying the Battle of Waterloo.[50] The details of the battle, scrupulously researched, are laid out methodically and 'scientifically'. This left little room for what was considered to be factually correct, and once the preliminary drawings were completed and transferred to the vast canvas, the problem was largely one of covering such an area with oil paint.[51] The colours, in particular the blues and greens, are the brilliant ones of Wyllie's later years which could, sadly, lack subtlety. In the case of the Panorama, however, they contribute to its success as a period piece. Wyllie almost certainly considered the Trafalgar Panorama the culminative achievement of his work in the historical genre, if not of his entire life's work, and it has, indeed, always been popular.

Nevertheless, it is for his watercolours, etchings and drypoints, rather than his oil paintings, that we may expect Wyllie eventually to be remembered. They stand in

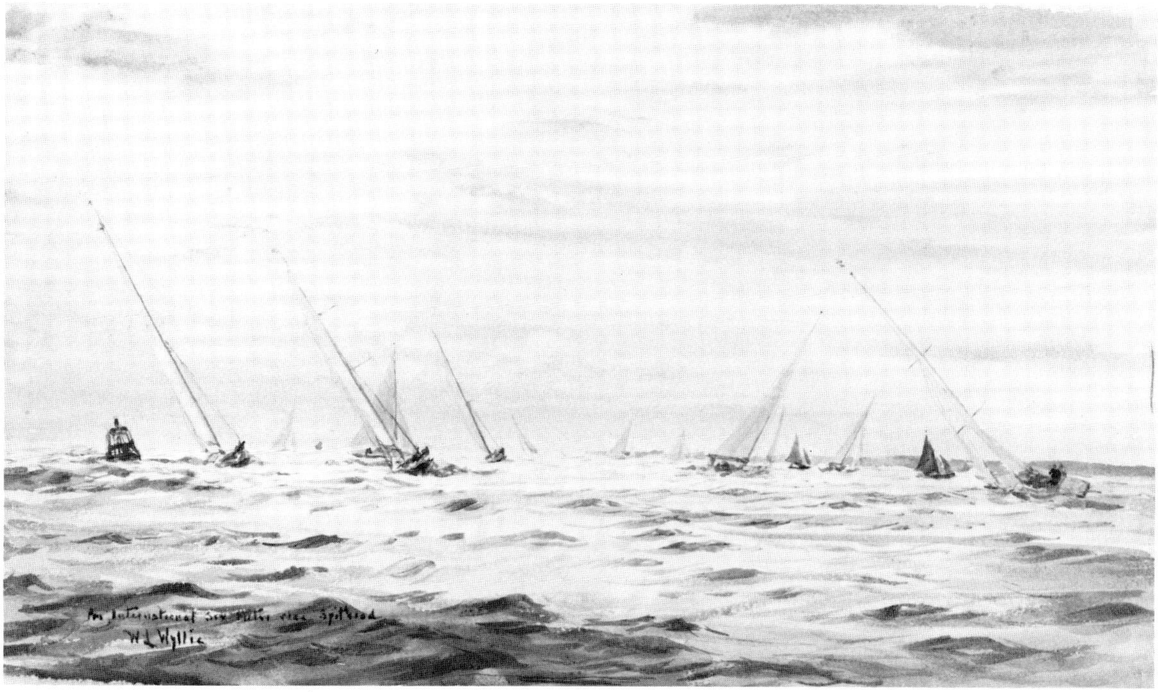

93. An International six metre race at Spithead, 1927
watercolour, $10\frac{7}{16} \times 17\frac{3}{8}$ (268×442)
National Maritime Museum, London

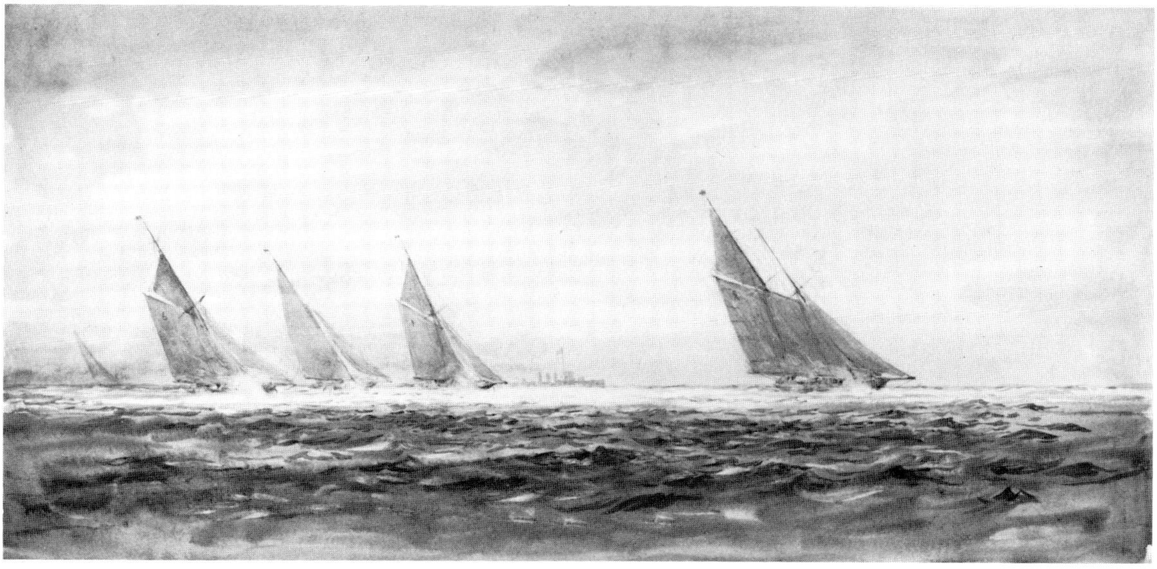

94. J Class yachts (including *Britannia*) and the American schooner *Westward*, *c.* 1920
pencil and watercolour, 14×20 (356×508)
National Maritime Museum, London

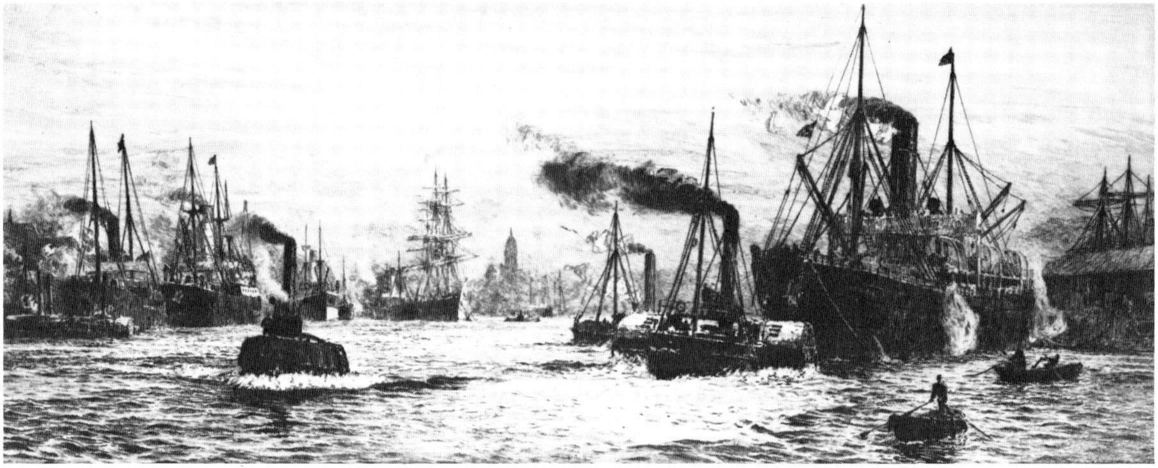

95. The Clyde at Govan, 1914
etching, roulette and drypoint, $8 \times 19\frac{1}{2}$ (203×496)
National Maritime Museum, London

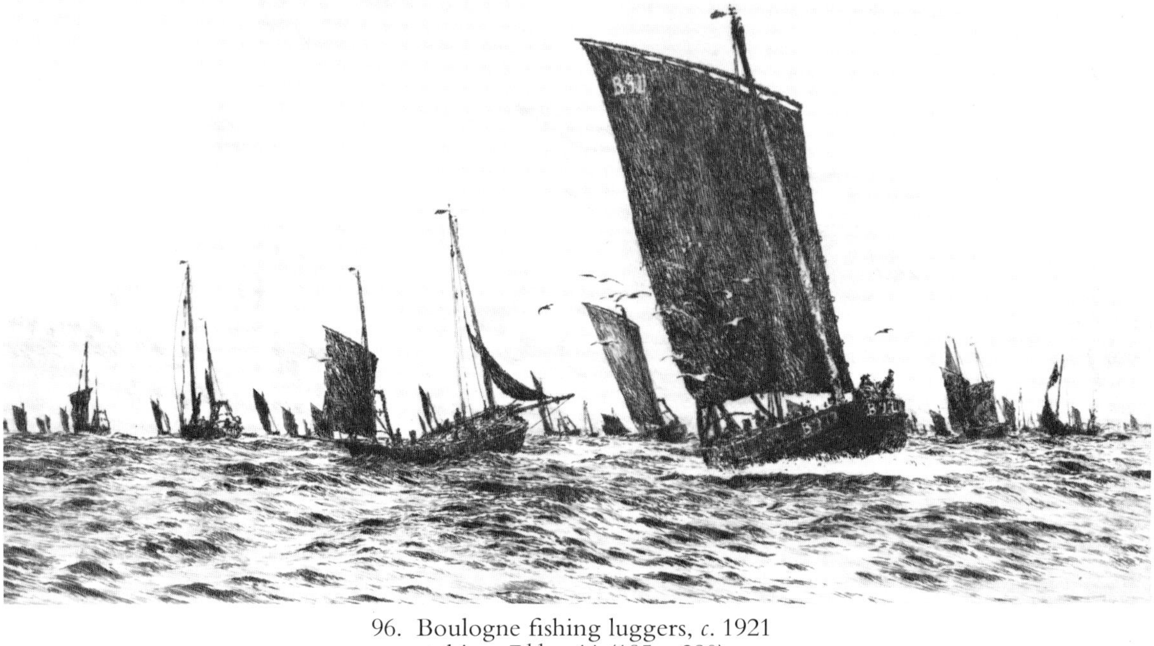

96. Boulogne fishing luggers, *c.* 1921
etching, $7\frac{11}{16} \times 11$ (195×280)
National Maritime Museum, London

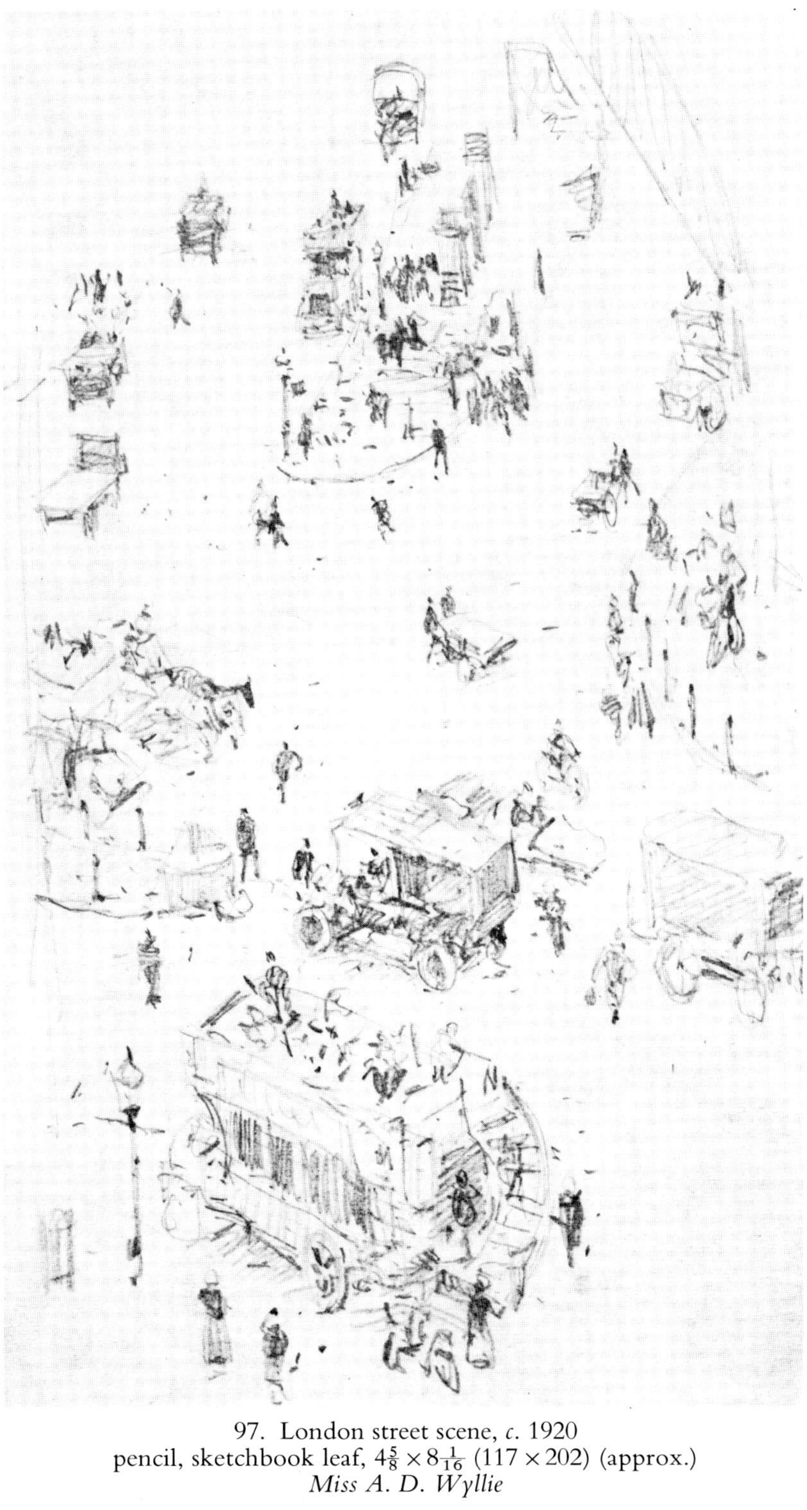

97. London street scene, *c.* 1920
pencil, sketchbook leaf, $4\frac{5}{8} \times 8\frac{1}{16}$ (117 × 202) (approx.)
Miss A. D. Wyllie

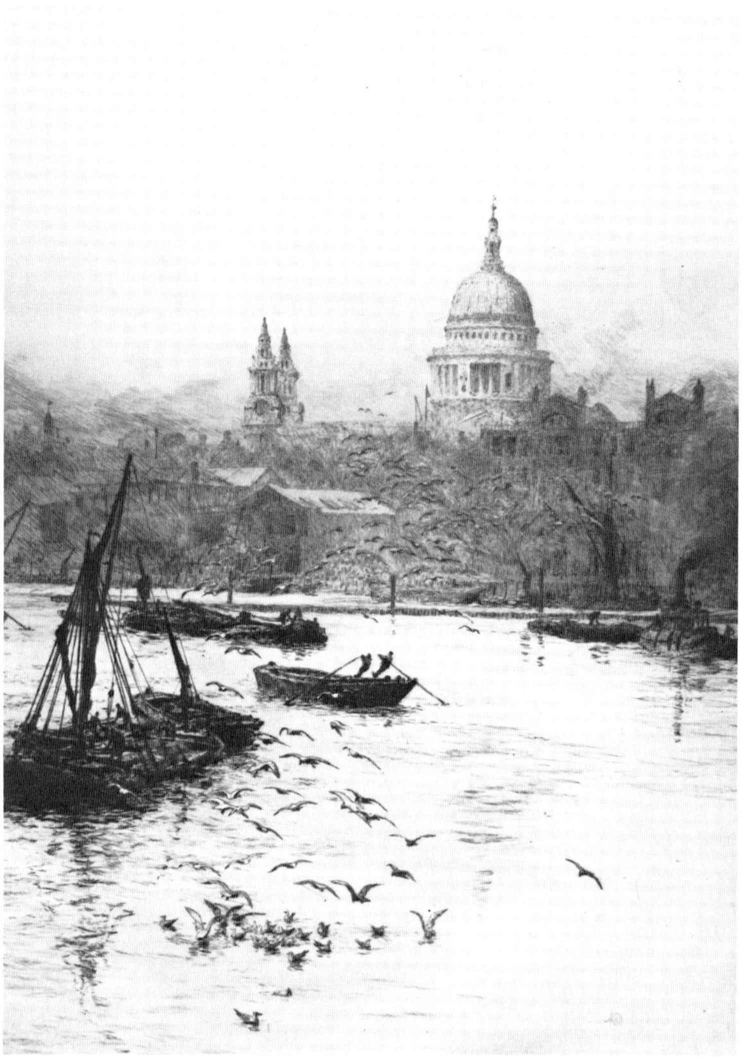

98. St Paul's Cathedral from the South Bank of the Thames, *c.* 1920–5
drypoint with roulette, $13\frac{15}{16} \times 9\frac{15}{16}$ (354 × 253)
National Maritime Museum, London

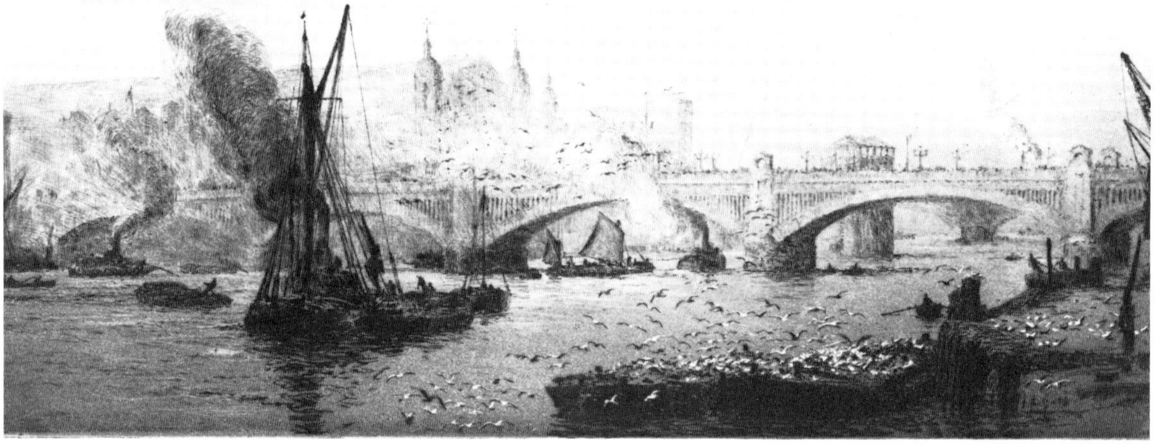

99. Southwark Bridge, *c.* 1920–5
aquatint, etching and drypoint, $4\frac{7}{8} \times 12\frac{3}{4}$ (123 × 324)
National Maritime Museum, London

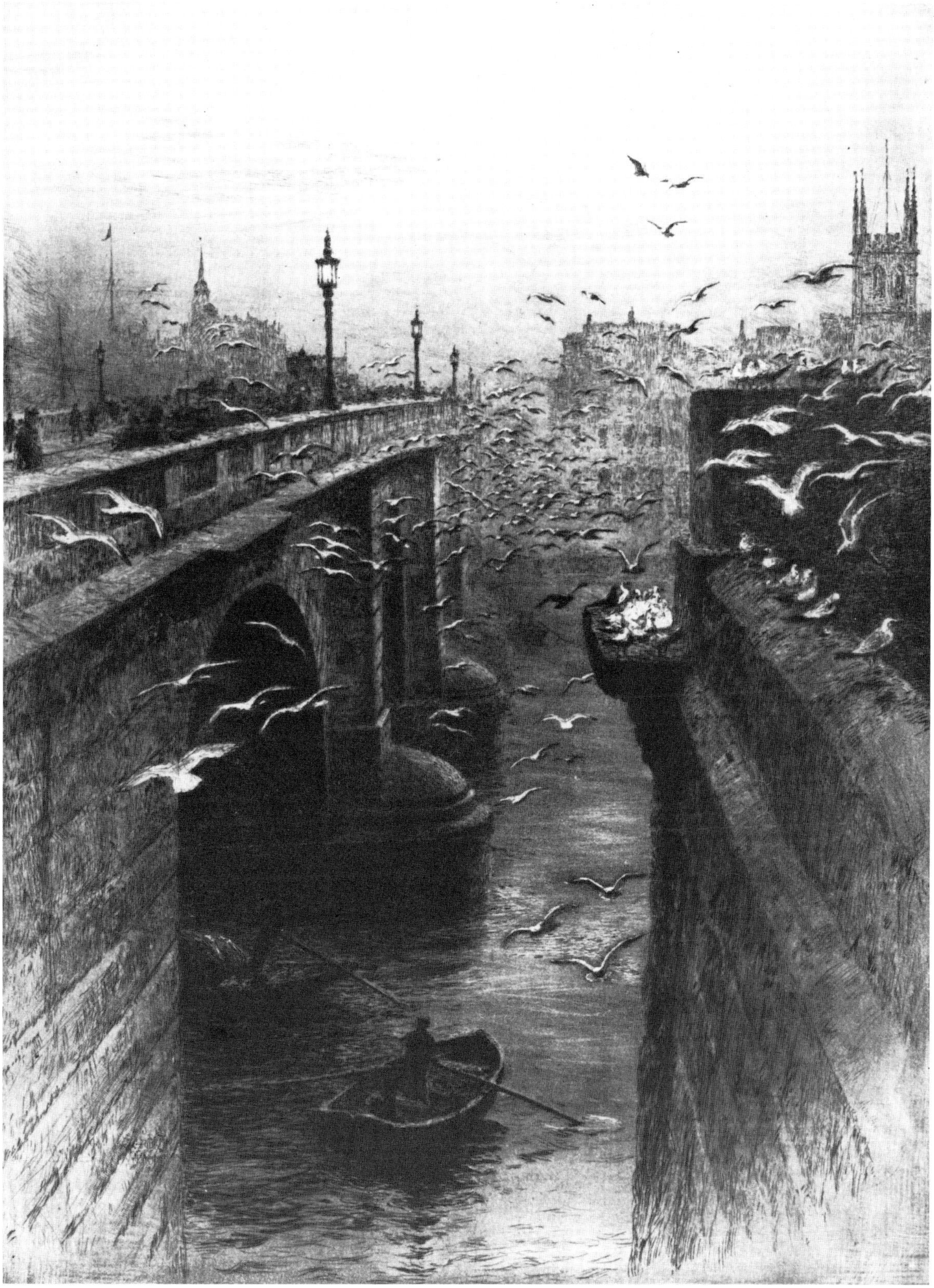

100. London Bridge looking towards Southwark Cathedral, *c.* 1920
aquatint, drypoint and roulette, 12 × 9 (306 × 229)
National Maritime Museum, London

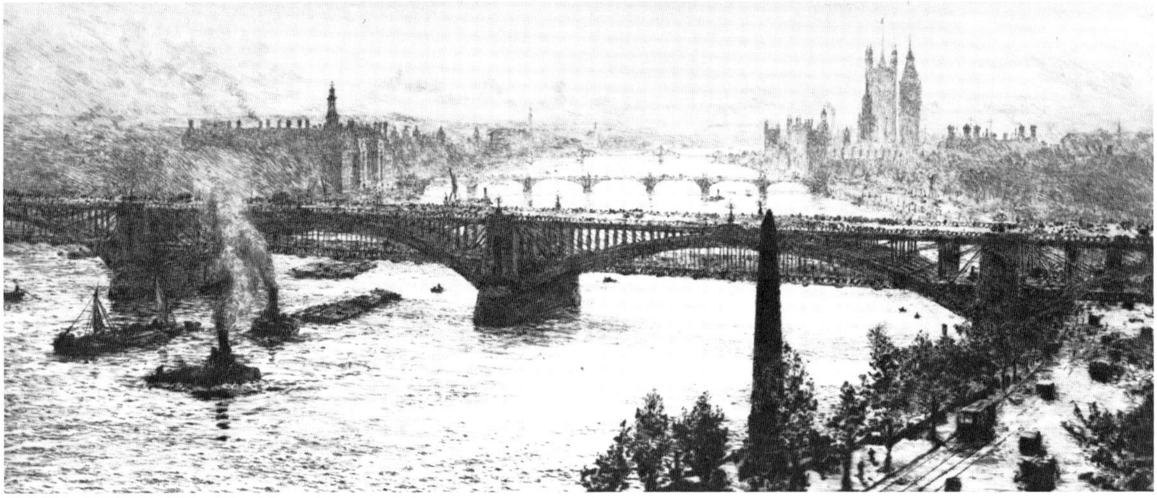

101. Westminster from St Paul's, *c.* 1920–5
drypoint and roulette, $6\frac{3}{8} \times 14\frac{7}{8}$ (163 × 376)
National Maritime Museum, London

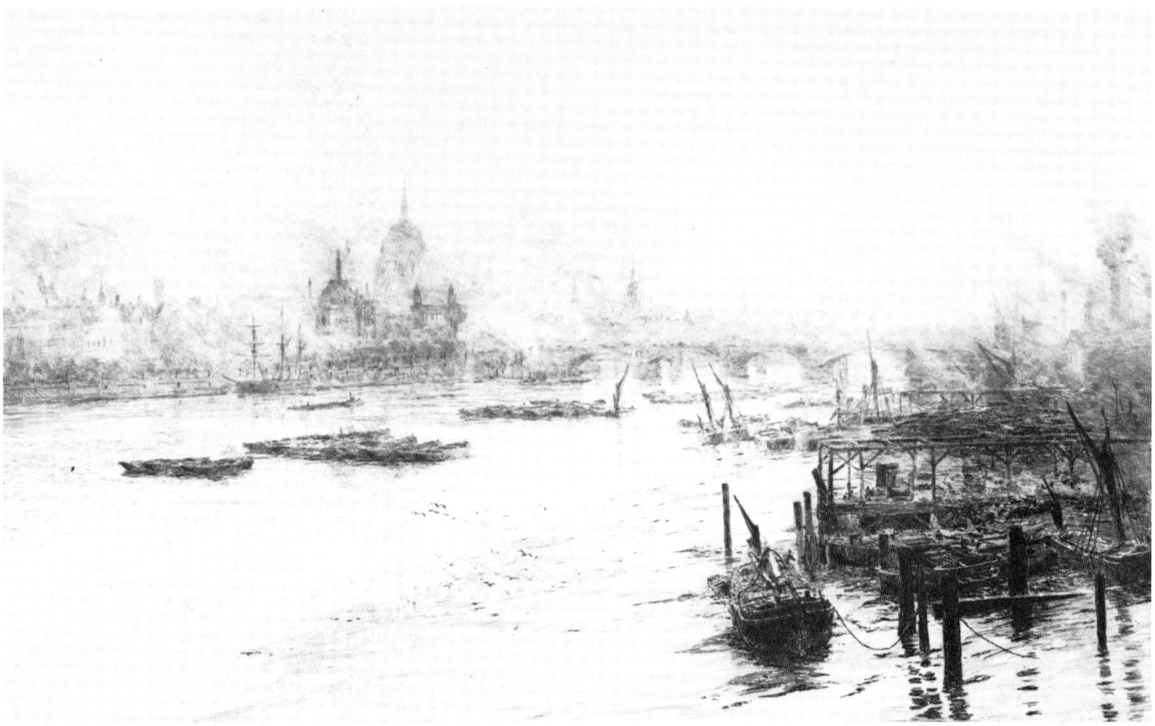

102. The Thames at Low Tide, *c.* 1910
etching, drypoint and roulette, $8\frac{15}{16} \times 13\frac{15}{16}$ (227 × 354)
National Maritime Museum, London

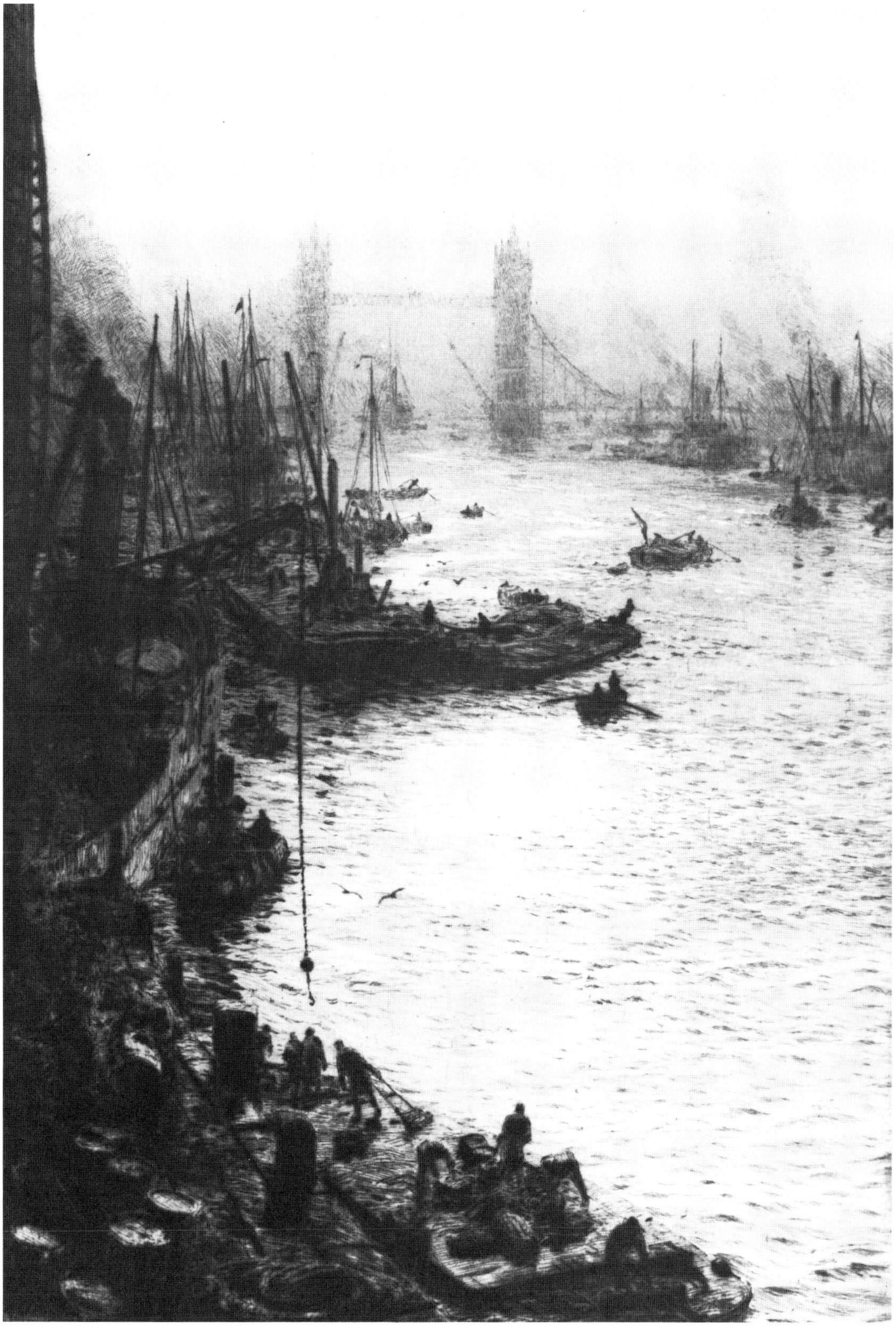

103. Tower Bridge, *c.* 1920–5
drypoint, roulette and aquatint, $10\frac{7}{8} \times 7\frac{3}{8}$ (277 × 187)
National Maritime Museum, London

terms of art as his finest achievement. Although the more specialist aspects of his work as a marine artist will always have a following, Wyllie's reputation will surely survive unscathed if assessed alone upon the finely wrought watercolours of *c.* 1900 (Plates 65, 69, 70, 77; Colour Plates 10, 11) or the technically superb London prints of the 1920s (Plates 98–103), in both of which is found an echo of the equally atmospheric 'sea and sky' beach scenes produced long before in France in the 1870s.

It could be said that Wyllie's excellence was achieved not in the first place by personal brilliance, but was born out of a love of the subjects which were part of his environment, and pursued with application and repetition. His art was founded upon rules and method, rather than on vision.

NOTES

1 R. M. Whitlaw and W. L. Wyllie, *Lionel P. Smythe, RA, RWS: His Life and Work*, 1923, p. 21.
2 Ibid., p. 22.
3 Ibid., p. 36.
4 Ibid., pp. 21–23.
5 M. Hardie, *Water-colour Painting in Britain*, III, 1968, p. 140.
6 Whitlaw and Wyllie, p. 9.
7 M. A. Wyllie, *We Were One*, 1935, p. 5.
8 Ibid., p. 6.
9 *Illustrated London News*, 4 December 1960, p. 570. Whitlaw and Wyllie, pp. 57–59.
10 *The Times*, 26 October 1869.
11 *Illustrated London News*, 15 January 1870, p. 74.
12 *Illustrated London News*, 22 November 1873, p. 473.
13 Ibid., 27 December 1884, p. 646.
14 Letter, M. Bennett – R. Quarm, 11 July 1980. I have been unable to discover where this picture was exhibited in Paris in 1878. It was neither in the Exposition Universelle nor in the Salon.
15 *The Times*, 1884.
16 *Illustrated London News*, 1 March 1884, p. 198.
17 Ibid., 14 November 1884, p. 572.
18 Ibid., 5 December 1885, p. 592. Institute of Painters in Oil Colours: 'Mr W. L. Wyllie's two works "The River of Gold" (215) and "The River of Silver" (502) represent the Thames below Greenwich by sunset and in evening grey, but for ideal treatment of the Thames, we must turn to Mr C. J. Lewis's "Old Battersea Bridge" (171) with its vained lights tingeing a London haze.'
19 H. V. Barnett, 'By River and Sea', *Magazine of Art*, May 1884, p. 314.
20 Ibid., pp. 314–15.
21 *Illustrated London News*, 21 June 1884, p. 594.
22 Ibid., 12 December 1885, p. 662.
23 *Magazine of Art*, May 1888, 'The Chronicle of Art', p. xxxii.
24 M. A. Wyllie, p. 263.
25 *Memoirs of Lord Charles Beresford*, II, 1914, p. 399.
26 H. V. Barnett, p. 310.
27 *Illustrated London News*, 7 June 1884.
28 Letter, H. Wyllie – E. Archibald, 19 July 1958.
29 *Illustrated London News*, 9 May 1885, p. 481.
30 *Magazine of Art*, 1889, p. 214.
31 Fine Art Society, London, Minute Book, 1882–3, 11 April 1883.
32 Royal Academy, London, July–September 1978, *Great Victorian Pictures*, cat. 38, illus. p. 61.
33 *Magazine of Art*, August 1889.
34 *Athenaeum*, 3354, 6 February 1892, pp. 186–7.
35 *Magazine of Art*, March 1892, 'The Chronicle of Art', p. xxii.
36 M. A. Wyllie, pp. 102–3.
37 W. L. Wyllie, *Marine Painting in Watercolour*, 1901, p. 9.
38 *Athenaeum*, 4140, 9 March 1907, p. 297.
39 Oliver Warner, *An Introduction to British Marine Painting*, 1948, p. 44.
40 M. A. Wyllie, p. 183.
41 *Magazine of Art*, 1889, Royal Academy Report II, p. 272.
42 W. L. Wyllie, *J. M. W. Turner*, 1905.
43 *Art Journal*, 1910, 'Passing Events', p. 159.

44 Ibid., 1904, p. 182
45 *Athenaeum*, 4140, 9 March 1907, p. 297.
46 M. A. Wyllie, p. 176.
47 H. V. Barnett, p. 315.
48 Letter, A. Wyllie – R. Quarm, 31 December 1980.
49 As note 39.
50 *The Panorama of the Battle of Trafalgar*, transcript of interview between J. Pack and A. Wyllie.
51 For an illustrated account of the production of the Trafalgar Panorama, see W. L. Wyllie, 'A panorama of the Battle of Trafalgar', Society for Nautical Research, Annual Report for the year 1929, pp. 35–6.

LIST OF WORKS EXHIBITED IN THE ROYAL ACADEMY

Medium is oil unless otherwise specified.
Titles are given as supplied in source, with spelling standardised.
Present ownership by galleries and other organisations is indicated where known.
Abbreviations: wc – watercolour; e – etching; d – drypoint; a – aquatint.

1868	Dover Castle and Town
1869	Outward Bound
1870	London from the Monument
1871	The old *Bellerophon*, Portsmouth Harbour Rotten Row, Portsmouth Harbour
1872	Ave Maria (Russell Cotes Art Gallery, Bournemouth)
1873	Landing fish at Ambleteuse 'She does no work by halves, yon raving ocean! Engulfing those she strangles.' – Scott
1874	The Goodwins (Russell Cotes Art Gallery, Bournemouth)
1876	A.B.; a floating sentinel Blessing the sea (Walker Art Gallery, Liverpool)
1877	Tracking in Holland
1878	The silent highway Summer clouds
1879	A land lost between sky and water
1880	Grelliers and Canterbury Wharves, Lambeth Coming up on the flood
1881	Beckton Gasworks The Rochester river

1882	Our river (Art Gallery of South Australia) The Port of London
1883	'Toil, glitter, grime and wealth on a flowing tide' (Tate Gallery, Chantrey Bequest)
1884	'Toil, glitter, grime and wealth on a flowing tide' (e) 'Heave Away': barges upward bound, shooting Rochester Bridge (e) Midwinter: the end of the story
1885	Storm and sunshine: a battle with the elements (National Maritime Museum) Debatable ground Rochester Bridge
1886	Work-a-day England 'Though thy tackle's torn, thou show'st a noble vessel' – Shakespeare
1887	In the wind's teeth King Coal Orient steamship *Ormuz*, fitting out The river of gold
1889	The phantom ship The homeward-bound pennant The highway of nations Towing up the Waal
1890	Davy Jones's locker The birth of a Titan The *Teutonic* leaving Liverpool HMS *Exmouth* Veere; a dead city (e) The Upper Pool, London Bridge (e)
1891	Spithead, 4th August, 1889; HIM the Emperor of Germany and HRH the Prince of Wales, inspecting the *Teutonic* mercantile armed cruiser, White Star Line The Battle of Trafalgar The glory of a dying day Brighton
1892	The Spanish Armada Kit's Hole Reach HMS *Calliope* at Samoa (e)
1893	'Robert and Susan to the rescue!' Newbiggin Bay Off to the Cape of Good Hope
1894	The Roaring Forties 'Yes sah! sixpence, sah!' 'At eventide there shall be light' Butterflies and working bees (Royal Corinthian Yacht Club)

1895	London's Water Gate
	The opening of the Tower Bridge
	The Union liner SS *Norman* leaving Southampton
	Bound for the Rio Grande
	A southerly gale, Brighton
1896	London Bridge
	Rearing the lion's whelps
	A silent highway
	Crippled, but unconquered (Army and Navy Club)
1897	The winding Medway
	Barry docks
	The liner's escort *Dunvegan Castle*, Union Castle Line (wc)
1898	Commerce and sea power
	Union liner *Briton* off Calshot
	The harbour bar
	Entrance to Barry Dock
	RYS *Valhalla*
1899	Peace and plenty
	The Battle of the Nile (Tate Gallery, Chantrey Bequest)
1900	Blake's great naval engagement with Van Tromp, 1653
1901	The passing of a great Queen (Walker Art Gallery, Liverpool)
	The City of London
	'Just a funnel and a mast lurching through the spray
	So we thrashed the *Bolivar* out across the bay'
1902	A whole gale of wind
	The Houses of Parliament (wc)
	Pushing down against the flood
1903	Peace driving away the horrors of war
	A stiff breeze
	June 1st, 1902; peace proclaimed
	The hub of the Empire
1904	Towing past the city
	Chatham Reach – midday
	St Paul's Cathedral (wc)
	A doomed valley: the water supply for Birmingham
1905	Trafalgar 2.30 p.m., Oct. 21st 1805
	Homeward Bound
	Fishing luggers: Dover
	Shrimpers: sea reach
1906	A Medway fleet
	L'Entente cordiale; arrival of the French fleet in Cowes Roads
	Low water Berck-sur-mer
	England's frontier

1907 Signals from the *Victory*
A royal salute
Spithead
Dreadnought and *Victory*
International courtesies, Portsmouth

1908 Lord Charles's liberty men
Spliced
A start of the Bird class on Belfast Lough
The breeze falls light (Diploma work)

1909 Tide race, Portsmouth Harbour
The Second Cruiser Squadron in the North Sea
The rosy morn: the mackerel fleet putting to sea

1910 Slipping out with the ebb
Hamilton Bank
From under the sea
Gosport
The mouth of the harbour

1911 New Zealand's gift to the old country (New Zealand Art Gallery)
Goat Fell, Arran
London from the Surrey side
P & O *Malwa* at Cronstadt

1912 Yachts hibernating, Gosport
Submarines and torpedo craft, old Portsmouth
In the nick of time
Stemming the ebb-tide
'A passage perilous maketh a port pleasant'

1913 The Home Fleet putting to sea
A distant thunder cloud
The King's Birthday
A friendly tow out against the flood
Snappers-up of unconsidered trifles

1914 Burning of the old Semaphore Tower, Portsmouth
The approach to St Petersburg
The launch of HMS *Iron Duke*
Windermere from Briery Close

1915 Bringing in the wounded *Lion*
Portsmouth in war-time: mine sweepers putting to sea
The fighting-line from Ypres to the sea
The armed liner *Carmania* engaging the *Cap Trafalgar* off Trinidade
Masters of the seas

1916 Spotting for the Fleet, Dardanelles
A fight to a finish: off Coronel, 1st November, 1914
The Hooge salient

1917 London Docks, 1916
Battle cruisers cheering ship after the Dogger Bank action
Battlefields of the Ancre and Somme from the north-west: altitude, 8,600 ft
Jutland 31st May, 1916: HM *Ships Warspite* and *Warrior*
Battle in the air: Ypres salient

1918 The battle of Bourlon Wood, 30th Nov. 1917
Admiral Beatty's battle cruisers, Windy Corner, 31st May, 1916
The wounded *Acasta* cheering the *Iron Duke* in battle, 31st May, 1916
Dawn, 20th Nov., 1917. The sunken road north of La Vacquerie: zero plus 102: our barrage lifts

1919 'Der Tag': the German High Seas Fleet coming in to be interned by Admiral Beatty
The German High Seas Fleet caged in Scapa Flow
The Battle of Villers-Bretonneux, 24th April, 1918

1920 To the glorious memory of Admiral the Hon. Horace Hood, Captain A. L. Cay, with 1,025 officers and men of HMS *Invincible* who gave their lives for King and Country on May 31st, 1916, off Jutland
His Majesty inspecting his Fleet off Rosyth on the eve of the German surrender
Spithead in peace
Destruction of the German raider *Leopard* by HM Ships *Achilles* and *Dundee*, 16th March, 1917

1921 The blocking of Zeebrugge waterway, St George's Day, 1918
An aftermath of the Great War (German destroyer in Portsmouth Harbour)
King George's river pageant, 1919

1922 'With drums and rolling music, like a Queen'; ships of the Atlantic Fleet play the *Victory* into dock
The South Cone
Whitby: low water
The Prince leaving Portsmouth for India
Greenwich Hospital (wc)

1923 Coastal motor-boats
A storm is coming
The Port of London

1924 The towers, spires, and bridges of our City
Scarborough Castle
'The flowing river winds past Palace, Park, and the homes of toiling millions' (London Borough of Greenwich: Woodlands Art Gallery)

1925 'The Nelson Touch': restoring HMS *Victory* (1805–1925), National Maritime Museum
King George V dock
The Fairway into Portsmouth
Mont St Michel
The gale, January 1915

1926	Jutland: attack of the 13th Flotilla St Ives: herring time Victory Bridge, Charing Cross: a vision	
1927	Waterloo: the doomed bridge A suggestion for the new Charing Cross Bridge The British Fleet of Jutland, 6.22 p.m. on 31st May, 1916 (United Service Club) 'Old Harry', between Swanage and Studland	
1928	Swaying up the mainyard Leaving Gibraltar (wc) Nile quarry boats (wc) The Pass of Glencoe (d with a)	
1929	The Temple of Pallas Athene from the sea Fifty north and forty west Action off Dover between HM Ships *Swift* and *Broke* and six enemy destroyers, 21st April, 1917	
1930	Collingwood in the *Royal Sovereign* engaging *Santa Ana*: Battle of Trafalgar *Victory, Redoubtable, Temeraire* and *Fougueux* locked together: Battle of Trafalgar *Santissima Trinidad* surrounded by *Leviathan, Neptune* and *Africa*: Battle of Trafalgar	Studies for the Panorama
	HMS *Laconia*, Course South 5° West, Speed $12\frac{1}{2}$ knots	
1931	Cape St Vincent Storming the Mole: St George's Day, 1918 Athens from the Gulf of Aegina	

LIST OF WORKS EXHIBITED AT LOCATIONS OTHER THAN THE ROYAL ACADEMY

This is a representative rather than a comprehensive list. Wyllie is also known to have exhibited at the French Gallery, the Royal Hibernian Gallery, the Royal Scottish Society of Painters in Water Colours and Manchester City Art Gallery. His etchings were advertised at the Fine Art Society and 'always on view' at Connel and Sons Gallery.

Titles of one-man shows are asterisked.

Medium is specified only where it is indicated in source, although it is sometimes implied by the nature of the exhibiting institution, e.g. Institute of Painters in Oil Colours.

Titles are given as supplied in source, with spelling standardised.

Abbreviations: wc – watercolour; e – etching; d – drypoint; a – aquatint.

1868	Dudley Gallery	Twilight (wc) Sunset (wc) The woods in spring (oil) The beach in winter (oil) Below bridge (oil) The sou'-wester (oil)
1869	Dudley Gallery	A twilight calm (oil) Wreck of the *Wheatsheaf* on the French Coast (oil)
	Agnews	In the downs A lee shore Going out with the tide
1870	Agnews	The rising tide Early summer Sketch for the Turner Medal Picture, RA, 1869 Dropping down with the tide The blessing of the sea before the herring fishery The herring fleet

		Coal barges in the Thames
		Bugsbys Reach
		Putting out
		Napoleon's ruined harbour at Ambleteuse
		Mid-day
		Evening
		The South Foreland
	Dudley Gallery	Berks and Bucks (oil)
		Aground (oil)
		Breakers (oil)
	Society of British Artists	A shoal in the offing
	Society of British Artists	The ebbing tide
		East London – A sketch
		A rift in the cloud
1870/1	Society of British Artists	The beach in winter
		The northern lights
		A back-water on the Thames
1871	Dudley Gallery	The Foreland (wc)
	Society of British Artists	Sunshine on the Solent
		'Tis an illwind that blows nobody good
		The Isle of Wight in winter from Southsea beach
		Off Boulogne
		Beaching thro the surf
	Agnews	Our Old Line of Battle Ships
		New Moon, with Old Moon in its arms
		Boats putting out
	Glasgow Institute of Fine Arts	The hay field
		Napoleon's ruined harbour at Ambleteuse
		The South Foreland
1871/2	Society of British Artists	Trawlers by moonlight
		The day before the gale
1872	Glasgow Institute of Fine Arts	Boulogne – boats beaching
		Winter sunshine – Isle of Wight in the distance
		Spithead
		Sea coast after a storm – time dawn (Turner Prize Picture)
		Boulogne – summer

	Agnews	The breaking wave A gleam of sunlight Moonlight
	Dudley Gallery	Windmill (wc) Barges beating up (wc) The Pent, Dover (oil) Whiting fishing (oil) Off with the ebb (oil) A store flock in Piccardy (*sic*) (oil)
1872/3	Society of British Artists	Barges at Chelsea (wc)
1873	Dudley Gallery	High Water Mark (wc) In Stays (wc) Abbeville (oil) Rouen (oil)
	Society of British Artists	Landing at low water Boulogne harbour Sea gulls Snow by the sea Noon (wc)
1873/4	Society of British Artists	Etaples – a good haul of fish Boulevard des Italiens, Paris A sandy spit Market day St Pierre on the Seine Roche Guyon from the cliffs
1874	Society of British Artists	Washing, on the Seine Berck boat beaching Early morning – Sheep Château Gaillard
	Dudley Gallery	Low water at Berh (*sic*) (wc) Boats at Berh (*sic*) (wc) Landing fish at Berh (*sic*) (wc) Antwerp Cathedral (oil) Blessing the sea (oil)
	Glasgow Institute of Fine Arts	'She does no work by halves. . .' Abbeville Boat building on the Cauche 'There is Society where none intrude, by the deep sea. . .'
1874/5	Society of British Artists	Le Palais du Franc, Bruges View of Ghent

1875	Society of British Artists	A high tide Low water Waiting for the ebb
	Dudley Gallery	Untitled (oil)
	Glasgow Institute of Fine Arts	The Goodwin Sands
1875/6	Society of British Artists	Holy Haven China clippers The Golden Age Boulogne pilot
1876	Society of British Artists	The end of a day Wreck of a Dutch fruiter Portel Sands – evening
1876/7	Society of British Artists	A dead city in Holland Enkhuizen, in the Zuyder Zee French Coast (wc) Amsterdam (wc) In Dock (wc)
1877	Society of British Artists	At 'the Good Intent' A Dutch canal
	Dudley Gallery	Boulogne pilots racing to a Vessel (black and white)
	Glasgow Institute of Fine Arts	Holy haven on the Thames Enk Huysen on the Zuyder Zee (oil)
1877/8	Society of British Artists	Whitstable, Kent The mouth of a river
1878	Society of British Artists	A Puffing Billy A lab'ring oar
	Paris	Blessing the sea
	Exposition Universelle, Paris	Sea birds
	Glasgow Institute of Fine Arts	Barges in a calm near Amsterdam At the Good Intent The village on the cliff
1879/80	Society of British Artists	Peaceful old age
1880	Society of British Artists	The Alps 'The moon is up and yet it is not night'

		Coming home Mont St Michel, Normandy (wc) The Roche de Naie (wc) The Dent du Midi (wc) The Valley of the Rhone (wc) Portsmouth Harbour (wc)
	Glasgow Institute of Fine Arts	The silent highway
1880/1	Society of British Artists	Twilight
1881	Society of British Artists	A fair wind A busy river
	Glasgow Institute of Fine Arts	The silent highway Steam colliers unloading – Atlas no. 1
1881/2	Society of British Artists	Corrie's coal derrick in Bagship Reach Ebb tide: Long Reach
1882	Society of British Artists	Equhien: low water Towing over the tide
1882/3	Society of British Artists	Ebb tide: Dordrecht Below Sunbury Lock
1883	Fine Art Society	The Bombardment of Alexandria (two oils)
	Society of British Artists	Timber ships towing to a berth
	Walker Art Gallery, Liverpool	'Toil, glitter, grime. . .'
1883/4	Institute of Painters in Oil Colours	Black Diamonds
1884	Fine Art Society	'The Tidal Thames'* (seventy-three wcs)
	Grosvenor Gallery	
	Institute of Painters in Oil Colours	
	Walker Art Gallery, Liverpool	Fort Ras-el-Tin, Alexandria A Cornish chasm Eunostus Point, Alexandria Barges upward bound
	Royal Institute of Painters in Water Colours	Funeral march of a hero Ras-el-Tin

		Eunostus Point Queenborough A Cornish chasm A West Country boat builder Falmouth
1884/5	Society of British Artists	The training ship *Exmouth*
	Institute of Painters in Oil Colours	High Water Mark Tide time
1885	Institute of Painters in Oil Colours	River of Silver River of Gold Gill's Yard
	Agnews	The *City of Rochester*
	Royal Institute of Painters in Water Colours	The *City of Rochester* discharging
	Walker Art Gallery, Liverpool	Gill's Yard
	Royal Institute of Painters in Water Colours	Gill's Yard The *City of Rochester* discharging 'Frost and Rime of Winter Time' The *Providence* repairing The mouth of the Medway
	Grosvenor Gallery	'Hard Times'. Dredging for coal
	St James Gallery	'Black and white exhibition' (contributions to)
	Tooth Galleries	Sheep dipping
	Society of British Artists	Fresh fish Portel The leisure hour (sketch for the engraved picture) A breezy day: Portel
1885/6	Society of British Artists	'O'er the Glad Waters of the Deep Blue Sea' Overhauling the Lines Guernsey Roads
	Institute of Painters in Oil Colours	River of Gold River of Silver
1886	Royal Institute of Painters in Water Colours	Gabriel's Wharf
1886/7	Institute of Painters in Oil Colours	Bumboats alongside White Star ss at Queenstown Riding it out

1887	Royal Institute of Painters in Water Colours	On the Medway On the Medway
	Agnews	The *City of Rochester*
1887/8	Institute of Painters in Oil Colours	Spithead, July 23rd, 1887 A spanking breeze
1888	Rembrandt Gallery (Dunthorne's)	'Netherland Waterways'* (wcs)
	Fine Art Society	
	Institute of Painters in Oil Colours	Spithead – July 23rd, 1887 A spanking breeze
	Walker Art Gallery, Liverpool	A Dutch bargain
	Grosvenor Gallery	A Dutch bargain Neptune's Garden
	Royal Institute of Painters in Water Colours	Neptune's Garden
	Royal Society of British Artists	
	Tooth Galleries	Winter on the Medway In the pool
1888/9	Institute of Painters in Oil Colours	The Highway of Nations
1889	Fine Art Society	'The Queen's Navy'* (wcs)
	Grosvenor Gallery	A Kentish river
	Institute of Painters in Oil Colours	Highway of Nations Lull before the storm
	Royal Institute of Painters in Water Colours	The Mersey from Liverpool A new colossus Sun Pier, Chatham
1889/90	Institute of Painters in Oil Colours	The lull before the storm
	Manchester Exhibition	
	New English Art Club	A rookery
	Exposition Universelle, Paris	The Goodwin Sands 'Toil, glitter, grime and wealth on a flowing tide' The Orient liner *Ormuz* off the Eddystone (wc) The training ship *Exmouth* (wc) Snappers up of unconsidered trifles (drawing) Southend Pier (drawing) The Highway of the Nations (e)

	Tooth Galleries	Harvest time in the Medway
1890	Great Exhibition, Chicago	A poster
	Glasgow Institute of Fine Arts	Phantom ship Davy Jones' Locker
	Institute of Painters in Oil Colours	Sou-wester
	New English Art Club	The Upper Pool, London Bridge HMS *Exmouth*
	Agnews	On the Thames (wc)
	Grosvenor Gallery	The Wreck Untitled
	Royal Institute of Painters in Water Colours	HMS *Devastation* and *Rodney*
	Brown's Gallery, Glasgow	The Shah arriving at Gravesend
	Munich Exhibition	Etchings, etc.
1890/1	Institute of Painters in Oil Colours	A sou' wester
1891	Royal Institute of Painters in Water Colours	The Bay of Naples Venice Mount Vesuvius
	The Maddocks Collection, Bradford	Bringing in the fish By the sea shore
1892	Fine Art Society	'Holiday Drawings in France and Italy'* (wcs) On the Medway The Battle of Trafalgar
1893	Royal Institute of Painters in Water Colours	North Atlantic Steam trials of the *Hood*, Sea Reach Off Erith
	New English Art Club	A calm on the Medway Three hundred miles from Sandy Hook Newbiggin-by-the-Sea
1893/4	Institute of Painters in Oil Colours	Long Reach
1894	Dowdeswell Galleries	'Oceans, Seas and Rivers'*
1896	Dowdeswell Galleries	'Salt Water Studies'*
1898	Dowdeswell Galleries	'Fair and Foul Weather from a Floating Studio'* (wcs)

	Agnews	Dordrecht (wc)
1899	Agnews	Dordrecht (wc)
	Walker Art Gallery, Liverpool	A land lost between sky and water
1900	Agnews	Taken at the flood ('English Art 1900')
	Exposition Universelle, Paris	The day's work
1901	Agnews (Manchester)	40 wcs, inc. 8 of Queen Victoria's funeral, and 9 of the Manchester Ship Canal and Docks (with Brangwyn, East, etc.)
1902	Dowdeswell Galleries	'On Many Waters'* (wcs)
1903	Royal Society of Painter Etchers and Engravers	On the last trickle of flood A stranded derelict Hauled up for repairs Unloading a leaky timber ship
1904	Royal Society of Painter Etchers and Engravers	Medway fishermen, barges and huffers (d) The City of Rochester A stiff breeze A Calm – Bawley shrimping barges waiting for the turn of the tide (d) Taking the tide at the flood
	Agnews	Elevator and timber stacks, Salford Bringing up in Queenborough Swale
	Leicester Galleries	Watercolours
1905	Royal Society of Painter Etchers and Engravers	Colchester sprat boats Coming out of dock
1906	Carfax and Co. Ltd	Towing past the City (oil)
	Royal Society of Painter Etchers and Engravers	Torpedo boats manoeuvring The Girdler lightship
1907	Royal Society of Painter Etchers and Engravers	HMS *Dreadnought* (d) Point, Portsmouth

		Victory (d) Destroyers (d)
	Fine Art Society	'Pleasure Cruises in a P & O from Spitsbergen to the Golden Horn'*
1908	Royal Society of Painter Etchers and Engravers	The City from Waterloo Bridge (e)
1909	Royal Society of Painter Etchers and Engravers	Portsmouth fishing boats Portsmouth Harbour Southampton Sheerness
1910	Royal Society of Painter Etchers and Engravers	*Britannia* at Dartmouth (d) Ryde (d) Plymouth (d) Devonport (d) Off Gravesend
	Agnews	The Pool of London
1911	Leicester Galleries	
	Royal Society of Painter Etchers and Engravers	The Tower of London St Paul's from Bankside
1912	Royal Society of Painter Etchers and Engravers	HMS *Orion* The Hot Walls, Portsmouth The *Victory*
1913	Royal Society of Painter Etchers and Engravers	HMS *Natal* leaving Portsmouth for America with the body of Mr Whitelaw Read
1914	Royal Society of Painter Etchers and Engravers	Porchester Castle Glasgow Newcastle-on-Tyne Extracts from Captain Scott's last Message to the Nation
1915	Royal Society of Painter Etchers and Engravers	An illustrated poem 'Our Fathers'
1916	Royal Society of Painter Etchers and Engravers	Minesweepers Seascouts, Portsmouth
	Rembrandt Gallery (Dunthorne's)	'The Sure Shield of Britain'* (wcs and drawings)

	Rembrandt Gallery (Dunthorne's)	The Battle of Bourlon Wood, 30th November, 1917
1918	Royal Society of Painter Etchers and Engravers	Battle cruisers off Jutland, May 31st 13th Flotilla leading the battle cruisers Lobster fishers Landing at low tide A swept channel in the North Sea
1919	Royal Society of Painter Etchers and Engravers	The convoy First in with the catch A bad time for Fritz The Battle of Jutland
1920	Royal Society of Painter Etchers and Engravers	The Embankment from the Savoy Hotel United States battle ships in the Forth The German fleet at Scapa Flow Probus and the U-boat
1921	Royal Society of Painter Etchers and Engravers	Running home in time Cherry Gardens, Rotherhithe Greenwich The 5th Battle Squadron
1923	Royal Society of Painter Etchers and Engravers	Tarbert The City of London Down stream from London Bridge White wings
1924	Royal Society of Painter Etchers and Engravers	London Bridge (d) A Royal Salute, the Tower of London (d) South Bay, Scarborough (d)
1925	Royal Society of Painter Etchers and Engravers	Yachts rounding the Warner light ship (d) London and Tower Bridge (d)
	The Abbey Gallery	
1926	Royal Society of Painter Etchers and Engravers	La Lieutenance, Honfleur (d)
1927	Royal Society of Painter Etchers and Engravers	The Duke and Duchess of York leaving Portsmouth for their

		Australian cruise (d) Racing in squally weather, Cowes Week (a, d)
1928	Royal Society of Painter Etchers and Engravers	Aberdeen Portobello and Arthur's Seat from Musselburgh (e)
1929	Royal Society of Painter Etchers and Engravers	HMS *Victory* (d) Portsmouth Dockyard (d)
1931	Royal Society of Painter Etchers and Engravers	The City of London (d) Black and Silver (d)
	Rembrandt Gallery (Dunthorne's)	'Etchings by the late W. L. Wyllie, RA'*

BIBLIOGRAPHY

A. BOOKS ILLUSTRATED, WRITTEN OR CO-AUTHORED BY W. L. WYLLIE

G. Allen, *The Tidal Thames*, London, 1884

W. L. Wyllie, *Marine Painting in Water-Colour*, London, 1901

W. L. Wyllie, *Nature's Laws and the Making of Pictures*, London, 1903

W. L. Wyllie, *J. M. W. Turner*, London, 1905

M. A. and W. L. Wyllie, *London to the Nore*, London, 1905

W. L. Wyllie, *Sketchbook*, London, 1908

M. A. Wyllie, *Norway and its Fjords*, London, 1909

M. F. Wren and W. L. Wyllie, *Sea Fights of the Great War*, London, 1918

W. D. Kirkpatrick, C. Owen and W. L. Wyllie, *More Sea Fights of the Great War*, London, 1919

R. M. Whitlaw and W. L. Wyllie, *Lionel P. Smythe RA, RWS*, London, 1923

W. L. Wyllie, 'A Panorama of the Battle of Trafalgar', *Society for Nautical Research, Annual Report for the year 1929*

W. L. Wyllie, *The Old Portsmouth and the New Southsea*, 1923

B. BOOKS AND ARTICLES ON OR REFERRING TO W. L. WYLLIE

H. V. Barnett, 'By River and Sea', *Magazine of Art*, May 1884

C. Beresford, *Memoirs*, London, 1914

C. Bridge, 'William Lionel Wyllie, RA', *Art Journal* (Christmas Number), 1907

Dictionary of National Biography 1931–1940, London, 1949

'E', 'Lionel Smythe's Place in the Cosmos', *Art Journal*, 1904

Fine Art Society, *Holiday Drawings in France and Italy*, Exhibition Catalogue with introduction by M. A. Wyllie, London, 1892

Fine Art Society, *The Queen's Navy*, Exhibition Catalogue with introduction by W. L. Wyllie, London, 1889

M. Hardie, *Water-colour Painting in Britain*, III, London, 1968

I. McAlister, *Alfred Gilbert*, London, 1929

Mariner's Mirror, April 1931

Rembrandt Gallery (Dunthorne's), *The Log of the Ladybird and Catalogue of Watercolours of Netherland Waterways*, London, 1888

Royal Academy of Arts, *Great Victorian Pictures*, Exhibition Catalogue, London, 1978

M. A. Wyllie, *We Were One*, London, 1935

INDEX